Build an Intranet

on a Shoestring

Maximum Technology at Minimum Cost

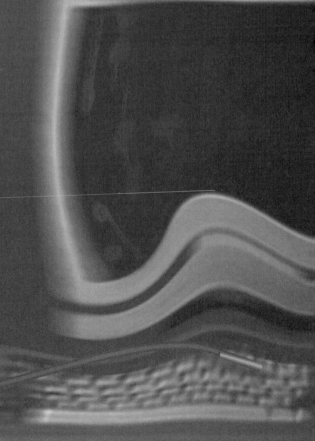

Build an Intranet

on a Shoestring

Maximum Technology at Minimum Cost

Paul Youngworth

VENTANA

Build an Intranet on a Shoestring
Copyright © 1997 by Paul Youngworth

Library of Congress Cataloging-in-Publication Data
Youngworth, Paul.
Build an intranet on a shoestring / Paul Youngworth. — 1st ed.
        p. cm.
        Includes index.
        ISBN 1-56604-521-5
        1. Intranets (Computer networks) I. Title.
TK5105.875.I6Y88 1996
651.7'9—dc20   96-27465
                                        CIP

First Edition 9 8 7 6 5 4 3 2 1

Printed in the United States of America

Ventana Communications Group, Inc.
P.O. Box 13964
Research Triangle Park, NC 27709-3964
919.544.9404
FAX 919.544.9472
http://www.vmedia.com

Chief Executive Officer
Josef Woodman

**Vice President of
Content Development**
Karen A. Bluestein

Managing Editor
Lois J. Principe

Production Manager
John Cotterman

**Technology Operations
Manager**
Kerry L. B. Foster

**Product Marketing
Manager**
Jamie Jaeger Fiocco

Creative Services Manager
Diane Lennox

Art Director
Marcia Webb

Acquisitions Editor
Neweleen A. Trebnik

Project Editor
Jennifer Rowe

Developmental Editor
Michelle Corbin Nichols

Copy Editor
Judy Flynn

Assistant Editor
Patrick Bragg

Technical Director
Dan Brown

Technical Reviewer
Robert Nichols

Desktop Publisher
Kristin Miller

Proofreader
Tom Collins

Indexer
Ann Norcross

Cover Illustrator
Elena Skrinak

About the Author

Paul Youngworth is an application developer and a freelance writer. He publishes a monthly column in *Internet Advisor* called "Building an Intranet." This series follows the experiences of a developer who is building an intranet for his corporation. Paul is also a contributing writer for *Data Based Advisor,* and has written for *ComputerWorld* and *PurePower*, a PowerBuilder magazine. He has written articles about using intranets to access corporate databases, bringing intranet technology to remote users, and Web development software. He is currently writing an overview of intranets that will be presented as a seminar to executives.

Acknowledgments

I'd like to acknowledge some very special people who helped me with this book.

First of all, I'd like to thank the intranet developers who took the time to answer my questions. A special thanks goes to Kyle Brown, an intranet developer with a lot of experience *and* patience. Thanks for all your help. I'd also like to send a special thank you to Dr. Lawrence Afrin, who took time from his busy schedule at the Hollings Cancer Institute to answer questions and put up with the trial and error of sending screenshots from one mail system to another.

I'd like to thank all of the wonderful intranet developers who helped me find information: Joe Meadows, John Swartzendruber, Russell Whitaker, Robert Hu, Aron Dutta, Jim Radford, Loke Crowfoot, Karilee Wirthlin, and Al Holmes. If I left anyone off of this list (unintentionally, I assure you), please forgive me.

A special thanks goes to Ted—you know who you are. Try not to get too much of that West Coast sun.

I'd like to thank the great crew at Ventana: Jennifer Rowe, who somehow made it all come together; Michelle Nichols, thanks for keeping me pointed in the right direction; and Neweleen Trebnik, Judy Flynn, Robert Nichols, Tom Collins, and Paul Cory.

Thanks also to David Kodama, who started it all by asking the question, "How would you like to write an article?"

To the beautiful Kathy Youngworth, thanks for putting up with all those late-night sessions at the keyboard—I love you.

Contents

Introduction

The network administrator for a billion dollar corporation recently had an amazing experience. He built a system that allowed employees to point and click through online manuals, procedure guides, product and customer information, and company newsletters. The system tied together related information and allowed users to search for documents containing a certain word or phrase.

The network administrator was most amazed by the cost of the new system. He was able to get the system up and running for less than $1,000.

The new system was an intranet. The term intranet is used to describe the structure that results from taking the technology of the Internet and applying it inside the organization.

The network administrator discovered that an intranet would sit on top of the company's existing network. It uses a communications protocol called Transmission Control Protocol/Internet Protocol, which the company already had in place. He added software called a web server to one of the company's existing network servers. Users connect using an inexpensive piece of software called a web browser.

An intranet is a set of computers (servers), connected through TCP/IP communications, that store data in various locations and formats. A client computer with a web browser can access this data using TCP/IP.

The "shoestring" in the title of this book is derived from the fact that it is possible to build an intranet for very little cost. Companies are also finding that intranets can yield significant business benefits from a small investment.

Build an Intranet on a Shoestring will show you how to build a low-cost intranet that can bring cost savings and other benefits to your organization. I'll present case studies that illustrate how companies are using this exciting technology, and walk you through the steps necessary to bring the advantages of an intranet to your corporation.

Who Needs This Book?

Anyone who wants to bring the benefits of an intranet to their organization without spending a fortune will find practical how-to guidance in this book. Even if you won't be the one who actually designs your company's intranet, you will find this book useful. It will show you how to reap big returns from this technology and what it takes to put it in place.

The book contains step-by-step information that will help network managers, system administrators, and developers put together an intranet. It will also help system managers and general business managers see what this much-reported technology is all about.

The book does not assume you have previous experience with an intranet or the World Wide Web. It uses examples from a real company to walk you step-by-step through the tasks needed to set up your own intranet. The book will show you how other companies are implementing big-payback intranet applications, and how you can do the same for your company. You'll learn from the advice of those who have successfully built an intranet.

What's Inside?

The book is divided into six sections.

The Basics of an Intranet

This section starts with case studies to show you how four companies built a low-cost intranet and what they are doing with the technology. It shows you how an intranet works and outline the components you'll need to start building one.

Building the Intranet Structure

You'll learn how to assemble the components you'll need for your intranet. You'll learn where to find low-cost TCP/IP software, web server software, and a web browser. You'll learn how to install and configure the building blocks of an intranet.

Putting Information in Your Intranet

You'll learn how to easily convert existing information to intranet documents. You'll also learn how to work with intranet graphics and forms.

This section reveals the secret of quickly building your intranet content by using web page templates.

Adding Value to Your Intranet

You'll learn how to add software to your intranet that will give your users powerful capabilities. Users will be able to search intranet documents, share information in an intranet forum, and query corporate data from intranet web pages.

Building a High-Payback Intranet

You'll learn what companies are doing with their intranets and where they are realizing significant benefits. Then you'll see how you can bring these same benefits to your organization.

Making Your Intranet Successful

You'll pick up tips for ensuring the success of your intranet. You'll learn how to implement a successful intranet pilot. You'll also learn from experienced intranet developers as they share their secrets for making an intranet a valued part of a company's information systems.

What You Need

The book assumes you have a network in place and already have or will acquire the hardware to host the intranet web server software. You'll also need to install Transmission Control Protocol/Internet Protocol (TCP/IP) communications if it isn't already in place. The book walks you through the process of installing TCP/IP communications.

The Companion CD includes a web server, a web browser, and tools to help you build intranet documents. It also includes example graphics and web pages so you can get started right away.

You can also get more information at the Web site for the *Build an Intranet on a Shoestring* Online updates. The site includes updates to chapters and links to other useful resources. You'll find the site at http://www.vmedia.com/updates.html.

Contacting the Author

Intranet technology changes rapidly. If you have any questions or comments about the material in the book, I'd like you hear from you.

Paul Youngworth
CompuServe address: 73324,3217.
Through the Internet send a note to: 73324.3217@compuserve.com.

SECTION 1

The Basics

This section starts by answering the question: Is it really possible to build a low cost intranet? The case studies in Chapter 1 show you how companies were able to deploy the web technology for relatively little expense. The rest of the section focuses on the technology itself. You'll see that intranets are popular because they take the easy-to-use features of the World Wide Web and apply them to applications inside the corporation. The section ends with an overview of the components you'll need to construct an intranet for your company.

Building a Low-Cost Intranet

Intranets are hot. The research firm International Data Corp. predicts that the annual sales of intranet web servers will grow from 70,000 in 1995 to an incredible 4,500,000 by the year 2000. A Forrester Research study said 22 percent of companies have an intranet in place and another 40 percent are considering adding the technology.

The interest in intranets is growing because they bring inside the corporation the easy, intuitive information access of the World Wide Web. The World Wide Web was designed to shield the user from the details of location, platform, and format. Data navigation is done with simple mouse clicks. Companies are finding that these advantages are just as useful inside the organization.

An intranet sits on top of a company's existing network, and it can use equipment that's already in place. This makes it possible to build an internal web for a low cost. That's why so many companies are starting intranets. They can do a proof of concept without spending a fortune. So can you.

Let's start our discussion of intranets by looking at four organizations that were each able to build an intranet for a relatively low cost. You'll see how they were able to use the technology to solve information-access problems without a huge expense.

The case studies will give you a framework that will help you understand intranet technology and what it can do for you.

Hollings Cancer Institute is a research center for testing cancer treatments. The institute built an intranet to convert a costly manual process to a paperless environment.

The Boeing Company is an aircraft manufacturer. Boeing uses an intranet to make it easy for employees to search through technical manuals and other documents to quickly find the information they need in order to do their jobs.

Eli Lilly is a pharmaceutical company that was having trouble coordinating projects in 300 countries around the world. Now they use an intranet to speed the flow of information across functions and geography.

Our last case study is a plastics company that used an intranet to facilitate collaboration throughout the organization. We'll use the experiences of this company throughout the book.

The software these organizations used to build an intranet included:

○ Transmission Control Protocol/Internet Protocol (TCP/IP) for communications.

○ Web server software to deliver intranet information.

○ Web browser software that allows employees to point and click through intranet documents.

The Hollings Cancer Institute

Dr. Lawrence Afrin knew there had to be a better way to distribute information. A clinical trial secretary had just finished her rounds, making sure each of 10 locations had the 100-page protocol that provided the details for one particular trial. When she returned she found an update on her desk. She had to turn around and do it all over again.

Dr. Afrin, a medical instructor at the Hollings Cancer Institute at the Medical University of South Carolina, had seen this happen far too often. Protocols provide the details of each clinical trial being conducted at the institute. They average between 50 and 100 pages and occasionally run up to 200 pages. They must be available to each location that has contact with a patient in the trial. This means constantly updating the huge shelves of binders at each location.

Dr. Afrin said the sheer amount of paper that had to be handled caused problems. "A number of times I discovered that a whole protocol would be missing or some pages I needed would be gone. Other times the copy wouldn't be legible."

The clinical trial protocols are crucial to the success of projects at the institute. Dr. Afrin knew something had to be done to speed the delivery and ensure the completeness of the information.

Requirements for the New System

Dr. Afrin wanted to automate the process of distributing medical research information, but he knew that he was facing a tough set of circumstances. For the system to be successful, it had to provide access to a single, electronic copy of each protocol at every location. The system had to make it possible for users to quickly find the precise information they needed. It also had to be available 24 hours a day, 7 days a week. And since the protocols were distributed to busy physicians around the state, the new system had to be easy to use and require little training.

A daunting set of requirements.

Searching for a Solution

Dr. Afrin said one possibility was to purchase an expensive fault-tolerant UNIX system that would use redundant hardware to provide 100 percent availability. "We couldn't afford that; it would probably cost several hundred thousand dollars. There were proprietary automation efforts, but they're hard coded and wouldn't extend from one trial to the next."

Dr. Afrin said a fault-tolerant UNIX machine with a proprietary document-handling system could approach one million dollars. He was looking for something that was low cost, but supported all the needs of a clinical trial.

Dr. Afrin was familiar with the Internet. It occurred to him that the solution to the institute's problem might be to use Internet technology inside the organization.

Building the Intranet

The benefit of using an intranet to solve the institute's information-distribution problem was that most of the structure was already in place. As Dr. Afrin said, "The infrastructure of the network already existed. We had a network with 5,000 machines spread throughout all of our buildings." The institute's network also already had TCP/IP communications, which is necessary for intranet connections.

The first step was deciding what kind of server to use. "The goal was mission-critical 24 by 7 operation," Dr. Afrin said. "I wanted two servers with identical copies of information, but I didn't want to have to post the documents in two places."

Dr. Afrin brought in two Dell servers with 100 MHz dual processors. The servers ran Windows NT 3.51 as the operating system.

For a web server, Dr. Afrin chose WebSite from O'Reilly Software. To provide document replication between the two servers, he used Octopus from Octopus Technologies. Octopus mirrors the file systems from primary to backup and even automatically switches over to the secondary server if the primary fails.

Dr. Afrin had the 24 by 7 capability he needed to make the system a success. "I've had the intranet up since June of 1995 and it hasn't crashed once," he said.

Client workstations use browsers from Netscape Communications. Because the intranet sits on top of the existing network and the browsers run on existing workstations, no further hardware or software was necessary to get the intranet up and running.

Dr. Afrin's cost to put the intranet in place would be $20,000 to $25,000 in today's prices. Quite a savings over the high-end UNIX setup.

From Paper to Online Information

Getting the protocols into the intranet was a challenge, since there were no electronic copies of the documents. To avoid retyping the information, the institute scanned the protocols using a flatbed scanner and a copy of OmniPage Pro from Caere. The scanned documents were saved as ASCII text and loaded into either WordPerfect or Windows Notepad. HyperText Markup Language (HTML) codes were inserted to turn the protocols into web page documents.

The new format of the protocols immediately enhanced its usefulness. If a protocol referenced another document, a hyperlink was inserted at that point to let the user jump to the referenced information with a single mouse click.

Tables of contents were set up so the protocols could be accessed by type of disease, by sponsoring department, or by university division. WebSite includes a search engine, so Dr. Afrin created the ability to search for protocols by keyword or the protocol ID.

Endless shelves of protocol binders had been replaced by an online, searchable system.

Figure 1-1 illustrates the intranet structure that Dr. Afrin put together.

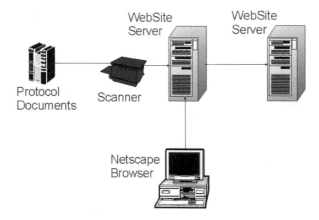

Figure 1-1: The Hollings Cancer Institute intranet.

The Benefits of the Intranet

The Hollings Cancer Institute intranet is used by 200 users spread around the university and 30 users from around the state. Under the previous system, users had to track down the appropriate binder and then page through 100 pages to find the information they needed. Now they fire up their browsers and just click.

The intranet has solved the information distribution problem. "Now we have a single, controlled, electronic copy of every document," Dr. Afrin said. "One copy serves everyone. This saves us paper, labor, and grief.

"There's incredible potential for savings and productivity gains," Dr. Afrin said. "The nifty thing about this technology is that it can automate other parts of the process. We could use it to track patients and collect data."

Dr. Afrin said that because an intranet uses standard technology, it can grow with the needs of the institute. "This all rides on an open architecture," he said. "If we ever need to scale things up, we can do it pretty transparently."

The Hollings Cancer Institute intranet was an immediate and dramatic success. "The intranet was officially available in October of 1995," Dr. Afrin said. "We burned all the protocol books in November.

"I haven't heard anyone ask for a paper copy in all the months the intranet has been in operation," Dr. Afrin said. "They love it. They click right to the information they need. They can search for whatever they want, and it's always readable. It's great."

Handling Remote Users

The intranet has also proved to be an ideal way for doctors from around the state to access the online information. The institute needs to recruit patients for its clinical trials. Physicians from various locations can connect to the intranet to check the status of a trial, then fill out an online referral form. This helps cut down the time it takes to recruit patients, thereby speeding up the whole process.

The intranet fulfills the requirement of being easy to use without requiring extensive training. Remote access on each physician's computer is set up to be as easy as possible. The doctor double-clicks an icon, and a script dials the institute and connects to the intranet. The doctor is prompted for an ID and password, and from that point on everything is accessible with a single mouse click. "We want to remove any barriers that users around the state might face," Dr. Afrin said.

Security is set up so that certain areas of the intranet can be accessed only by selected users. The security check is done behind the scenes, using the ID and password entered by each user.

Future Uses of the Intranet

The intranet is currently being used for cancer trials only. Dr. Afrin said this will be extended to other divisions of the university. He is also planning to set up a parallel site for patients. This new site will contain documents with more patient-friendly terminology.

Dr. Afrin said intranet technology could have a significant effect on medical research across the country.

The Hollings Cancer Institute might be one of several institutions in a clinical trial group. "There might be 30 institutions in a study," Dr. Afrin said. "Thirty copies of the protocols need to be made and sent to individual institutions. Then each institution makes more photocopies and distributes them internally. A single intranet server could hold one copy of the protocol.

"The cost of bringing drugs to market includes the cost of clinical trials," Dr. Afrin said. An intranet shared among the institutions could lower this cost. It could also cut the lead time. "The same technology could be used to speed proposals for new drugs," he said.

The Hollings Cancer Institute's intranet is proof that you can eliminate mountains of paper without spending a fortune to do it.

The Boeing Company

It's possible to build an intranet for a low cost, but is it possible to put one together for nothing?

Boeing did just that. In late 1993, some employees at the aircraft company wanted to experiment with an intranet as a way to share information across platforms. The company already had a network and TCP/IP communications in place, so the internal web would just sit on top of the existing structure. Boeing's intranet pioneers decided to use freeware servers and browsers to test the concept before asking for money.

Joe Meadows is product manager for proxy services at Boeing's Information Support Services division and one of the intranet's founders. He explained the strategy of those early days: "The price had to be $0 initially, since it would have been impossible to show any cost justification for it at the time."

Meadows and the rest of the intranet pioneers used freeware web servers and web browsers from the National Center for Supercomputer Applications (NCSA). This software allowed users to share information regardless of platform.

Building Intranet Content

In the early days, getting information into Boeing's intranet was a no-frills operation. "Initially we did manual conversions using whatever text editors were available to us," Meadows said. "A lot of information was already just flat text, so it was left that way or prettied up a little with title tags and so forth. We had a few early pilots with CGI scripts accessing various databases and a directory service." Meadows said they got permission from a software developer to use his search engine for the Boeing intranet.

The team had a working intranet and had built it for no cost. Figure 1-2 shows the design of the Boeing intranet.

BOEING INTRANET

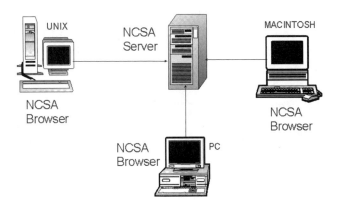

Figure 1-2: The Boeing intranet.

The first mission of the Boeing intranet was to prove that the technology was worth it. Meadows explained, "We used it to prototype various applications, such as a search engine and links to databases, as proof that it could be used for a wide range of things."

The intranet is now being used for database access, workteam collaboration, and as a front end to legacy applications.

The Intranet Catches On

"The benefits were clear to many of us right from the start," Meadows said. "I couldn't say when it became clear that it would become the success that it did, but we thought selling management would be harder than it turned out to be."

Meadows said what helped sell the intranet was its ability to maximize the investment in current computer technology. "Some people bought into it very early," he said, "seeing that we could finally share a piece of information across all of our platforms. Prior to the web we had several different text-based systems, and information had to be released to all of them."

Meadows said the number of intranet users has grown steadily. "Our internal web environment started with just a dozen users. By the end of 1994 we probably had one or two thousand. By the end of May of 1996 there were probably 20,000 users."

The Boeing intranet is now being used for just about any type of information. Business units are encouraged to build their own web sites to share information with the rest of the company.

First You Try, Then You Buy

As the number of users climbed, Boeing decided to take a look at commercial web software, especially for user authentication and document encryption capabilities. "We recently negotiated a corporate license for a commercial browser," Meadows said, "though I expect we'll continue to see some variety of browsers in use. We have a wide variety of servers. The last I knew we had around 300 web servers." Boeing is also using a commercial web search engine, Topic, from Verity, Inc.

Boeing's experience has been duplicated at a number of other companies. People have found that it's possible to build a test intranet for little or no cost, then move on to commercial software if the internal web proves to be beneficial.

Eli Lilly & Company

The story of Eli Lilly's intranet has been reported often in both computer industry publications and business magazines. The company's internal web receives a lot of coverage because it achieved three notable accomplishments:

○ It started out as a small experiment, then was quickly scaled up to 3,000 users.

○ It clearly demonstrated business benefits that touched almost every part of the business.

○ The company rolled the intranet out to the first 3,000 users at a low cost per person.

Eli Lilly is a $7 billion pharmaceutical company with over 30,000 employees and sales to 120 countries. The company was suffering from some of the same information access problems as the Hollings Cancer Institute, but on a global scale. Not only did they have to dig through the paperwork necessary to introduce new drugs, but they also had to do it across time zones around the world.

The Problem

Eli Lilly administrators had to deal with the different regulatory processes of 120 countries. Scheduling clinical trials and gathering the paperwork necessary to submit drugs for approval was a nightmare for regulatory coordinators at the company's Indianapolis headquarters.

Each market has unique legal requirements for pharmaceuticals. Keeping track of regulations and paperwork required a tedious exchange of e-mail messages and phone calls. Teams of administrators, doctors, clinical researchers, and legal personnel were often frustrated as they tried to pull the information together. They knew it was somewhere in the company, but where?

It was also frustrating dealing with coworkers whose work day ended just as yours was beginning.

Keeping a global sales force up-to-date was another challenge. The company had to get current information to 300 sales people around the world. Sales and marketing colleagues would distribute presentations and other sales materials to the field, but it would sometimes become outdated before it could be used.

Eli Lilly wanted to build an information system that could solve the problem of collaborating across borders and time zones.

Trying an Intranet

Eli Lilly information consultant John Swartzendruber started experimenting with an internal web in the fall of 1994. He started with freeware servers and browsers from NCSA and used existing equipment to house the intranet.

The company started converting Microsoft Word documents to HTML-based web pages. As more information was added to the intranet, it became apparent that this would be an ideal way to foster information sharing across the company.

In the spring of 1995, Eli Lilly licensed Netscape Navigator web browsers and rolled the intranet out to 3,000 users in 20 countries. Figure 1-3 shows the structure of the Eli Lilly intranet.

ELI LILLY INTRANET

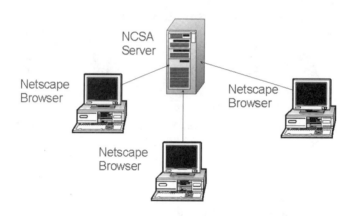

Figure 1-3: The components of the Eli Lilly intranet.

The Cost

Swartzendruber estimated that Eli Lilly spent only $80,000 to build the intranet for the first 3,000 users. "We used existing hardware and freeware servers from the NCSA," he said. "Most of the cost was for the browser software."

This meant Lilly was able to connect workers in 20 countries for a cost of less than $27 per person.

Information for Everyone

Eli Lilly calls its intranet ELVIS, which stands for Eli Lilly Virtual Information Service. Figure 1-4 shows the ELVIS home page.

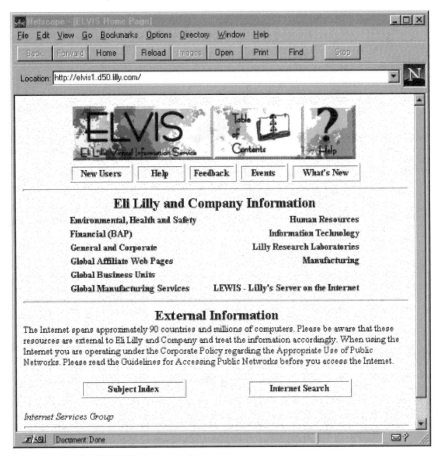

Figure 1-4: The Eli Lilly intranet home page.

From the intranet home page employees can access regulatory data, lab information, human resources documents, press releases, a daily newsletter, news about the industry—even the latest stock price.

There is also an online, searchable personnel directory containing phone numbers, locations, and mail addresses—no small feature for a company with over 30,000 employees.

Regulatory information is stored on centralized servers. The servers contain constantly updated information and can be accessed by anyone 24 hours a day.

Sales partners spread across the globe can access the latest sales presentations by clicking in their browsers. They can download information to take with them or print out selected data for use with a customer.

The Benefits of the Intranet

The intranet speeds up the process of introducing new products. The administrator coordinating the introduction of a new product can refer to the relevant web page during a meeting, and anyone throughout the company can bring up that same information.

Employees can find what they need without time-consuming phone calls or e-mail exchanges. Everyone shares the same information, regardless of location.

Swartzendruber said there are certainly cost savings from the intranet, but this is not the top benefit to the company. "The main thing is the information we can access," he said. "The big advantage is the speed and the ease of use."

The company was able to use web technology on top of their existing network to keep the cost of a global document system low. "You don't have to have a proprietary client to get at the data," Swartzendruber said.

Expanding the Internal Web

Lilly has been steadily rolling out the intranet to more and more users. The company wants to connect 16,000 employees by the end of 1996.

Lilly has moved from using only freeware servers to using commercial servers. Swartzendruber said they are now using Netscape Communications Servers and a couple of Netscape Commerce Servers. There are over 20 intranet servers spread around the world.

A Piece of Advice

Swartzendruber and his colleagues were successful in demonstrating the benefits of an intranet before investing a great deal of money in the concept. He had some advice for companies who want to try out the technology. "Figure out what you're doing before you start," he said. "Otherwise you'll eat up way too much time fooling around. Make sure you have goals for your intranet from the beginning."

A West Coast Plastics Company

The last intranet we'll talk about in this chapter is a case study we'll use throughout the rest of the book. It's an internal web developed by a West Coast company who manufactures and distributes plastic components. The company has chosen to remain anonymous, but we'll follow the experiences of Ted, the project manager.

We'll see how Ted and his coworkers assembled the company's intranet piece by piece. As each chapter discusses a component of an intranet, you'll see the steps Ted went through to install and configure that component.

The Need to Share & Manage Information

The need for an intranet started with a simple newsletter. The company has production facilities spread across the United States. These plants produce a variety of products but share a common set of manufacturing procedures. Production managers wanted to promote the idea of sharing best practices among the plants, so they asked each site to produce a newsletter. Each facility was asked to distribute their newsletter to all other plants.

The concept was simple. When someone came across a good idea for cutting costs or improving the product, it would go into a newsletter, which would be distributed everywhere. The plants would share their best ideas and the whole company would benefit.

The problem with this idea is that it created the same challenge faced by almost every organization; you soon have a mound of paper and no efficient way to find information when you need it.

The newsletter from each production site typically ended up in some kind of rack in each plant's lunchroom. As the months went by, the sheer amount of paper climbed. It didn't take long for it to grow into an unmanageable stack of information.

The real problem wasn't so much the amount of material but the way the information was collected. Say you work on one of the processes in a facility. You suddenly start having problems with stains on one particular component. You remember reading about a solution to this problem in one of the newsletters. The problem, obviously, is remembering which plant's newsletter contains the information you need and which issue contains the article.

The information has been collected. It's very valuable data. You just can't find it.

That was the problem facing the plastics company. Production managers went to Ted and asked for a better way to access the gold mine of information contained in the plant newsletters.

Time for an Intranet

Ted got this request at a very appropriate moment. He had been reading about companies that were using the technology of the Internet's World Wide Web to simplify information access inside their corporations.

The company already had an extensive network connecting personnel at headquarters, the plants, and sales offices across the country. They also had UNIX servers at many locations. Desktops had the necessary TCP/IP communications to connect to these UNIX servers.

Ted was able to find an under-utilized PC-based server to hold the intranet's web server. He knew he could start building an intranet pilot right away, since it would use existing equipment.

Keeping the Cost Low

Ted was fairly sure that the intranet would pay for itself, but he wanted to keep the cost of the pilot as low as possible. He didn't have a lot of experience with Internet software, so he didn't want to cut costs by using freeware products that sometimes came with skimpy documentation and little support. He decided to use evaluation copies of software wherever possible. He would then buy the commercial version once verified that the products would work and benefit the company.

Putting the Intranet Together

Several people in the company already had Netscape browsers to connect to the Internet. Ted looked at some information about the different web clients and made the decision to standardize on the Netscape product.

Ted installed Windows NT 3.51 on the PC server, then got an evaluation copy of the Netscape Communications Server. After he got the web server up and running, he wanted to find some documents to start testing the intranet concept.

Ted downloaded an evaluation copy of an HTML editor, HoTMetaL Pro from SoftQuad, and used it to convert HR policies to web pages. The plant newsletters were designed using Microsoft Word, so he also downloaded the Word Internet Assistant. Ted used this freeware add-on to convert the plant newsletters to web page documents.

As Ted started to build the content of the intranet, he wanted to make it look appealing, and he also wanted it to be easy to use. He got an evaluation copy of Paint Shop Pro, from JASC, Inc., to work with web page graphics. He also got a copy of Mapedit to create the ability to navigate by clicking on buttons or other graphics. Mapedit is a shareware program developed by Thomas Boutell.

Ted wanted to give intranet users the ability to search for information, so he downloaded an evaluation copy of the Excite search engine from Excite, Inc.

There are a number of case studies of companies using discussion group software on their intranets to enhance the collaboration between workgroups. Ted thought this technology would be a good match for sharing manufacturing best practices, so he got a trial copy of Digital's Workgroup Web Forum. Figure 1-5 shows the intranet that Ted assembled.

> *Note*
> We'll cover the details of the software Ted used as we cover each component in future chapters.

PLASTICS COMPANY INTRANET

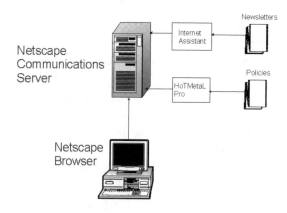

Figure 1-5: The plastics company's intranet.

Adding Up the Costs

Ted kept the cost of the intranet pilot low by using existing equipment and evaluation copies of web software. The only expense in the early days of the pilot was $700 for a copy of Microsoft's NT Server, and the IS department would have purchased this anyway. The initial version of the intranet was either free or $700, depending on how you look at it.

Ted quickly decided to purchase the Netscape Communications Server and the web page development software. He estimated that this cost around $800 total, but would be less at today's prices.

The plastics company had a prototype intranet for around $1,500. Ted said that even if existing PC hardware for the server wasn't available and he had to add that expense, the total cost would be under $5,000.

Selling the Intranet

Ted had the applications he needed to show the benefits of the intranet. He used the hyperlink capability of the web technology and the search engine to show how product personnel could find the best practices information from the newsletters. He surveyed other functional areas and built applications based on their input.

Ted presented the intranet to the plastics company's top executives. It was a hit. The CEO asked Ted to take the intranet from pilot to production.

Learning From the Case Studies

The case studies show how four companies used four different approaches to build a low-cost intranet:

○ Dr. Afrin started with new hardware and commercial software. He also brought in special software for 24-hour availability.

○ Boeing built their initial intranet for no cost using freeware web server and browser software.

○ Eli Lilly started with freeware web software, then quickly moved to commercial browsers.

○ The plastics company used existing equipment and evaluation copies of software to test the benefits before incurring expense.

The approach you take to build your intranet will depend on circumstances. Dr. Afrin knew that the Hollings Cancer Institute intranet had to be available 100 percent of the time from the start. He kept costs low, but decided to buy commercial products from the beginning. The intranet pioneers at Boeing weren't sure they could justify spending money on their internal web, so they started with freeware products. Eli Lilly and the plastics company fall in between the two strategies.

The case studies show that it's possible to use freeware web server software and freeware web browsers to create an intranet that is truly built on a shoestring. These intranets are fully operational and functional systems.

You've also seen that these companies moved from freeware to commercial products in some cases. The companies wanted some of the extra features that come with the commercial products.

You can build your intranet with freeware software and realize the benefits of the technology without upgrading to commercial products. But there are some benefits to commercial versions of the intranet components. I'll cover these as I talk about each component.

But Is It a Shoestring?

The purpose of this book is to show you how to build an intranet on a "shoestring." How can $20,000 or $80,000 qualify as a shoestring?

Let's look at the Eli Lilly $80,000 investment first. Remember that John Swartzendruber started out by using freeware web servers and freeware browsers, so he put together the initial pilot for close to no cost. He decided to use a commercial web browser to roll the intranet out to 3,000 users around the world. The cost to implement the internal web to that number of users was $80,000, but that's a cost of only $27 per user. If you scale the user count back to the smaller number of users typically included in the early phase of an intranet, it truly is a shoestring.

Dr. Afrin implemented the Hollings Cancer Institute's internal web for $20,000 to $25,000. This is a shoestring for a system that met the strict requirements of 100 percent availability that Dr. Afrin faced.

The key point is that you can build a low-cost intranet, then scale it up after you've demonstrated the business benefits. This is one of the most attractive qualities of intranets.

Moving On

Companies are finding intranets hard to resist. It's possible to test the concept of an internal web without spending a lot of money, and they often bring significant business benefits to a corporation.

An intranet borrows features from the World Wide Web to make it easy for employees to access information without worrying about the messy details of location, platform, and format. The next chapter shows how the World Wide Web accomplishes this and how you can apply this capability to the information in your organization.

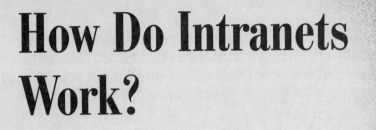

How Do Intranets Work?

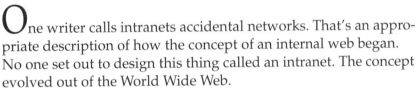

2

One writer calls intranets accidental networks. That's an appropriate description of how the concept of an internal web began. No one set out to design this thing called an intranet. The concept evolved out of the World Wide Web.

The best way to understand how an intranet works, and why the idea is hot, is to look at the beginnings of the World Wide Web. You'll see that the founders of the Web had the same information-access problems that you face. They put together an architecture that overcomes these problems and makes it easy to share information across the world. You can use this same technology to improve the flow of information inside your organization.

We'll start out by seeing exactly how the World Wide Web designers put together a structure that solves age-old information access problems. Then we'll look at how companies are using the technology to display information on the public Web. From there we'll examine how companies take the same technology and apply it to internal information needs.

Finally, we'll return to a couple of the case studies from Chapter 1. We'll see how Dr. Afrin used intranet architecture to eliminate a labor-intensive paper system. We'll also start looking at how the plastics company used the technology to accomplish its objectives.

The Design of the World Wide Web

In the late 1980s, a group of scientists in a Swedish organization known as CERN wanted to design a system that would make it possible to share research and ideas with colleagues around the world. They faced a problem most organizations share. Information was stored in a variety of locations, platforms, and formats.

Many scientists were using the Internet to exchange information with others, but this had its problems. You still had to know where the information was and how to retrieve and display it.

The experience could be frustrating. You would log onto someone's computer, issue change directory commands until you found the file you wanted, copy the document to your system, and log off. Later, as you read through the information, if you discovered a reference to another document, you'd have to go through the same sequence all over again.

The scientists knew there had to be a better way. They wanted a system that would provide an intuitive map to information stored around the world. They wanted to concentrate on the data itself, not on how to get to the data.

Goals of the World Wide Web

The scientists at CERN wanted to design a system that met these goals:

○ Hide the details of location, platform, and format.

○ Allow anyone, anywhere, to make information available throughout the system.

○ Provide a method to jump to related information so a user can effortlessly follow a train of thought.

○ Provide intuitive navigation that does not require extensive training to use.

A group of people at CERN, led by Tim Berners-Lee, came up with a design that met these objectives. The story of how they overcame the limitations faced by other information systems is key to how you can realize the same benefits.

Linking Computers on the Web

The scientists who designed the World Wide Web wanted the new system to link computers around the world. They wanted this link to be a buffer so that users didn't have to know where the computers were located or what platform they were linking to. Fortunately, a communications standard already existed that provided this very capability.

The Internet uses a communications standard called Transmission Control Protocol/Internet Protocol, commonly known as TCP/IP. This standard assigns a unique numeric address to every computer connected to a network. When you want to connect to another computer using TCP/IP, the protocol just sees two numbers; it doesn't care where the computer is located or what type of system it has. So, when you use the Internet, you just request information and the network figures out how to get it to you.

The scientists designed the Web to use the same communications protocol, TCP/IP, as the Internet. This meant they could use existing hardware and communications software. The same is true for your internal network. TCP/IP lets you use an existing network and hardware to build your intranet.

We'll cover TCP/IP in a little more detail in Chapter 3. In Chapter 4 we'll walk through how Ted's company set up TCP/IP and how it relates to the intranet they built.

Finding & Retrieving Information

The TCP/IP standard allowed the World Wide Web to hide the details of location and platform from users. There was still the problem of finding and retrieving information.

The World Wide Web founders wanted to design a way to find information without having to tediously issue change directory commands. They wanted to refer to information by name, and let the system translate this name into the location of the document.

They also wanted to easily link related information, so a user could intuitively follow the chain of information from one document to another.

The URL

The Web founders came up with a standard called the Uniform Resource Locator (URL). The URL could contain the address of the computer holding the information, the directory containing the data, and the file name itself. TCP/IP communications already had a mechanism that allowed users to assign an alias name to IP addresses. The URL could use this as well.

If Ford Motor Company has a Web page that lets customers navigate through Ford's products, the URL might look something like this:

```
http://www.ford.com/products/contents.html
```

This URL translates into the document named contents.html, in the products directory, on a computer whose IP address has the alias www.ford.com.

It would seem that the user still had to know directory names and file names. The CERN group created a feature for this new system to shield users from even this detail. The feature is called a hyperlink.

Navigating With Hyperlinks

The CERN group wanted a way to tie together related information. They accomplished this by giving users the ability to navigate by selecting URLs that were embedded in the information itself. These hyperlinks could be highlighted text; or, later when graphic capabilities were added to the Web, hyperlinks could be some graphic element such as a button. Users could jump to the related information by clicking on the hyperlink.

Hyperlinks made it possible for scientists to simplify the instructions for finding documents on their computers. They could just give someone the address of the highest level document on a Web site, then use hyperlinks to point colleagues to other information. This was much easier than having to issue change directory commands for each document.

Hyperlinking is the most significant feature of the World Wide Web. Chapters 7 and 8 cover building intranet documents and take you through the process of putting hyperlinks in your intranet information.

The HTTP Standard

The concepts of a URL and hyperlinks made it possible to give easy access to information. The CERN designers developed standards for client and server software to use URLs to exchange information. They called this standard the HyperText Transport Protocol (HTTP).

You can set up an intranet over a TCP/IP network by installing an HTTP server and HTTP clients. The HTTP server is called a web server. HTTP clients are known as web browsers. This software knows how to process information using URLs.

We'll cover web servers in Chapter 5 and web browsers in Chapter 6.

A Universal Document

The most critical problem for the Web founders to solve was the dilemma of the information itself. If everyone uses a different platform and different software, how can it be possible to exchange documents?

The founders designed a document standard that was platform independent. The standard called for a document that was plain text. Formatting was accomplished by using simple, "human-readable" codes.

This eliminated the headaches caused by trying to format something on a Mac, for instance, that could be read on a UNIX workstation. If you wanted a line of text, say a heading, to be in a large font, you just used a code like H1. The client software would decide what font to use to display H1 text.

The HTML Standard

The document standard of the World Wide Web is called HyperText Markup Language (HTML).

As we've already mentioned, the initial standard was for text only, but the ability to include graphics was soon added. The graphics are not stored in the HTML documents themselves. You use a code that points to the graphics in their native format.

The HTTP client, the web browser, interprets the simple codes in the HTML document, assembles all the elements into one document, and displays the document on the client machine.

The Advantages of HTML

HTML greatly simplified the process of making information available on the World Wide Web and can do the same for an internal web on an intranet. The advantages are:

○ You don't need special software to create a document—a plain text editor will do.

○ The format isn't proprietary. Anyone can add information.

○ You can convert existing documents by adding a few HTML codes.

○ Since HTML documents are text files, it's relatively easy to write programs that automatically create them.

You'll learn to use software that makes it possible to create HTML documents without coding in Chapter 7.

A Revolutionary Information System

The World Wide Web was designed using standards that are deceptively simple. The combination of these standards results in an information system that is extremely powerful.

You can use URLs to retrieve platform-independent documents from any computer on a TCP/IP network. This network can be the World Wide Web or your own internal network—an intranet.

If you set up your users' browsers to automatically load your intranet's home page, users never have to enter a URL at all. They just click to navigate through information. Later in the chapter we'll look at how Dr. Afrin did this to set up the Hollings Cancer Institute intranet.

Using Web Technology

The World Wide Web was created to make it easier for scientists to exchange information. The system hides the details of location, platform, and format. A scientist can just point to the information he or she wants, and the system handles the details.

It didn't take long for companies to realize that this same technology could be used to communicate with customers. A corporation can put information about products and locations on the Web and not worry about what platform their customers use to connect to the Web site. Companies can't provide training to customers before they link to the Web site, but this doesn't matter because the World Wide Web offers intuitive navigation.

Organizations moved to the World Wide Web at a rapid pace. They designed Web sites that served as maps to a wealth of information. All users had to do was click a mouse.

Silicon Graphics

Silicon Graphics, Inc. (SGI) makes graphics workstations and high-performance computers that are used for engineering, scientific, graphic design, and entertainment applications. The company is a good example of how companies are using Web technology for both external customers and for internal data access.

SGI offers a wide range of hardware and software. Their World Wide Web site allows potential customers to explore the products they offer, see case studies of products in action, and find the nearest dealer.

SGI has moved the Web technology inside to build an intranet. Let's take a look at how SGI uses the technology for it's World Wide Web site, then compare this to how they use the same software for their intranet.

The next several screens show SGI's Internet World Wide Web pages. As for the intranet, most corporations won't allow an author to publish much more than their intranet home page because the rest of their intranet screens contain sensitive information. I'll use SGI's World Wide Web screens to illustrate some points about the technology. The same design considerations apply to intranet web pages.

Silicon Surf

SGI's public Web site, called Silicon Surf, is designed to be a map to the variety of information that's available.

The Home Page

Figure 2-1 shows the Silicon Surf home page. This document is attractive and provides intuitive navigation. There is a navigation area in the upper right portion of the screen that has text labeled News & Events, Search, How to Buy, and Help. Users can click on a label to immediately jump to one of these functions.

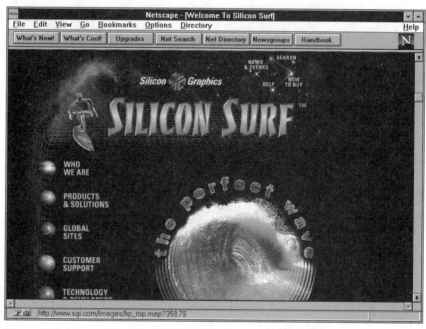

Figure 2-1: Silicon Graphics World Wide Web home page.

On the left edge of the screen there are colorful buttons labeled Who We Are, Products & Solutions, Global Sites, Customer Support, and Technology & Developers. These buttons are used to navigate to specific content on the Web site.

In the lower middle area of the screen there is a large graphic titled, "the perfect wave." SGI uses this area of the home page to highlight some new product or service they want to feature. This part of the home page changes frequently. You can access the document behind this graphic by clicking on the image.

SGI takes full advantage of the ability to use graphics as a hyperlink. Even a person with little exposure to the World Wide Web would quickly understand what information is available and how to get to it.

A Hyperlinked Directory

Clicking on Who We Are in the home page brings up the screen shown in Figure 2-2. This screen uses simple text hyperlinks to provide navigation to information about the company, products, case studies, and employment opportunities as well as other information. This screen is formatted like a traditional table of contents because it clearly identifies what information is available and how to find it.

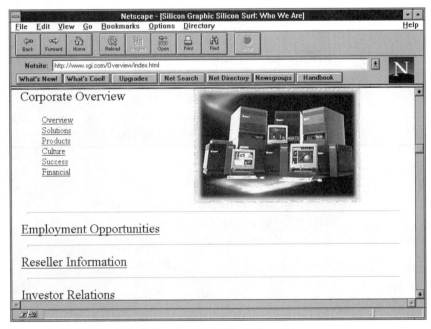

Figure 2-2: A hyperlinked directory to SGI's information.

Drilling Down to Product Data

When you click on the Products hyperlink from the directory, you see the screen shown in Figure 2-3. This screen gives an overview of each product. A button on the lower right lets you drill down into more detail, including a photograph of the product. This same technique allows sales and marketing personnel to drill down into product information on an intranet.

Figure 2-3: Drilling down into product information.

Finding the Nearest Sales Office

SGI's Web site has a document that lets you find the nearest sales office or dealer (see Figure 2-4).

Figure 2-4: Drilling down into dealer locations.

SGI has sales offices around the world. This page divides the dealers into six regions and also offers a list of international resellers. Clicking on a region brings up a list of sales offices or dealer locations including contact, address, phone, fax, and e-mail.

Notice the button bar on the bottom of the screen. This bar lets users jump to other sections of the Web site. It acts as an overview map to the entire site, and lets users skip the steps involved in going back to the table of contents to choose another section.

TIP

Use navigation bars on your intranet pages to give users a way to go directly to the information they are interested in.

Clear & Simple Navigation

Silicon Surf contains a lot of information on SGI's product, Exchange, so they created a Web page to map this subset of information.

Figure 2-5 shows the Exchange navigation page. Although there's an extensive amount of information on Exchange, this page clearly and intuitively shows what's available.

Figure 2-5: A navigation page for a subsection of information.

There are two other features worth mentioning on this navigation page. First, at the top of the screen there is a text hyperlink to the newly released white paper on the product. This shows how it's possible to add new information to a web site, then instantly make it available to your users. You don't have to send out a notice; just add a hyperlink to one of your intranet pages.

TIP

Use eye-catching hyperlinks to draw attention to new information on your intranet.

The other feature worth mentioning is the button bar at the bottom of the screen. The buttons are used to provide navigation to more general information, such as a glossary and a table of contents. You can structure a navigation page so that it clearly delineates the different kinds of information available.

Letting Users Search for Data

Sometimes users want to go right to a piece of data without navigating through the hierarchy to get there. SGI includes a search program on their Web site and makes it available from the home screen and from button bars throughout the site.

Figure 2-6 shows the screen that lets you search for specific information. You can search for a keyword or phrase in entire documents or only in the title of documents. You can limit the size of the list of matching documents, and there is a drop-down list of options for sorting the list.

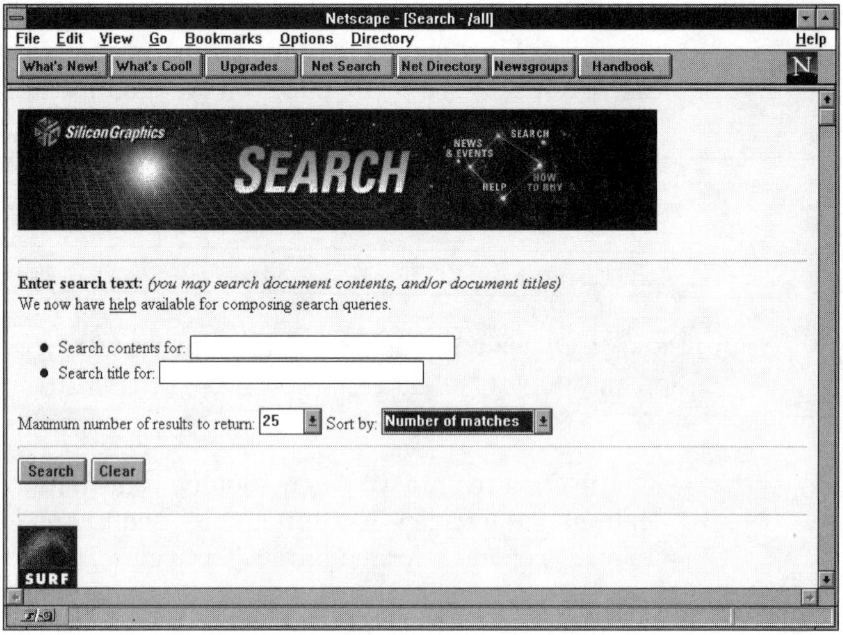

Figure 2-6: Searching for information in Silicon Surf.

The search program is designed to find documents containing the keyword or phrase you entered. When you click on Search, the program looks through an index of documents on the site, then returns the matches as hyperlinks to the documents themselves. You merely indicate what kind of information you're looking for. The system returns not only a customized table of contents to that data, but the way to navigate to the data as well.

TIP

A search capability adds value to the your intranet.

We'll show you how to add a search engine to your intranet in Chapter 11.

Retrieving a White Paper

If you enter the word "intranet" into the Silicon Surf search program, one of the hyperlinks it returns points to a white paper about intranet technology (see Figure 2-7).

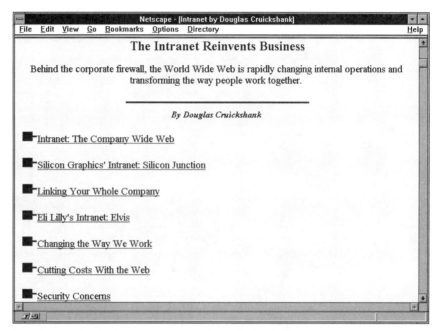

Figure 2-7: Retrieving a white paper from the Web site.

The intranet white paper in the SGI Web site starts off with a table of contents, which is a list of hyperlinks that jump to the appropriate section in the same document. This makes it easy for you to jump around in a long document, and it also keeps all the information in one file. This also allows you to print the white paper or save it to your local hard drive without having to follow links between documents.

You can use the ability of a web browser to print or save documents to your advantage by storing electronic versions of a document, but still allowing your users to create their own copy of the information.

The Silicon Graphics Intranet

Silicon Graphics uses the World Wide Web to give their customers information about the company, its products, and locations. SGI also uses Web technology to give their employees a map to data stored inside the corporation.

Figure 2-8 shows the home page of the Silicon Graphics intranet, called Silicon Junction.

Figure 2-8: Silicon Graphics' intranet home page.

The Silicon Junction home page is laid out like a newspaper. In the upper left-hand corner are buttons labeled Employee Services, Computer Tools, Internal SGI Sites, and External Web Sites. These buttons let SGI employees jump right to various sections of the intranet or go out to the Internet to access relevant information.

Linking an Intranet to the Internet

Silicon Graphics' intranet contains hyperlinks pointing to information out on the Internet. Many companies link the internal web to customer, competitor, or industry information stored on the Internet. This lets employees use one system to access related internal and external data.

You can link intranet users to the Internet in one of two ways. You can purchase dial-up connections to an Internet Service Provider (ISP) or you can acquire a direct connection to the Internet through a leased line or other method.

If you link your intranet to the Internet, you'll have to add security measures to prevent unauthorized users from connecting to your internal data. We'll talk about security in more detail in Chapter 19.

Underneath the Silicon Junction banner is another row of buttons. One of these takes the user to a Table of Contents page. Another is marked Recent Hot Items. This button lets SGI draw attention to newly added documents.

There is a banner marked Search in the upper right corner. An employee can sign on to the intranet and immediately begin a search for specific documents.

The home page also shows the current stock price; underneath this is a hyperlink to stock information. There is a button marked On-line News that jumps to internal company news.

In the center of the page is a colorful graphic that draws attention to some newly added or important information. This graphic can change daily. It's an easy way to make employees constantly aware of new data stored on the network.

A Map to Corporate Data

Silicon Graphics' intranet touches every area of the business. Work teams post status reports so others can follow the progress of key projects. Employees can use web page forms to submit requisitions to purchasing. Silicon Junction contains the latest product and marketing information so sales personnel can drill down to current data, including pricing.

Employees can even install software from the intranet. They click to select the software they want and the intranet handles the installation, then automatically charges the proper cost center. If an approval process is required, the intranet handles that too.

Speeding Data to Sales Partners

SGI has created a subsection of their intranet to speed the flow of information to sales reps and resellers. This section is called Channel City.

Channel City has sales information and sales tools. For example, the quote configurator is a tool that taps into a database of product configurations and pricing. The rep puts together a configuration to match a customer's needs, then clicks a button to send a quote directly to the customer's fax machine.

Collaborating With Suppliers

Silicon Junction also provides critical data to suppliers. There is a special section of the intranet that provides access to technical specifications and the manufacturing schedule, and lets users change orders. Suppliers can see changes in requirements instantly, and this speeds the response to a change in business needs.

Benefits of Silicon Junction

SGI makes extensive use of web technology to give employees easy access to data stored on the internal network. Employees have direct access to the data they need to do their jobs, and can avoid time-consuming phone calls to hunt down information.

Silicon Junction fosters collaboration across the organization. This makes it easy for work teams to share information within the team and with the rest of the company. SGI also uses heavily secured areas of the intranet to share information with resellers and suppliers.

Silicon Junction puts a user-friendly map on top of SGI's network, and gives employees a central location to find constantly updated information.

The Hollings Intranet Home Page

When Dr. Afrin designed the Hollings Cancer Institute intranet, he faced a tough set of requirements. He had to create a system that contained a ton of information, yet made it extremely easy for users to find the exact data they wanted. The new system also had to be intuitive enough for busy doctors around the state to quickly get the information they needed.

Dr. Afrin had to design a point-and-click map to data that was previously stored in row upon row of thick binders. He used the architecture of the World Wide Web to create the easy-to-use interface to the institute's critical data.

The institute set up each client browser to automatically load the intranet home page (see Figure 2-9). The home page divides the intranet into two sections: information for physicians and information for patients. Once the home page appears, the user navigates the entire site with mouseclicks.

Figure 2-9: The Hollings Cancer Institute intranet home page.

The Table of Contents

When users click on the line marked "information for physicians," they jump to a high-level table of contents (see Figure 2-10). This screen gives users three ways to access a protocol: by sponsoring department, disease, or protocol number.

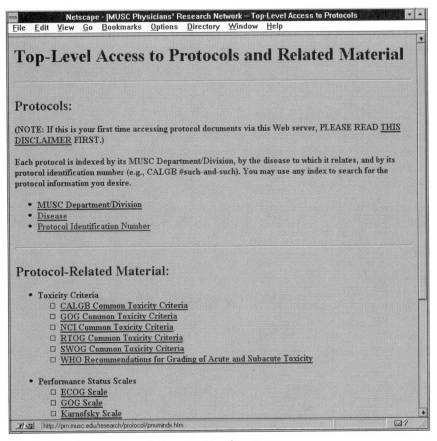

Figure 2-10: The Hollings intranet table of contents.

The internal web greatly improves how information can be accessed. Before the system went online, there was one binder for each protocol. When you wanted to access information, you had no choice but to hunt down the relevant protocol numbers and find the associated binders.

A web-based system lets you use hyperlinks to organize information any way you want. You can even use the same hyperlink in multiple contexts, giving users more than one perspective on the information.

The table of contents screen also contains hyperlinks to related information.

Drilling Into Categories of Data

Figure 2-11 shows the protocols organized by disease. Users can drill down to the protocol itself by clicking on the hyperlinked list of documents. This screen is useful when the institute is trying to recruit patients for a trial because it allows doctors around the state to easily see what trials are being scheduled for a particular disease.

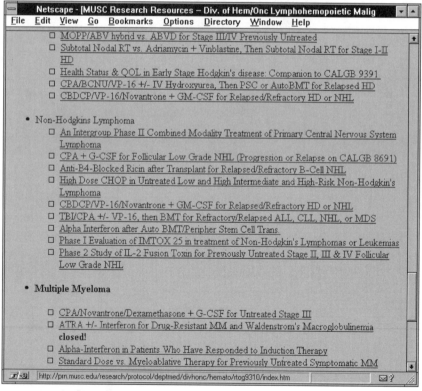

Figure 2-11: Drilling into data by category.

Finding Data by ID

Sometimes you know exactly what data you want and don't want to go through unnecessary navigation to get there. The web page in Figure 2-12 duplicates the way protocols were stored before—by ID.

The document divides the protocols into the upper-level qualifier of the protocol IDs. Within each group of protocols the IDs are in ascending order. There is a hyperlink at the top of the page that allows users to jump directly to a particular section of protocols, or users can just use the scroll bar to page through the list.

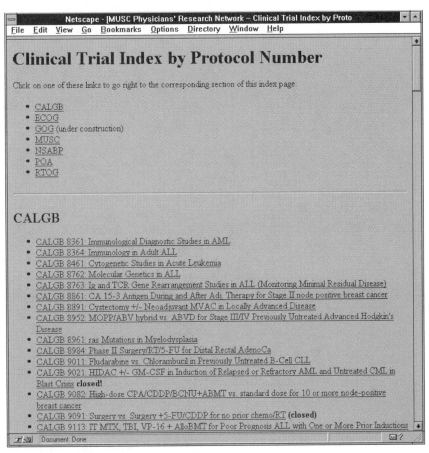

Figure 2-12: Finding a protocol by ID.

Build an Intranet on a Shoestring

Getting the Details

Web technology let Dr. Afrin apply another useful feature to the protocols themselves. He divided the protocols into sections, and provided a table of contents into this divided information. Figure 2-13 shows a table of contents for one protocol.

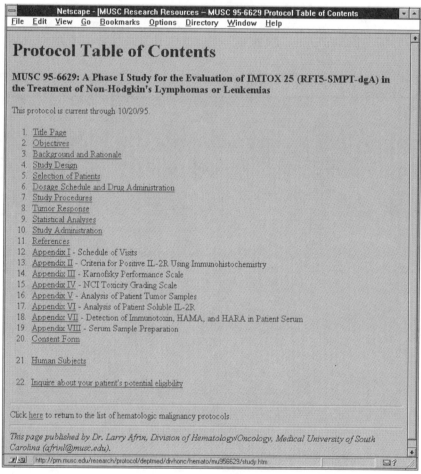

Figure 2-13: A table of contents for one protocol.

Dr. Afrin used the power of hyperlinks to take a 50 to 100 page document and provide a clickable map into the information itself. He used web technology to greatly reduce the time it takes to find a protocol or a particular page within that lengthy document.

Figure 2-14 shows a section within one of the protocols. This particular section contains the instructions for administering the drugs used for this trial. The instructions contain some text, along with a table of numbers.

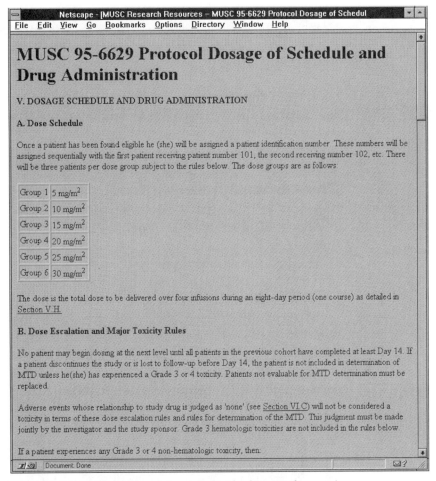

Figure 2-14: Drilling down into an individual protocol.

Notice the hyperlink at the end of section A in Figure 2-14. This link is embedded in a sentence that refers to another section of the protocol. Dr. Afrin was able to make a protocol a living document.

If some text references another part of either the same or a different document, the user can click on that reference and jump to the related information.

> **TIP**
> Use hyperlinks whenever documents reference other material so that users can follow the chain of information.

The Hollings Cancer Institute intranet is structured so users can quickly find the shortest path to a piece of data. The interface was so intuitive that the institute was able to burn the paper copies of the data and never look back.

The Plastics Company Intranet

We'll use the plastics company intranet as an example throughout the book. We'll see the details of how Ted built the company's intranet.

We can't use screens from the company's real intranet, but we can build web pages that show how they designed intranet documents to meet their objectives.

In upcoming chapters, we'll build web pages for a fictional company called KLP Industries. These screens will represent the design used by our anonymous case study corporation. KLP Industries is a totally fictitious corporation and any similarity to a real organization is completely unintentional.

Searching Plant Newsletters

One of the driving forces behind the plastics company intranet was the need for production facilities to share practices and procedures. (As you'll remember from Chapter 1, each of the company's production facilities produced a newsletter to share best practices among the plants.) The company included a search engine in its internal web to allow employees to find information. This enabled production personnel to find information without having to remember which issue of the newsletter it was in or which plant published the relevant article. Figure 2-15 shows a prototype of this search screen.

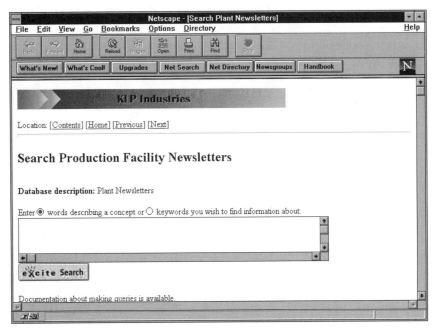

Figure 2-15: Searching for information across locations.

The search page lets employees search by concept or by keyword. A search by concept finds information that matches a topic even if that word or phrase is not in the matching document.

This screen also has a simple navigation bar at the top. Near the bottom of the screen there is a hyperlink to a document that provides help on using the search software.

We'll see how the plastics company built this screen when we cover search engines in Chapter 11.

Creating Online Reports

The plastics company also wanted to use the intranet as a sort of decision-support system. They wanted to put reports online, then let users drill down into the details behind those reports.

Figure 2-16 shows an example of a report that is designed so users can click on the report itself to drill down into the data behind that part of the report.

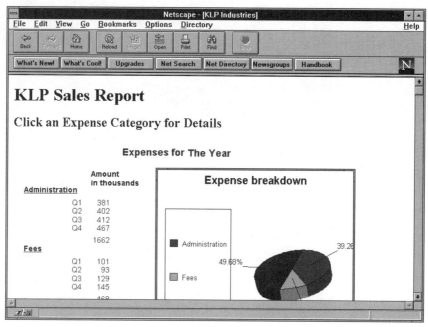

Figure 2-16: Drilling down into a report.

This report shows sales expenses in both the raw numbers and as a pie chart. It's possible to create a hyperlink from the expense category names on the left side of the screen. You can also make the wedges of the pie chart into hyperlinks.

Clicking on an expense category brings up a document detailing the data behind the summary information.

This is not as hard to do as it might seem. We'll cover this technique when we talk about web graphics in Chapter 8.

Moving On

You've seen how you can use web technology to provide easy access to your internal information. You can borrow from the standards behind the World Wide Web to put an intuitive map on top of your network.

The next chapter lists the components you'll need to build your intranet. The chapter paves the way for a detailed explanation of how you can start putting together an internal web.

3

What You Need to Get Started

You've seen how the scientists from CERN put together the World Wide Web by designing a set of simple standards. And you've seen how to apply that technology to your internal data, so now it's time to start putting together an intranet.

The World Wide Web is based on an open architecture. When you bring this architecture inside your corporation, you're free to choose any mixture of products that meet the standards. Since the standards were made freely available from the start, there are a wide range of products to choose from.

This chapter introduces the components you need to build your intranet. Then Chapters 4, 5, and 6 show you how the plastics company assembled the components and where you can get the products you need.

To see what components you'll need for your intranet, let's start with a simple example. What would it take for you to connect one client workstation to a web server and give that workstation the ability to retrieve and view web-page documents?

Figure 3-1 shows this simple example. The client workstation makes a request for information, and the server returns a web page in response.

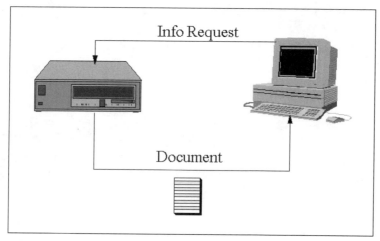

Figure 3-1: A simple intranet example.

The components needed to put together an intranet are:

❍ One or more server machines

❍ Client workstations

❍ A network

❍ TCP/IP software

❍ Web-server software

❍ Web-browser software

❍ Intranet documents

If you want to reference servers by name instead of a numeric address you'll need a Domain Name Server. We'll cover that later in this chapter.

The Client & Server Machines

The simple intranet in Figure 3-1 has one client and one server. The intranet can have any combination of platforms.

The Client

The client can be a PC, Mac, or UNIX workstation. Users get the most out of an intranet when they can use a mouse, but you can set up intranet documents to be viewed on a text-only workstation.

The clients don't have to be high-end computers. Some popular web browsers recommend 8MB of RAM, but you can use a low-end browser on workstations with less memory. The clients don't need a lot of hard disk for the intranet since they'll be accessing documents that reside on the server.

A key advantage of intranet technology is that you can use almost any existing workstation to access the information.

The Server

The intranet server can also be any platform. There is web-server software for UNIX, Windows, and Macintosh hardware.

For your initial intranet, start with at least 32MB of RAM on the server and sufficient hard disk space to hold intranet documents and software. As an example, for your server you could use a PC with 32MB of RAM, a gigabyte of hard disk, and a Pentium processor for around $2,500 to $3,000.

The open standards of the web enable you to use almost any existing server for your intranet.

A Network & TCP/IP

The component that allows you to connect a variety of platforms to your intranet is a network with TCP/IP communications.

The Network

Any network that supports TCP/IP protocols can be used for an intranet. This book assumes that you either already have a network or will install one before building the intranet, so we will not cover network installation.

TCP/IP Communications

Transmission Control Protocol and Internet Protocol are two communications protocols developed in the 1970s. The goal was to design a mechanism that would allow any computers and networks to be connected.

The TCP/IP standard was structured to send data from one point on a network to another without regard to platform. It does this by dividing a message into subsets called packets and putting an envelope around each packet. The TCP/IP software at the receiver knows how to deal with each packet received from a sender.

TCP/IP is really two protocols. Under the IP protocol, every computer on a network is given a unique numeric IP address. This address is made up of 4 numbers, each less than 256. When you type an IP address, you separate these numbers with a period. For example, the IP address of my Internet Service Provider is 198.70.64.2.

Every packet of data that is sent across a TCP/IP network is given an IP envelope that identifies the IP address of both the sender and the receiver.

The TCP protocol is what divides large messages into packets and puts a TCP envelope on the packets. This TCP envelope includes a number that is calculated based on the data in the packet. The TCP/IP software on the receiver uses this checksum number to verify the completeness of the incoming data.

As data arrives at the receiver, TCP checks each packet. If data is missing or corrupted, TCP triggers a request to the sender to retransmit that packet.

It's possible that packets will arrive out of order. TCP reorders the packets and assembles them back into the original message.

TCP/IP & an Intranet

What services does TCP/IP provide for an intranet? First, since it is an open standard, it allows you to connect any combination of platforms. Client workstations and intranet servers can be totally different kinds of systems. After all, each computer on the intranet is just a number to TCP/IP.

TCP/IP also lets you connect computers over a long distance. You can build your own network routing or even use the routing of the Internet to deliver intranet documents. TCP/IP knows how to handle the unpredictable nature of long distance routing, and will verify the accuracy of the transmission and assemble the pieces back into one document.

Figure 3-2 shows our example intranet with TCP/IP added. We have to install TCP/IP software on the server and on every client that connects to the intranet.

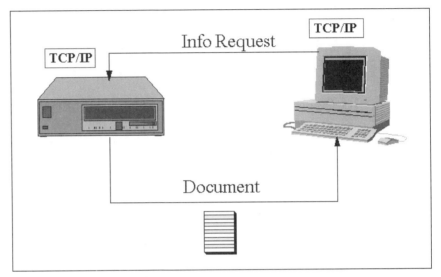

Figure 3-2: Adding TCP/IP.

When the client user requests the document, TCP/IP routes this request from the IP address of the client to the IP address of the server. When the server returns a document, TCP/IP checks it to ensure it arrives correctly, and reassembles the individual packets into our intranet document.

Chapter 4 walks you through the process of adding TCP/IP to a network.

A Domain Name Server

A TCP/IP network uses a numeric address to deliver information, but it would be tedious if you always had to refer to computers by their four-place address. The Internet has a technology that lets you use a name instead of a number to locate a server. This technology is called the *Domain Name Service* (DNS).

You can reach the Silicon Graphics World Wide Web server by using the name www.sgi.com. The DNS looks this name up in a table and returns the numeric address. The address is what is actually used to route your request.

You'll probably want to use this capability for your intranet. You can get by without it, but that means that calls to the intranet will have to be made using the raw IP address. As you add servers to your intranet, this will become tiresome in a hurry.

Figure 3-3 shows our example intranet with a domain name server. This can be a low-end PC, which is what the plastics company uses. When intranet clients send a request to the server, a call is made to the domain name server to translate the name back to an IP address.

Some operating systems automatically include domain name servers. UNIX systems in particular usually have DNS as part of the package. But it's not difficult or expensive to add it, as we'll see in Chapter 4.

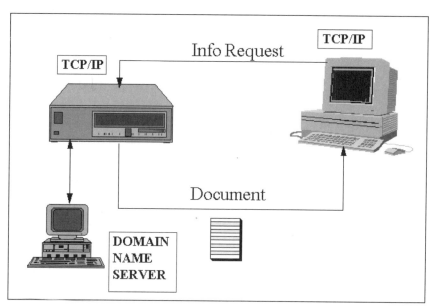

Figure 3-3: Adding a domain name server.

The Web-Browser & Web-Server Software

When the CERN group created the World Wide Web, they came up with a protocol called HTTP. For a web client and server to exchange information, both must have software that follows the HTTP standard. This software knows how to handle a request from the client and return a document.

For the client, this software is called a web browser. For the server it's called a web server.

Figure 3-4 shows our intranet with a web browser installed on the client and a web server on the server hardware.

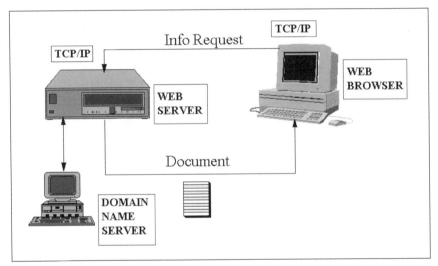

Figure 3-4: Adding a web browser and web server to the intranet.

Once again we can thank the people who designed the World Wide Web for the decisions they made. Not only did they create open standards for the web browser and web server, but they made sure these standards were widely circulated. They also made the browser and server software they developed available for free.

This openness encouraged organizations and individuals to develop web software for every platform. There are dozens of different web servers and web browsers available today.

The standard was designed so that a web browser and web server would work together even if they were on different platforms and from different software companies. As a result, you have a lot of freedom in configuring the software for your intranet.

The Web Server

The primary role of the web-server software is processing a request from the HTTP client browser and returning a document. But web servers have other important tasks in an intranet.

A web server can be configured to recognize different types of files, such as audio and video. The web server sends a sort of envelope to the browser letting it know what type of file is coming.

A key feature of a web server is the ability to invoke processing. A web page can contain a form that serves as a data entry template. An example would be a survey that the user fills out. The web server has the ability to send the contents of this survey to a program for further processing. We'll cover forms in Chapter 9.

A very important feature of a web server is security. You can configure many web servers to secure the whole site, document directories, even individual documents. There are a couple of different ways web servers provide intranet security. We'll discuss security in more detail in Chapter 19.

Web servers also serve as hosts to add-on products such as search engines or discussion-group software. The web server software acts as a kind of a mediator between the browser and the add-on software.

Web servers also perform a valuable auditing service. They can be set up to log all the transactions coming from clients. This enables you to keep track of the load on the intranet. It also gives you an indication of problems, such as users timing out or requesting a nonexistent document that may have been inadvertently deleted.

In Chapter 5, we'll look at how the plastics company installed and configured a web server. Then we'll talk about the different servers available and how you can get an evaluation copy of many different packages.

The Web Browser

When you start the web browser in our example intranet, the browser knows how to send a request to the server to retrieve the intranet home page. When the home page is returned to the client, the browser knows how to interpret the HTML codes and pulls together the text and any graphics into one document for display. The browser knows how to highlight any hyperlinks in the document and knows what action to take when a user clicks on one of the hyperlinks.

The web server can also recognize non-HTML formats and send a message to the browser letting it know what type of file is about to arrive. Many browsers let you indicate how you want them to handle this non-HTML format.

You can set up a web browser to play audio or video, for example. You can also set up a web browser to handle a spreadsheet or word processing document. This is a handy feature for an intranet, and one that we'll cover in Chapter 13.

Beyond the basics of retrieving and displaying a document, web browsers have a wide range of features. Some of the most common are:

○ A Back button that allows users to return to the previous document without reentering the URL.

○ The ability to print a document.

○ A history function that shows users the URLs of recently retrieved documents.

○ The ability to save URLs as bookmarks or hotlist so you can retrieve them again without typing.

○ The capability of viewing the source HTML of the current document.

Beyond these common features, web browsers vary greatly. The features of the web browser you select will determine how easy it is for intranet users to find and manipulate information. Choosing a web browser is an important step in the intranet design process.

We'll talk about browsers in more detail in Chapter 6. We'll explore the details of the browser the plastics company is using, then tell you how to acquire a browser.

Intranet Documents

Once you have all the intranet components in place, you're ready to start serving up information. The next step is to create HTML documents.

The HTML standard was designed to eliminate the need for special software to create documents. You can create intranet documents by adding a few simple codes to text files. There are software packages that can automate this process for you.

You don't need HTML-authoring software to create an intranet, but it sure makes things easier. Chapter 7 shows you how to create intranet documents the easy way. Chapter 8 shows you how to add graphics to your documents. Chapter 9 shows you how to embed web-page forms in your intranet documents. Chapter 10 discusses the idea of web-page templates: using existing HTML skeleton pages and merely adding the specific content for that document.

Hopefully, we'll take some of the mystery out of creating web pages.

Moving On

The straightforward standards of Web technology mean that you can assemble an intranet using a few widely available components. You've seen what you need to build your internal web. Now it's time to start digging into the details.

The next chapter shows you the details of adding TCP/IP and a domain name server to a network as the first step in building an intranet.

SECTION 2

Building the Intranet Structure

The technical terminology used for Internet/intranet hardware and software can sometimes make it sound more complex than it really is. The purpose of this section is to take the mystery out of building an intranet. In Section One you learned what components you need to assemble an intranet. This section uses the experiences of our example plastics company to walk you through the steps necessary to install those components.

Installing TCP/IP & a Domain Name Server

Your intranet will rely on TCP/IP communications to connect your intranet clients and servers. This chapter takes the mystery out of installing TCP/IP. I'll show you how Ted installed the necessary TCP/IP software for the plastics company. Then I'll show you where to get the software you need and point you to helpful resources on the World Wide Web.

Setting Up the TCP/IP Client

When you set up each client workstation in a TCP/IP network, you have to tell the software three things:

○ The IP address of the workstation.

○ The IP address of at least one network router.

○ The IP address of the domain name server.

Let's look at these one at a time.

Workstation IP Addresses

We've already discussed the function of the IP address. Each computer on a TCP/IP network is assigned a unique IP address. The address is used to allow connections between any two computers on the network, regardless of their platform.

Your network may already be set up for TCP/IP. If so, workstations may already have IP addresses, and you won't have to assign them.

If your network hasn't been configured for TCP/IP, you'll have to get valid IP addresses for each workstation. To do this, you have to contact the Internet Network Information Center (InterNIC). InterNIC will give you an IP address that identifies your network.

An IP address is four bytes and is written as four segments divided by periods. Each segment is a number from 1 to 255. An IP address might look like this:

    212.33.187.10

IP addresses are assigned in one of three classes: Class A, B, or C. Which class is used depends on how many of the four segments of the address refer to the network. This determines the upper limit on the number of computers that can be connected to that network.

Class A IP addresses use the first of the four segments to refer to the network, leaving three segments for the individual computers. This means there can be over 16 million computers connected to a single Class A network.

For example, a Class A address of 27.* means the InterNIC has given your network an address of 27. The remaining bytes can be used to identify each computer on the network, up to the 16-million limit.

The InterNIC only gives Class A addresses to extremely large companies and Internet Service Providers.

Class B IP addresses use the first two segments to refer to the network, which leaves the second two segments for the individual computers. There can be a little over 65 thousand computers connected to this class of network.

Class B addresses are reserved for large corporations and organizations such as universities.

Class C uses the first three segments to identify the network, leaving only the last segment to identify the connected machines. This limits the network to 255 machines.

Class C is the most common address class, so InterNIC is more likely to give a company multiple Class C addresses than a single Class B address, unless the company is very large.

You can request IP addresses by contacting InterNIC. Current fees are $100 for each domain name, which is a group of IP addresses, and $50 a year thereafter. For details, see the InterNIC's WWW page (http://rs.internic.net/index.html).

Real or Fake IP Addresses?

If you never plan to connect your intranet to the Internet, you can make up your own IP addresses, but this is generally not a good idea. If you ever decide to connect to the Internet you'll have to change all your addresses because they will conflict with numbers that have been already assigned.

Even though you can set up your intranet by using any valid IP addresses internally, you should plan ahead and contact the InterNIC for your IP addresses.

Network Router IP Addresses

A TCP/IP network moves information from sender to receiver by using the TCP/IP address. If all of your intranet users are at one location, the system merely maps IP addresses to physical network addresses. But what if you have users in various locations across the country or the world?

Companies with multiple locations typically have multiple networks, one at each site. Networks handle internetwork data transfers by using a hardware device called a router.

Figure 4-1 shows how routers work. Suppose the source computer in this diagram is in Chicago and the destination system is in San Francisco. The data has to travel through multiple networks to go from source to destination. Each network in this example has a router.

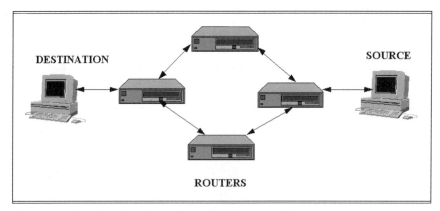

Figure 4-1: Routing data through a multiple network intranet.

In a multiple location TCP/IP network, the job of the router is to direct TCP/IP packets through the interconnected networks to the destination. Each router has a table containing a list of other routers, their addresses, and how far away they are.

When you set up your TCP/IP clients, you'll have to tell the client software the IP address of at least one router. This allows the system to direct intranet documents between your various locations.

Domain Name Server IP Addresses

The previous chapter discussed the role of a domain name server. This device lets you use names instead of IP addresses when requesting intranet information. The server then translates the names into the numeric IP addresses that are used by TCP/IP.

When you configure your TCP/IP clients you'll have to enter the IP address of the primary domain name server. You can also enter the IP address of a secondary domain name server. The secondary domain name server acts as a backup so the intranet can still resolve IP addresses if the primary server goes down.

A Secondary DNS

When a company sets up a domain name server, they can designate a primary and secondary server. The secondary domain name server is a second machine that is set up to take over if the primary server fails.

Domain name resolution is important enough to your intranet that you'll probably want a secondary domain name server. The reason is that if the primary domain name server fails, and you don't have a backup, users will have to enter the numeric IP addresses of your web servers instead of the name. Hyperlinks that are coded to use the web server name instead of the address will fail, because the system can't resolve the names into the equivalent addresses. The intranet will stop functioning.

Domain name server software doesn't need much in the way of resources, so the secondary machine can be any existing server or even a low-end PC. You'll just want something that can serve in a pinch until the primary server is back up.

Example: Setting Up TCP/IP

Throughout the book we'll use the plastics company's intranet as an example and show you how Ted, the intranet project leader, set up each component.

Setting up intranet clients for TCP/IP communications is fairly simple. Ted installed TCP/IP software on each intranet workstation, then entered an IP address, the IP address of a router, and the IP address of the domain name server.

Let's take a look at the details.

Selecting TCP/IP Software

The plastics company has a mix of computing platforms, including Windows desktops, UNIX mid-range systems, and a couple of IBM mainframes. The various platforms were connected through Novell NetWare Networks. There was a Novell LAN at each location.

The company recently began moving applications off the mainframe to the UNIX platform. Ted wanted to find TCP/IP client software to fill two roles: provide the TCP/IP stack needed for the intranet and enable desktop users to log in to UNIX systems.

The plastics company used Novell NetWare for their network. Ted decided to use a Novell product, called Novell LAN Workplace, to provide the TCP/IP stack.

Configuring IP Addresses Using LAN Workplace

Ted installed LAN Workplace by running a setup program on each client. After the software was installed, he set it up for TCP/IP by making entries in two files on the desktop, net.cfg and resolve.cfg.

The files net.cfg and resolve.cfg are part of the LAN Workplace install. There will be equivalent TCP/IP configuration files on every TCP/IP network. These files are typically found in a directory called NET or something similar.

The connection parameters for LAN Workplace are in net.cfg. Ted entered the IP address of the workstation and the IP address of the company's network router that was closest to the web server into a section of net.cfg labeled "Protocol TCPIP."

The resolve.cfg file tells LAN Workplace how to resolve IP addresses entered as names. The file has two entries: one for the primary domain name server and another for the secondary. Ted entered the IP address of each in the appropriate section.

At this point the client workstation has the TCP/IP stack that the intranet requires. The setting in the configuration files tells TCP/IP how to route intranet documents between locations and how to resolve intranet URLs that use a name instead of a TCP/IP address.

For more information on LAN Workplace visit Novell's Web site (http://www.novell.com/).

Setting Up the Domain Name Server

Domain name servers typically don't require a lot of system resources. Ted found a low-end PC that had OS/2 installed. He bought IBM's Domain Name Server for OS/2 for around $300 and installed it. The Domain Name Server PC is kept in the computer room and operates 24 hours a day.

The server uses a table called named.dom to resolve IP addresses. This table is really a flat file containing each server's IP address and one or more aliases for that address.

The plastics company assigned each server a name that followed a standard, such as IT01. They also gave meaningful nicknames to systems. The UNIX box that holds sales databases is called SALES, for example. This naming standard lets intranet developers create URLs that users can recognize and remember.

> ### TIP
> Use the alias capability of a domain name server to assign meaningful aliases to your intranet servers.

Whenever a new host is added to the network or there is an update to a host's alias, Ted makes an entry in a file on the LAN called hosts.txt. Figure 4-2 shows the LAN Workplace help screen that describes this table.

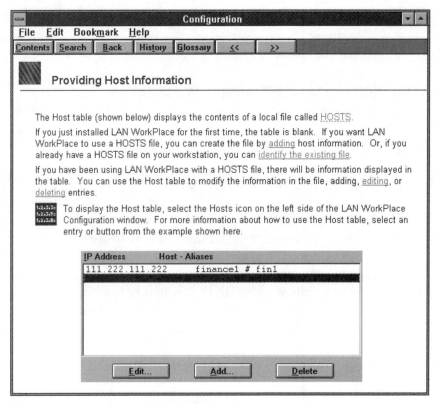

Figure 4-2: An example of a Host table.

The Host table is just a text file containing the IP address of each host on the TCP/IP network, followed by the aliases assigned to that host. When the Host file on the LAN is updated, Ted runs a program that submits the entries to the DNS.

It may seem like double work, but there is a good reason to do this. If the DNS goes down or the connection is broken, LAN Workplace can switch to the hosts.txt file to resolve IP addresses. This is especially critical for users at remote facilities. Both the primary and secondary domain name servers are at headquarters. If the connection is lost, the Host table on the local network is key to continuing operations.

The Intranet has TCP/IP

The operating system Ted used for the intranet server, Windows NT 3.51, comes with TCP/IP capability. Most server operating systems include this as part of the base software. With TCP/IP installed on the clients and the domain name server ready to go, Ted had the TCP/IP infrastructure he needed for the intranet.

TCP/IP Software on a Shoestring

To build an intranet, you need to have TCP/IP software on each workstation. Fortunately, there are several ways you can add this software to all of your clients for a relatively low cost.

Recent desktop operating systems already include TCP/IP software. All you have to do is set it up. If your workstations don't already have this capability, you can choose from among several software solutions.

Let's take a look at how you would set up TCP/IP on three desktop operating systems: Windows 95, Mac OS, and Windows 3.1.

Note
We're not going to discuss TCP/IP installation on UNIX systems. TCP/IP has been an integrated part of UNIX for a long time, and is usually defined during the initial configuration of a UNIX system.

Windows 95

TCP/IP software is included with Microsoft's Windows 95. It's not automatically installed during setup, so you'll have to use the Control Panel to install and configure the TCP/IP stack on the Windows 95 desktop.

The steps to set up the Microsoft TCP/IP stack are:

1. Use the Network option in the Control Panel to add the Microsoft TCP/IP to the list of installed protocols.

2. Select TCP/IP from the list of network components and click on Properties.

3. Use the tabbed Properties dialog box to add the workstation's IP address, the IP address of the domain name server, and the IP address of a network router.

There is a Web site (http://www.windows95.com/connect/tcp.html) that guides you step-by-step through the process of installing TCP/IP on Windows 95 systems. Figure 4-3 shows the graphical interface into this online tutorial.

Figure 4-3: Online help for setting up Windows 95 TCP/IP.

The tutorial shows you how to set up a Windows 95 system for an intranet (choose the LAN Connections icon), for the Internet, and other configurations.

Macintosh

Apple began including MacTCP with System 7.5. MacTCP is a TCP/IP stack for the Macintosh. You can also get MacTCP as an add-on to earlier versions of Mac OS.

The steps to configure MacTCP are:

1. Open the Controls Panel.

2. Open the MacTCP Panel.

3. Click the PPP icon, then the More button.

4. Enter the IP address of the workstation, the IP address of the domain name server, and the IP address of your network router.

There is an online tutorial for configuring Mac TCP/IP (http://www.winternet.com/~kae/wnet_faq/connecting/mac/index.html). Figure 4-4 shows the table of contents for this online guide.

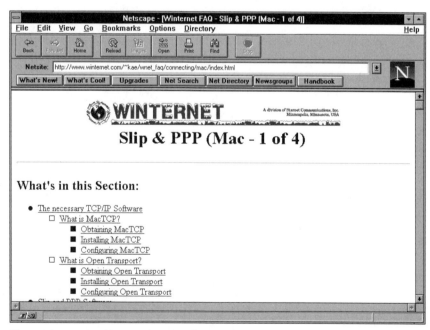

Figure 4-4: An online guide to configuring Mac TCP/IP.

Windows 3.1

Microsoft Windows 3.1 does not include a TCP/IP stack, so you'll have to find your own. Fortunately, you have several software packages to choose from.

When you select a TCP/IP stack for Windows 3.1, you can go with a bare-bones package that supplies just the TCP/IP stack or choose a TCP/IP suite that includes other software.

Let's look at an example of both types of products.

Trumpet Winsock

A popular TCP/IP stack for Windows is Trumpet Winsock, from Trumpet Software International. You can obtain Trumpet Winsock for a 30-day evaluation. A single-user license costs $25, but with a large number of users you can purchase a site license that runs somewhere between $5 and $10 per user.

Visit the Trumpet Software International Web site (http://www.trumpet.com.au/) for more information.

NetManage Chameleon

An example of a software suite that provides both a TCP/IP stack and various TCP/IP programs is NetManage's Chameleon.

Figure 4-5 shows the Chameleon program group. Among the programs Chameleon includes are a web browser, a File Transfer Protocol (FTP) client, a mail program, and Archie and Gopher services.

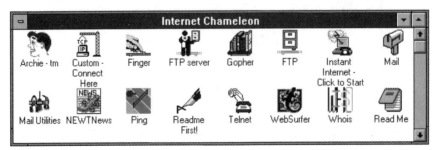

Figure 4-5: The TCP/IP programs available in NetManage's Chameleon.

Figure 4-6 shows the Chameleon FTP client. This program provides a visual interface to file transfers, making it easy to navigate through the directories and files of the client and server.

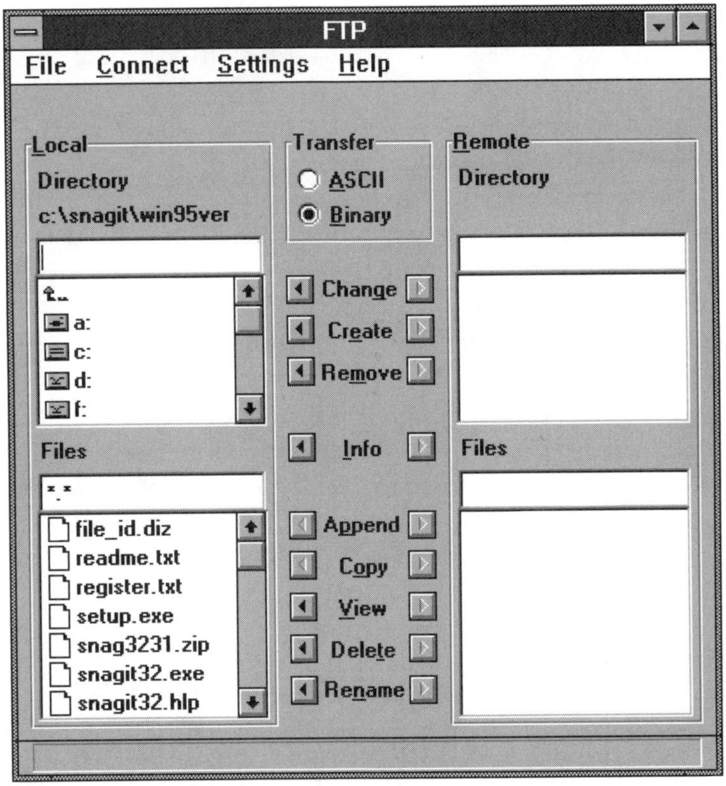

Figure 4-6: Chameleon's FTP client.

A product like Chameleon will be more expensive than a plain TCP/IP stack, but your users may be able to make good use of the additional software.

NetManage offers a range of products with varying prices. Visit the NetManage Web site (http://www.netmanage.com/) for more information.

A Domain Name Server on a Shoestring

You can add domain name server software to your TCP/IP network for a relatively modest cost.

You may already have a domain name server on one of your systems. Most UNIX mid-range computers include this capability. Apple's MacDNS comes free with the Apple Internet Server Solution.

If you don't already have a domain name server, you can choose from several products on the market.

A company called FBLI makes a domain name server for Windows NT. The software is called FBLI DNS. The cost of this product is $100 for just a primary DNS, or $150 for primary and secondary capabilities. Visit the FBLI Web site (http://www.fbli.com/dnspage.htm) for more information.

Microsoft maintains a Web page (http://internet.microsoft.com/tools/dns.htm) that contains a list of domain name servers that run on Windows NT.

QuickDNS Pro is a DNS for the Apple Internet Server Solution. The product is from Men & Mice and lists for $290. See the Web site (http://www.menandmice.is/) for more details.

Moving On

TCP/IP is an essential component of an intranet. You can obtain the necessary software for your intranet clients at a modest cost. You can also add a domain name server to your TCP/IP network without spending a lot of money.

With our intranet TCP/IP structure in place, it's time to select a web server. The next chapter walks through the steps Ted took to get a web server up and running. We'll also look at some of the web servers that are available and talk about sources of information about web servers on the World Wide Web.

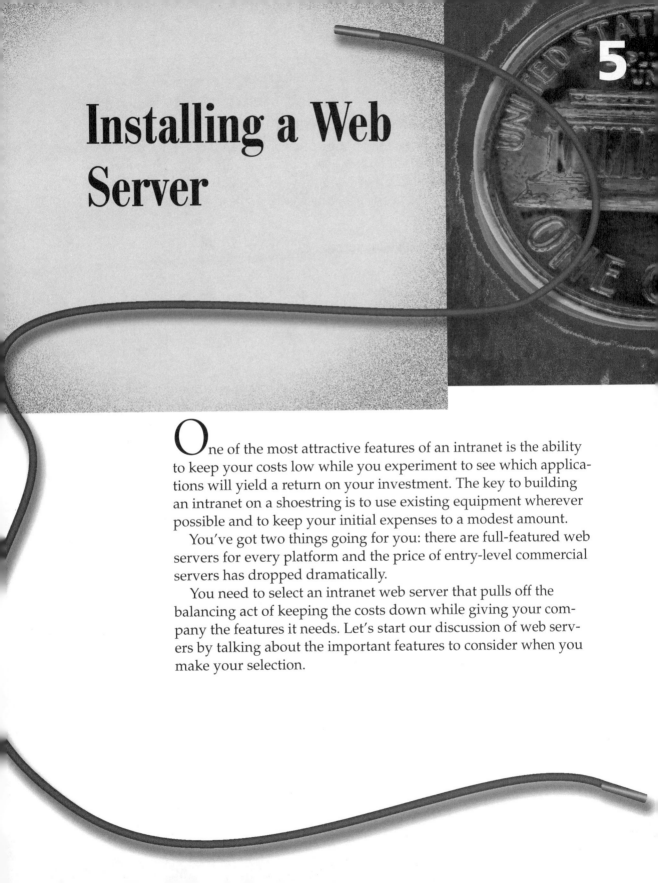

Installing a Web Server

5

One of the most attractive features of an intranet is the ability to keep your costs low while you experiment to see which applications will yield a return on your investment. The key to building an intranet on a shoestring is to use existing equipment wherever possible and to keep your initial expenses to a modest amount.

You've got two things going for you: there are full-featured web servers for every platform and the price of entry-level commercial servers has dropped dramatically.

You need to select an intranet web server that pulls off the balancing act of keeping the costs down while giving your company the features it needs. Let's start our discussion of web servers by talking about the important features to consider when you make your selection.

Web Server Selection Criteria

All web servers follow the same HTTP standards. They do differ in which systems they can run on, how easy they are to manage, and what capabilities they have for working with information. You'll want to evaluate web servers based on these criteria:

- ○ Platform
- ○ Setup & Maintenance
- ○ Available Software
- ○ Documentation and Support
- ○ Security
- ○ Image maps
- ○ Cost

At the end of the chapter I'll give you some resources that you can use to see how the various web servers compare in these categories.

Platform

The first decision to make is what platform will host the intranet server software. You may have to decide between using hardware that's already in place and using a platform that is familiar to the people who will build and run the internal web.

> **Note**
> I'll be using the phrase "internal web" throughout the book. This phrase is often used to refer to an intranet, since it brings the technology of the external World Wide Web into an organization

Suppose you have some UNIX servers, but the network department is more comfortable with Windows NT or a Mac server. You want to use existing equipment where possible but not if it causes a long learning curve. You can start by purchasing a PC server and still keep the cost relatively modest. It's better to start with what you know and build from there.

Another factor to consider is whether you want to have web servers on more than one platform. If you have departmental servers from a mixed computing environment, you may want to go with a web server that is available for multiple platforms. There are several of these.

Setup & Maintenance

How easy is it to install, configure, and maintain the server? Some web servers can be set up and maintained through a GUI interface. Others require expert knowledge of system commands and configuration files. The key here is to consider the skills of the people who will run the intranet and choose a web server to match.

Available Software

When you choose web-server software, it's very important to consider what add-on software it supports. You'll certainly want a search engine, for example. Make sure the web server software you select either includes a full-featured search engine or can support a third-party product.

At some point you'll probably want to give your intranet users the ability to post messages to discussion groups, query databases, and even develop and manage their own web pages. Be sure you understand what software runs on a particular web server before you commit.

Users will judge your intranet for the features it delivers long after they've forgotten that you saved $200 on a server.

Documentation & Support

Some freeware or shareware servers are skimpy on documentation. Others offer extensive manuals that either come with the product or can be downloaded from a Web site. Support varies from product to product as well. Be sure you understand what kind of support and documentation is available for your web server.

Security

The initial content on your intranet might be information like procedural manuals and policy guides. You might not have a need to secure this information, but eventually you'll add confidential data to your internal web. Therefore, you need to be able to restrict access to selected data on the system.

Security is one feature that separates web servers. Some low-end servers have almost no ability to block access to intranet content. Other modestly priced servers have extensive security features such as the ability to protect individual documents or provide security by groups of users.

Give a lot of weight to security features when selecting a web server.

Image Maps

An image map is used to assign hyperlinks to sections of a graphic image. It is a text file that contains coordinates and the hyperlink URL assigned to those coordinates.

An example of this is a row of buttons on a web page. These buttons are often one graphic image. An image map allows the developer to assign a different hyperlink to each individual button on the row. A user might click on a button marked "Products" that retrieves an HTML document serving as a table of contents pointing to product information.

The Products button might actually be part of a long graphic containing several buttons. The image map also allows the developer to code different actions for each subset of the image—in this case a button.

Image maps simplify the task of designing web-page navigation. There are a few web servers that do not have this capability, so be aware of this when making your selection.

Cost

The cost of a web server is not always a good indication of how well it will meet your needs. There are some freeware or shareware products that are fairly robust. There are also some mid-range web servers that may not have the features you need. We'll talk about this when we compare some products. I'll also give you some places to go online to find thorough comparisons of web servers.

Now let's see how Ted selected and implemented a web server for the plastics company's intranet.

Example: Using the Netscape Communications Server

The plastics company had several UNIX servers, but Ted didn't have experience in this environment. He decided to use an existing PC with Windows NT 3.51 to host the intranet web server.

Ted looked at some of the web servers on the market and decided to bring in an evaluation copy of the Netscape Communications Server. Ted knew he would be putting some sensitive data on the intranet, and he liked the security features that came with the product. Also he was pleased with the amount of third-party support the server had. He knew he would have more than one choice for products like a search engine and discussion-group software.

Declining Web Server Prices
When Ted first brought in the Netscape Communications Server, it was priced at $595. The price has now been reduced to $295, and it is being replaced by the Netscape FastTrack Server—which also lists for $295.

Let's walk through what it took to install and configure the Netscape Communications Server on the Windows NT server.

Installing the Web Server

Installation was easy. Ted downloaded the installation files from the Netscape Web site (http://www.netscape.com). Then he installed the zipped files in a working directory and unzipped them. The last step in the installation was to run setup.exe from the working directory. This created the appropriate directories and installed the software.

The next step was to go through the various settings needed to properly configure the server.

Setting Up Server Addresses

When the server was installed, Ted fired up his web browser and brought up the server's administration web page. You manage the Netscape Communications Server completely from a graphical, point-and-click interface.

Figure 5-1 shows one of the web pages that lets you navigate through the various server configurations.

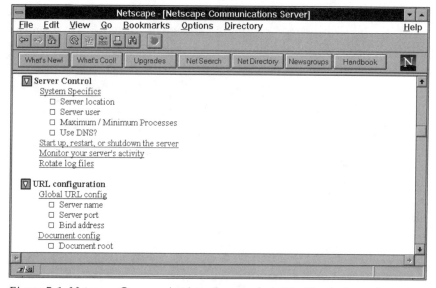

Figure 5-1: Netscape Communications Server administration is done via web pages.

Ted set up an administrator ID and password for the server. He entered the server's IP address, then told the server to use a domain name server for IP address resolution and entered the IP address of the DNS. Next, he set up a default port number, 80, and an administrator port. This last address is any unused port number. The server only goes into the administration mode when it receives a request for this port.

Web Server Ports

A server port is not hardware, it's the method used by the server to tell what kind of service is being requested. The default port for the HTTP protocol used for web services is 80. The default port for File Transfer Protocol (FTP) is 21. This is how requests for different services can be sent through the same connection.

A port can be any number from 0 to 65535. Some numbers are reserved and have special meaning, but there are many unused port numbers. Since the standard for the HTTP protocol of the Web is 80, if you use a different port number for the web server administrator only that person will be able to connect to the server in administrative mode.

Clicking on any option usually brings up a dialog box with step-by-step instructions and appropriate data entry fields. Figure 5-2 shows the dialog box used to enter the port number.

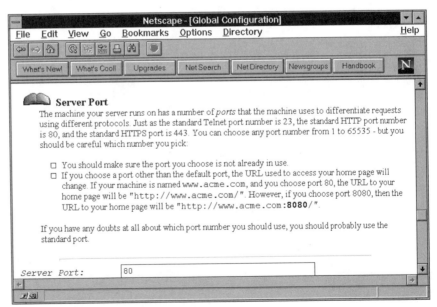

Figure 5-2: Netscape Communications Server administration screens contain step-by-step instructions.

Configuring the Documents

Ted's next step was to configure the document parameters of the server. Figure 5-3 shows the screen used to do this. Ted set up the document root directory. This is used to indicate what directories users can access. Another screen later in the process let Ted set up the server root. This is a directory that only the administrator can access.

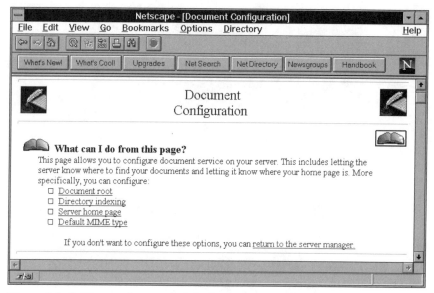

Figure 5-3: Setting up document defaults.

Ted also used this screen to name the server home page. If he didn't specify a name, the home page would be a file called index.html that resided in the document root. Whether he used the default name of index.html or assigned a different name, Ted had to create an HTML document of that name to serve as the intranet's home page.

> ### Note
> To specify the name of the default document in a web server directory, use the appropriate configuration setting. This parameter is usually called DirectoryIndex, or something similar. Many web servers use index.html (or index.htm, depending on the operating system) as the default.
>
> The ability of the web server to use a default document allows you to code a link to a home page by just referring to the server name. Thus, http://www.acme.com refers to the default document in the root directory of the Acme company's web server.

Remapping Directories

When Ted set up the Netscape Communications Server document configuration, he specified the document root directory. At this point, the Netscape server could only serve documents from the root directory or directories below the document root.

The web server has to know all the directories containing intranet documents so that it can apply global security rules to documents. Ted wanted access to documents stored in directories outside of the document root, so he used directory remapping to configure this.

Figure 5-4 shows the screen that is used to add a directory to the document path. This is used for two purposes. First, it allowed Ted to point to directories outside of the document root and even gave those directories an alias. Second, some web software requires that you map to a directory outside the normal document tree. The discussion-group software that Ted installed required this kind of mapping.

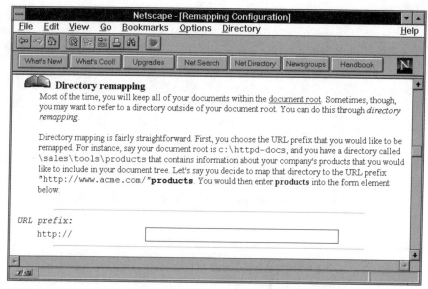

Figure 5-4: Mapping to a directory outside of the document tree.

Setting Up Security

Figure 5-5 shows the options Ted had in setting up access controls. He could limit access to directories or documents by IP address, by name and password, or by referencing document-access rules stored in each directory.

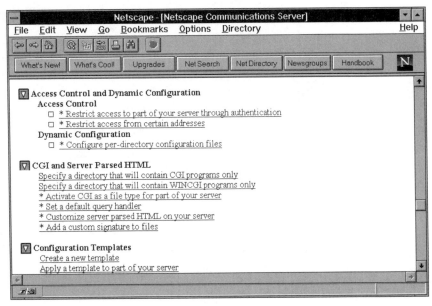

Figure 5-5: The web server security options.

Ted chose the option to restrict access through user ID and password, which brought up the dialog box shown in Figure 5-6. Ted could use this screen to require user authentication for the entire server, for selected files, for files determined by a wildcard, or for a file pattern contained in a template. If Ted wanted to set up authentication for the intranet, he'd have to build a database of valid usernames and passwords.

Figure 5-6: Setting up user authentication.

Web Servers on a Shoestring

There are full-featured, low-cost web servers for any computing
platform. Let's take a look at example web servers for UNIX,
Windows NT, the Mac, and Windows 95.

Popular Web Servers

The WebCrawler search engine keeps tabs on the host computers on
the World Wide Web and constantly updates a couple of pie charts
showing which platforms and which web servers are being used.

Figure 5-7 shows how World Wide Web servers are divided by platform. This chart shows that a little over 84 percent of WWW servers are running on a UNIX platform, almost 7 percent are on Windows NT, and nearly 5 percent are on Mac servers. These statistics show the Web servers that stand up to heavy Internet hit counts, and are used to handle companies critical WWW online communications with customers.

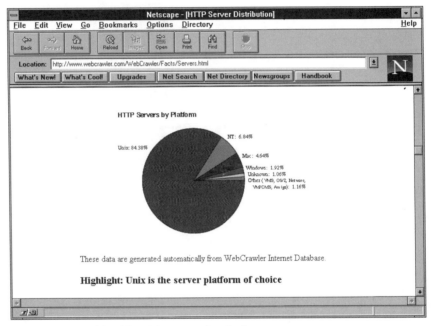

Figure 5-7: World Wide Web servers by platform.

Figure 5-8 shows World Wide Web servers by the Web server software used. Over 70 percent of the WWW servers in use today are free Web servers! The NCSA server is used at 26 percent of the sites. You can also use freeware servers for your internal web.

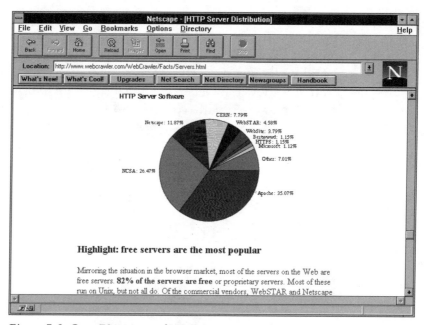

Figure 5-8: Over 70 percent of WWW servers are freeware.

You can view the latest versions of these pie charts at http://
www.webcrawler.com/WebCrawler/Facts/Servers.html. The
WebCrawler search engine can be found at http://
www.webcrawler.com.

UNIX Web Server

Two of the case studies we looked at in the opening chapter,
Boeing and Eli Lilly, started their intranets with freeware servers
from the National Center for Supercomputer Applications
(NCSA).

The NCSA web server has a lot of the features that we talked
about when we discussed the server selection criteria. The proof
that it's still a popular server comes from some interesting statistics about the World Wide Web.

The NCSA server can secure web site documents by IP address,
domain name, an access file in individual directories, or user
authentication by user ID or user groups. It comes with a search

engine and can be set up to use the freeWAIS search software. The server can handle image maps.

To install the NCSA web server, you download it from an NCSA FTP site, and uncompress the files. Then you copy files to the correct directories and edit configuration, resource, and access files.

See the NCSA web server documentation (http://hoohoo.ncsa.uiuc.edu/docs/Overview.html) for more information.

Figure 5-9 shows the table of contents for the online installation instructions for the NCSA server. This is a step-by-step guide to getting the server up and running. See the NCSA Web page (http://hoohoo.ncsa.uiuc.edu/) for more information.

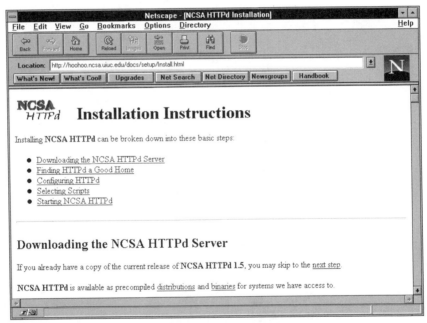

Figure 5-9: Online installation instructions for the NCSA web server.

Another popular web server for UNIX environments is the Apache server (http://www.apache.org/). The latest WebCrawler report shows that Apache servers are being used by 35 percent of WWW sites.

The Apache server runs on most UNIX variants. It provides security by IP address, domain name, and user group. It is a fast and robust server that is being used for a lot of World Wide Web sites.

Windows NT Web Server

We've already seen how Ted installed and configured the Netscape Communications Server for Windows NT. Netscape is replacing this product with the Netscape FastTrack Server. The FastTrack Server lists for $295 and comes with the Netscape Navigator Gold web browser and a GUI HTML-authoring tool. Navigator Gold comes with a nice set of web-page templates, a collection of web-page graphics, and a web-page generator.

The FastTrack Server is a full-featured web server on a shoestring. It's also available for numerous UNIX platforms.

For more information and to download an evaluation copy of Netscape FastTrack Server, visit the Netscape Web site (http://www.netscape.com/).

Microsoft has a web server for Windows NT called the Internet Information Server that is available for free. You can find out more about the Microsoft Internet Information Server at Microsoft's Web site (http://www.microsoft.com/).

Macintosh Web Server

MacHTTP was a shareware web server for the Macintosh that was acquired by StarNine Technology, Inc. It's now available in two versions.

MacHTTP is still a shareware product. You can register the software for $95. It comes with the MacTCP TCP/IP stack, has most security features, includes the AppleSearch search software, and supports image maps.

WebSTAR is an enhanced version of MacHTTP that includes more security options, adds GUI setup and maintenance, and allows more user connections. WebSTAR lists for $495.

You can get more information and download the shareware version of MacHTTP at the StarNine Technology Web site (http://www.starnine.com/).

Windows 95 Web Server

WebSite from O'Reilly & Associates is a full-featured web server that runs in both the Windows NT and Windows 95 platforms. It offers many security options including user groups, GUI setup and maintenance, and a search engine; it can also handle image maps.

O'Reilly offers two other products that can be useful for your intranet. WebBoard is a discussion-group product, and PolyForm is used to simplify the building and processing of HTML forms. The price for each was recently dropped to $149. Figure 5-10 shows the download screen for these products.

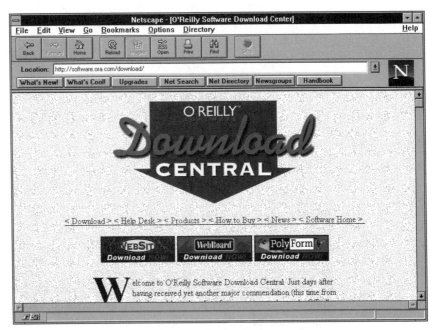

Figure 5-10: You can download WebSite and other products at http://software.ora.com/download/.

Great Resources for Web Server Information

We've only covered a few of the numerous web servers on the market. Fortunately there are some great sources of web server information on the World Wide Web.

Web Compare

There is an extensive comparison of web servers at a Web site called Web Compare. Figure 5-11 shows an example of the thorough comparison you'll find there. This list changes from month to month as Web Compare adds new software and deletes products that are no longer supported. The last time I visited this site, it compared 55 web servers.

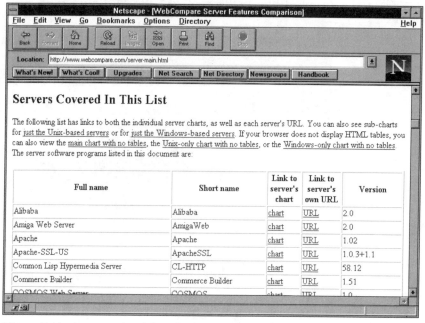

Figure 5-11: An example of the extensive web server comparison at http://www.webcompare.iworld.com/server-main.html.

Web Compare lists nearly 80 criteria for each server, including price when it's available. You can view the 80 criteria two ways: by each individual server or by all the servers that meet certain criteria. You can use this feature to find valuable information such as a list of servers that run on each platform or which web servers include search engines.

Yahoo!

The Yahoo! search software displays World Wide Web documents by category. Yahoo! has a category for web servers (http://www.yahoo.com/Computers_and_Internet/Internet/World_Wide_Web/HTTP/Servers/). Figure 5-12 shows the table of contents, which groups information by platform and other categories.

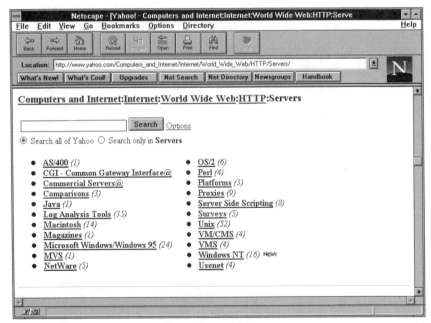

Figure 5-12: Web server information by platform at Yahoo!'s search site.

Web Server FAQ

An excellent source of web server information is the list of Frequently Asked Questions maintained by Thomas Boutell (http://www.boutell.com/faq/). Figure 5-13 shows some of the information at this site.

> ### *Note*
> A Frequently Asked Questions list (FAQ) is a format that has evolved for collecting useful tips and hints. It's often used by hardware and software vendors, online forums, or users' groups to display helpful information in a question-and-answer format. These types of lists are often intended to provide answers to questions heard frequently by support personnel.

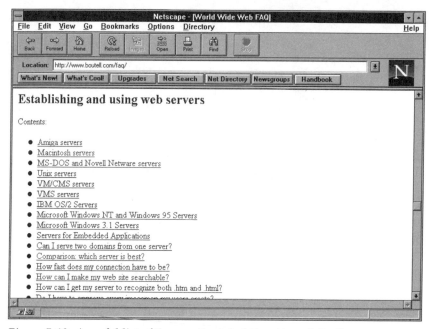

Figure 5-13: A useful list of Frequently Asked Questions (http://www.boutell.com/faq/).

Get the Support You Need

You can implement a web server on a shoestring for any platform. Just be sure to select software that will meet your needs.

I would recommend that, at a minimum, you find a web server that has adequate support. The installation instructions for one of the freeware packages available across the Internet lists six steps to install and configure the software. The sentence that follows the list reads something like: "To start the server, double-click on the icon in the program group. There is a chance that the server won't work. If that happens to you, contact the author at his e-mail address."

While some freeware web servers have good support, if your choice comes down to a freeware product that has questionable support and a commercial $300 package, spend the money. It's worth it.

Moving On

You've seen how to select and install the server side of an intranet. In the next chapter we're going to look at the client side of the system—web browsers.

There are a large number of web browsers on the market with a wide range of features. We'll look at this category of software in terms of how it helps you deliver the benefits of an intranet.

6

Selecting a Web Browser

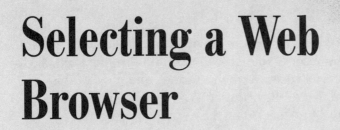

In some ways the web browser is the most important component of your intranet. To your users it *is* the intranet. It determines how they see the information and what they can do with it.

This chapter looks at web browsers in terms of what they do for your intranet users and what value they add to your internal web. You'll learn what to look for in a browser and how to compare the products that are on the market. You'll also discover some good sources of online information about web browsers.

The web browser you select will determine what your users can get out of your intranet. It's an important decision, but this chapter will help you make that decision.

Aren't They All Alike?

A browser is software that reads simple HTML codes and uses those codes to format a document. In the early days of the World Wide Web, browsers were all pretty much the same. They followed the same HTML standards and offered a few minor variations.

So why did Eli Lilly and Boeing switch from freeware browsers to commercial browsers? You'll recall that Eli Lilly spent $80,000 to connect the first 3,000 users to their intranet; and most of this expense was the cost of the browser. Why would companies spend money on a browser when they can get one for free?

These companies switched to a commercial browser because it offered significantly enhanced features. There's a somewhat controversial history behind this. Let's take a look.

Going Beyond the Standards

Committees have maintained HTML standards since their development. These committees draft proposed changes, put them out for review, then issue a revised standard. The standard determines what HTML codes are allowed and therefore limit how Internet and intranet documents can be formatted. This determines how your users will see the information.

Document Formatting in Standard HTML

The initial standard and the HTML 1.0 revision really didn't allow for much formatting in documents. Besides the body text, you could have headings, bullets, numbered lists, and indentation. It was enough to get by, but it was hard to make documents look like their printed counterparts.

HTML 2.0 added inline graphics and interactive forms. These were significant improvements, but still didn't do much for document formatting. Netscape changed that.

The Netscape Extensions

Because a browser simply reads and interprets the HTML codes, there is nothing to prevent a company from adding codes that go beyond the HTML standard, then programming the browser to interpret and act on those codes. That's exactly what Netscape did.

Netscape's web browser, called Navigator, supported the existing HTML codes, but added new capabilities—in effect creating a superset of the HTML standards.

Netscape gave web-page designers the capability to center text, divide sections of documents with horizontal rule lines, add numbers or differently shaped bullets to lists, and change font size.

For graphics, Netscape added the ability to have a colored background, to use a graphic image as a background, and to wrap text around graphics. They also added new ways to align and format graphic images.

The codes that Netscape added to HTML are typically referred to as the Netscape extensions. For the most part, these extensions give developers more control over document appearance. They make it possible for documents viewed through a browser to look more like the typical paper documents that users see in their daily work processes.

Figure 6-1 shows a page from the Netscape Web site that makes use of several Netscape extensions to the HTML standards.

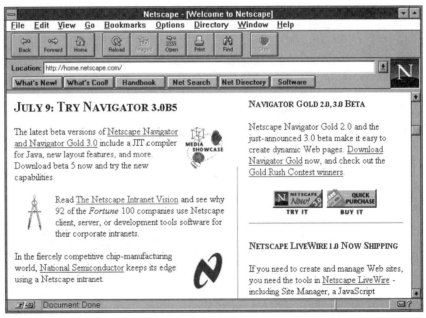

Figure 6-1: A Web page that uses several Netscape extensions to the HTML standard.

In Figure 6-1, text wraps around graphics. Sometimes the graphic image is aligned on the right, sometimes on the left. The page contains both a horizontal and a vertical rule line.

The page also makes subtle use of fonts. Notice that in the three headlines on the page, the first letter of each word is in a larger font than the remaining letters in the word. This is done by changing the font tag at the start of each word, then changing it again before the second letter of the word.

The next release of Netscape Navigator, version 2.0, added another significant extension to HTML—the ability to display information in multiple frames. Figure 6-2 shows how frames might be used in an intranet.

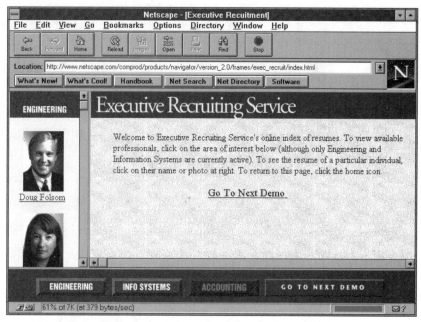

Figure 6-2: Using HTML frames in an intranet.

This example, from Netscape's Web site, is a page for a fictitious recruiting service. It divides the screen into three frames. On the bottom is a button bar that lets users pick the category of employee they're looking for. Clicking on one of the buttons changes the document that's displayed in the left side of the screen. Clicking on a hyperlink for an individual retrieves that person's resume and displays it in the center frame on the screen.

The frames operate independently. Users can scroll through a resume or the list of candidates without affecting the other frames. The frame across the bottom keeps the navigation buttons on the screen at all times, no matter how you scroll the other information.

This is a powerful feature and a good choice for some applications. It cuts down on the amount of navigation users have to do between documents. It also lets users keep vital information, such as a navigation bar, on the screen while other information changes.

The net effect of these extensions is a document that is easier to use and easier to read. Netscape extensions became popular because they allowed developers to create online documents that looked more like the real thing. This is one reason why Eli Lilly, Boeing, and other companies have moved away from freeware browsers and invested in commercial software.

So what happens when someone uses a browser that strictly adheres to the official HTML standards and does not allow the Netscape extensions?

When Standards Collide

Figure 6-3 shows another page at the Netscape Web site. This page uses Netscape extensions to align hyperlinked text into groups. Let's see what happens when you use a browser that doesn't have these extensions.

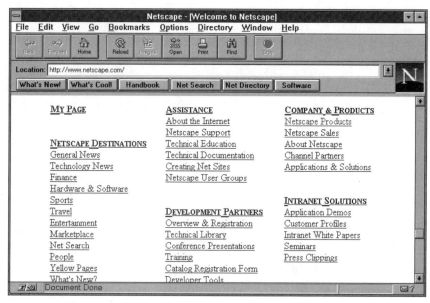

Figure 6-3: Using Netscape extensions to create groups of hyperlinks.

Figure 6-4 shows the same screen that Figure 6-3 does, only this time it's viewed through an older version of a web browser called WebSurfer. This version of WebSurfer doesn't support the Netscape text alignment extensions. All of the text is displayed flush left, and you lose the ability to have multiple groups of hyperlinks on the screen at the same time.

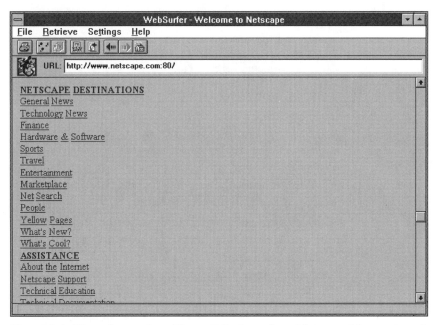

Figure 6-4: The web page from Figure 6-3 when viewed from an older version of a browser that doesn't have the Netscape extensions.

The difference becomes more dramatic as web pages use a mix of extensions. The document in Figure 6-1 would not only lose its newsletter appearance when seen with a browser without extensions, it would also become unattractive and difficult to read.

HTML Extensions & Your Intranet

The HTML extensions allow more control over the appearance of intranet documents, giving you the ability to format data to look like typical business documents. One criteria to use when selecting a web browser is how much it supports the extensions to the HTML standards.

There was a time when few browsers supported the HTML extensions. Now software companies are updating their browsers rapidly. You still want to confirm that the browser you select will handle the more popular extensions to HTML, but this is less of a problem than it once was.

Adding Functions With Plug-ins

Another innovation Netscape brought to Web browsers was the plug-in concept. A plug-in is some piece of software that extends the behavior of a browser.

When a browser without a plug-in encounters a reference to a video in a web page, it looks for software called a helper app and, if it finds it, hands control over to that program. A separate window opens and obscures the browser. This disrupts the natural flow of processing.

With a video player plug-in, the video is played inline, right inside of the browser window itself. The video appears to be a seamless part of the intranet information. The plug-in extends the native capability of the browser to functions it couldn't normally handle.

Examples of plug-ins include a spreadsheet program that puts a working spreadsheet inside of a web page, and plug-ins that can display word processing documents and other file types in their native format. There are over 50 plug-ins available for Netscape Navigator.

Plug-ins are a way to add value to your intranet. We'll discuss this technology in detail in Chapter 13.

Web Browsers & Programming Languages

In the initial design of web technology, the web browser was an inactive partner. Any processing was done on the server. The browser merely interpreted and displayed the HTML documents.

This was true even for data entry forms. The web browser accepted input and sent that input back to the server, but didn't process the data on the client.

This arrangement causes problems in some situations. You might have a data entry form that requires validation. Since the web browser can't do any processing, the validation is done on the server. This might cause a tedious cycle of submitting the data, correcting errors, submitting the data, and so on. You wouldn't know the input was incorrect until after it hit the server.

Another situation where the lack of client processing causes a problem is when you want something to be dynamically displayed in the browser. Say you have a web page that displays a loan payment after the user types in the loan amount, number of months, and interest rate. If the web browser has no processing capability, the input has to be sent to the server, the loan payment has to be calculated by the server, and the result sent back to the browser. This is a lot of overhead to display one number.

Java

Sun Microsystems, Inc. changed the dynamics of web technology. They introduced a programming language called Java. A Java program is called an applet.

Java applets are handled like graphic images. When a web browser encounters a reference to an image in a web page, it retrieves that image and adds it to the document. When a browser encounters a reference to a Java applet, it retrieves that program from the server and runs the program as part of the document.

A Java program can validate input, dynamically display information, run animation, and perform other tasks on the client.

JavaScript

Netscape Navigator 2.0 supports Java applets. Netscape also added a new programming language with Navigator 2.0 called JavaScript.

JavaScript is a much simpler language than Java and is also less powerful. But it has the capability to do client-side processing like validation and dynamic display. JavaScript is designed to carry out simple client-side processing without requiring a steep learning curve.

Let's look at an example. Figure 6-5 is another example from Netscape's Web site. This one shows how JavaScript makes the web browser interactive.

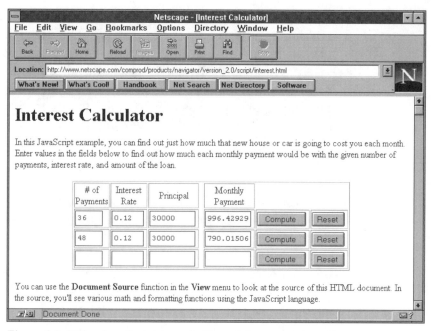

Figure 6-5: Using JavaScript to make the web browser interactive.

The Web page in the example includes a calculator that computes a loan payment given the details of the loan. Users can enter up to three scenarios and compare monthly payments. When they click on Compute, the browser doesn't send the input back to the server for processing. A JavaScript program runs on the client to calculate the loan payment and displays the result in the appropriate area.

What Does This Do for You?

Client-side processing is another feature that you can offer your intranet users. Even if you don't take advantage of this capability in the first iteration of your internal web, you should consider this feature when you select a web browser. You might have a need for it in the future, and you can avoid changing software if you plan ahead.

We'll compare web browsers in a bit. Before we do that, let's see how Ted selected a web browser and then see what the product he selected offers his intranet users.

Example: Selecting a Web Browser

In our plastics company example, Ted compared some of the web browsers on the market, then selected Netscape Navigator for the plastics company's intranet. Ted's decision was based primarily on three factors: cross-platform capability, HTML extensions, and plug-ins. Ted also liked the look and feel of Netscape Navigator, not to mention its performance.

Cross-Platform Capability

The plastics company has a mix of platforms. The dominant desktop operating system is Microsoft Windows, but there are some engineers with UNIX workstations and some graphic designers who use Macs. Navigator runs on all three platforms.

HTML Extensions

When Ted selected a browser, Netscape had the lead in introducing HTML extensions. Ted knew he was going to convert newsletters and other documents to the intranet, and wanted the ability to make the information look as much like the originals as possible. He liked the fact that Netscape continually added HTML extensions that gave him more control over document appearance.

Plug-ins

Ted had an application for at least two Netscape Navigator plug-ins. The first was for engineers who use Autodesk's AutoCAD for their drawings. Autodesk created a Netscape plug-in called WHIP! that enabled the browser to display and manipulate AutoCAD drawings. Ted knew this plug-in would allow corporate-based engineers to use the intranet to share drawings with their counterparts at each facility.

The other application for a plug-in was for the sales department. They wanted to use the intranet to display product labels. The marketing department could convert scanned labels into the Adobe Portable Document Format (PDF) so that they could be displayed by Adobe's Acrobat Reader. Adobe recently introduced a plug-in called Amber. This plug-in on the intranet would allow sales partners to view the labels using the browser without having to launch a separate program.

Installing Netscape Navigator

Installing Navigator was easy. When Ted was evaluating the product, he downloaded the self-extracting file from Netscape's Web site. Then he extracted the programs and ran setup.exe. The program walked him through the installation.

Comparing Browsers

So far we've only covered Netscape's web browser. At one time, Netscape had over 80 percent of the web-browser market, according to some estimates. Netscape took the lead in introducing HTML extensions and innovations like browser plug-ins and programming language support. That's why many companies that started out using freeware browsers purchased Netscape Navigator for their intranet clients.

Other companies, however, are starting to catch up with Netscape. This is particularly true of Microsoft, whose Microsoft Internet Explorer web browser has many of the same features as Netscape Navigator. Microsoft stirred up the browser market by offering Internet Explorer as a completely free product. It's not shareware or evaluation software—it's free.

At one time, your web browser choice was straightforward. If you wanted the latest features, you bought Netscape Navigator. Now the choice isn't as clear.

Netscape Navigator vs. Microsoft Internet Explorer

Microsoft recently released the latest version of Internet Explorer 3.0. Internet Explorer now supports most of the Netscape HTML extensions and offers a few extensions of its own.

Microsoft countered Netscape's plug-ins by including ActiveX in the latest version of Internet Explorer. ActiveX is Microsoft's new name for Object Linking & Embedding (OLE). Just as Netscape plug-ins extend the capabilities of the Navigator browser, ActiveX objects extend the functionality of Internet Explorer. The latest version of Internet Explorer also adds Java and JavaScript capabilities.

The latest release of Internet Explorer is currently only available for Windows 95 and Windows NT, while Navigator runs on Windows, Mac, and UNIX systems. This gives Netscape an edge for companies that have Macintosh and UNIX workstations among their computing platforms.

Netscape also still seems to have the edge based on its lead in third-party support and the maturity of the Navigator technology. This lead is getting thinner, however.

To download an evaluation copy of Netscape Navigator, visit the Netscape Web site (http://www.netscape.com/). To get a free copy of Microsoft Explorer, visit their Web site (http://www.microsoft.com/).

Internet Explorer: Browser on a Shoestring?

Microsoft's Internet Explorer would seem to be the ideal browser if you're building an intranet on a shoestring. With the latest release, 3.0, Internet Explorer seems to have caught up with Netscape Navigator—and Internet Explorer is free.

At the time of this writing, Internet Explorer is only available for Window 95 and Windows NT. This means that it's not a free browser for corporations that use Windows 3.1 desktops. Those companies would have to upgrade the operating system to take advantage of the "free" browser. Companies with a mix of Windows platforms along with Mac and UNIX workstations will need multiple browsers if they want to use Internet Explorer on their Windows desktops.

Microsoft has announced plans to port Internet Explorer to other platforms, but until that happens, choosing between Internet Explorer and other browsers is not an easy decision for many companies.

Other Browsers

The battle between Netscape and Microsoft is getting a lot of attention, but those are not the only browsers on the market. There are over 60 browsers available for various platforms.

The following are a few browsers that run on multiple platforms:

○ **GNNpress** supports many of the HTML extensions and is available for the Windows, Mac, and UNIX platforms. GNNpress is free. For more information on GNNpress, see the GNNpress' Web page (http://www.tools.gnn.com/press/index.html).

○ **Spyglass Mosaic** is a commercial browser available for Windows, Macintosh, and UNIX systems. It also supports many of the HTML extensions. To download an evaluation copy or to get more information, visit Spyglass Mosaic's Web site (http://www.spyglass.com/).

○ **NCSA Mosaic** is a multiplatform freeware browser available from the University of Illinois at Urbana-Champaign. To find out more about this product or to download a copy, visit NCSA's Web site (http://www.ncsa.uiuc.edu/).

Browser Selection Criteria

Selecting a browser really comes down to answering two questions: What platforms will you have to support? and What capabilities do you want to offer to your users? You can use the following criteria to see how browsers meet your requirements for platforms and user capabilities.

Platform

If you have a mix of computing platforms, you may want to use the same browsers across the various systems. This minimizes the training and support for the browsers. It also allows you to avoid the problems that can occur if your company uses browsers with different HTML capabilities.

HTML Extensions

You'll want as much control over the appearance of intranet documents as you can get. This means you need a browser that supports many, if not all, of the HTML extensions.

The features that a browser supports affect the way intranet documents can be created. For example, if a browser does not have the ability to align text, content creators won't be able to create documents that look like multiple column newsletters.

If your company wants to use the intranet to display simple text, this may not be as big of a factor to you. You might be able to select any browser that runs on your platforms. The tradeoff here, however, is that you might outgrow the browser as the company gets more sophisticated about formatting web pages.

Standard Features

The built-in features of web browsers vary greatly from product to product. You'll want a web browser that prints documents and saves them to disk. You'll also want a browser that gives users some way to bookmark valuable intranet pages so that they can return to them with a single click.

Some web browsers keep a running list of the pages a user has visited. This lets a user review the hierarchy of information and skip intermediate levels when returning to an upper level of the intranet.

You'll want to choose a browser whose features give intranet clients both a lot of control over navigation and the ability to manipulate intranet information.

Add-in Products

A web browser with the ability to support third-party add-ins, such as the Netscape plug-ins or Microsoft ActiveX objects, extends the functionality of your intranet. You should consider this technology when selecting a browser.

There are browser add-ons that let you display spreadsheets and reports in their original formats, without conversion to HTML. There are other add-ons that handle specialized functions, such as engineering drawings. You'll see more about this in Chapter 13.

Web Programming Languages

Java and JavaScript give you the capability of adding interactive processing to your intranet. You might not take advantage of this technology in the early stages of your intranet, but selecting a browser that supports client-side programs gives you the ability to extend the capabilities of your intranet clients in the future.

Ease-of-Use

Browsers' interfaces vary greatly. Play around with the features of the web browsers you evaluate to get a feel for how intuitive they are.

Do your employees already connect to the Internet? If so, they already have web browsers (ones they really like, too). Consider the software that's already being used when making your decision.

Web Browser on a Shoestring

When you build a low-cost intranet, you'll want a web browser that keeps the cost down, but still provides the features you need. Where there was once a wide difference in the features browsers offered, this gap is closing. Select a browser for your intranet that balances cost with the capabilities you can give your users.

Remember, the browser is the user's only window into the intranet. Keep the cost of your intranet reasonable, but don't focus on price alone. Here are a few things to consider.

Per Client or Total?

A single copy of a web browser is a relatively inexpensive piece of software. Netscape Navigator lists for $49, but the street price is less than that. Site licenses reduce the per unit cost even more.

In my opinion, price alone isn't enough to drive the browser decision *on a per user basis*. Navigator provides a lot of functionality for the price, as do other commercial browsers.

The problem is how the browser cost affects the total cost of your intranet. If you roll your intranet out to thousands of users, the total amount spent on the browser will add up to a significant expense.

You'll recall that Eli Lilly's initial intranet expense of $80,000 was almost entirely due to the browser cost. This worked out to a per user cost of $27. Is this a shoestring or not? It depends on how you view the costs to implement computer technology.

You Have a Choice

There was a time when your decision would be to either purchase Netscape Navigator or go without some features. Microsoft Explorer has changed that. You can now add a full-featured browser to your intranet for free. Some of the other browsers have added many of the Netscape features as well.

Your Goal

Your goal when selecting a web browser is to keep the costs down while delivering the full benefits of an intranet. You'll want to select a browser that offers the features and the interface that lets your users get the most out of your internal web.

Selecting a browser can be a difficult decision. I recommend that you get a free copy of Microsoft Internet Explorer, an evaluation copy of Netscape Navigator, and maybe a couple of other browsers. Select a group of evaluators, then have them explore the World Wide Web with the different products.

Make sure that your evaluators visit a number of different Web sites to learn how the browser formats the display and how easy it is to navigate using each product. Generally, you want them to get a feel for the software's ease of use and utility.

Gather feedback on the browsers you test and use this as one of your selection criteria. The browser you select will have a significant impact on how users accept your intranet. Take the time to make an informed decision.

Resources for More Information

Web browsers are moving targets. Netscape and Microsoft continue to compete by adding new features to their products. Other vendors are trying to keep up by enhancing their software.

Fortunately there are sources on the World Wide Web that you can use to track the web browser market.

BrowserWatch

There is a Web site called BrowserWatch that follows developments in the browser market. Figure 6-6 shows the BrowserWatch home page (http://browserwatch.iworld.com/).

Figure 6-6: BrowserWatch is a good source of information on web browsers.

BrowserWatch has an archive of browser news stories, a list of plug-ins, and a list of browsers. Figure 6-7 shows a sample of their browser list.

The BrowserWatch list contains almost 70 browsers. It shows you what platforms the browsers run on and gives hyperlinks to the sites where you can download a particular browser or get more information.

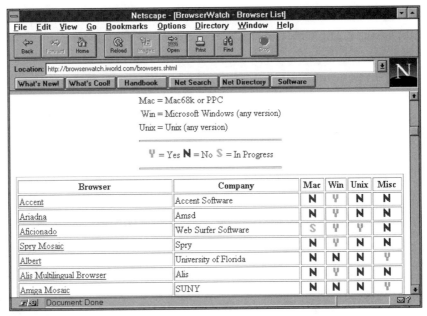

Figure 6-7: Browser Watch maintains a list of web browsers.

webreference.com

Another excellent source of information on web browsers is a Web site called webreference.com. Figure 6-8 shows the browser page at the this site.

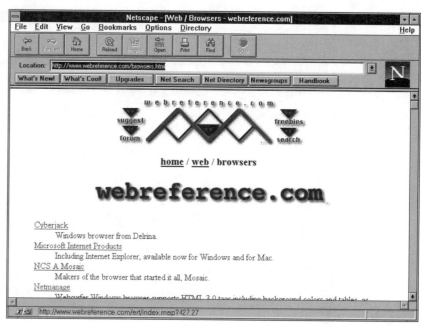

Figure 6-8: webreference.com is another good source of web browser information.

The webreference.com site has an extensive list of hyperlinks to sources of information on browsers. There are links to comparisons of browsers, plug-in lists, and there's even a link to a Web site that shows examples of the same HTML document when viewed by different browsers.

For more information, check out the webreference.com browser page (http://www.webreference.com/browsers.html).

Others

Yahoo! has an extensive collection of hyperlinks to browser information (http://www.yahoo.com/Computers_and_Internet/ Internet/World_Wide_Web/Browsers/).

Web Compare maintains a comparison of web browsers at its Web site (http://www.webcompare.com/). This list is not as comprehensive as their web server comparison, but it does group browsers by feature.

Moving On

Now you've assembled the components you need to build your intranet. The component covered in this chapter, the web browser, is the software that determines how employees see and work with the intranet. It's very important to select a browser that offers the features that unlock the potential of the intranet.

The next chapter shows you how to create intranet documents. You'll learn how to convert existing information to web pages and how to build an intranet document from scratch. I'll show you some software that simplifies the process of turning company information into live, clickable intranet documents.

SECTION 3

Sharing Your Information—Putting It in the Intranet

The last few chapters showed you how to build your intranet. Now it's time to reap the benefits of the technology. Chapter 7 through 10 walk you through the process of turning your company's information into live, clickable intranet documents.

Chapter 7 shows you how to use free or inexpensive software to convert existing information into intranet web pages. You also learn how to enhance the value of existing documents using the features of HTML.

In Chapter 8 you learn how to use web page graphics to make intranet documents more attractive and to make navigation easier.

Chapter 9 covers intranet forms. You learn how intranet forms allow you to automate work processes across the organization.

You don't have to design each intranet document from scratch. Chapter 10 introduces the concept of web-page templates. You learn how to use templates to speed the development of your intranet content.

When you finish this section of the book, you'll be able to start moving information into your internal web. You will be able to build the information structure that can provide the business benefits this promising technology can deliver.

A Quick & Easy Intranet

Just click. That was the headline of a recent article about intranets. The technology has generated a lot of excitement because it makes it possible for your users to navigate through your company's information with simple mouseclicks.

The big benefits of an intranet come from the ability to create live, clickable documents—documents that guide users to related information.

Most companies start building their intranets by converting existing information to web-page documents, then enhancing these online documents with the features of web technology. Some companies reap significant business benefits just from converting a few of their key documents to an intranet. The benefits include:

○ Dollar savings gained from eliminating the cost of printed information.

○ Productivity gains realized from making information easy to find and navigate.

○ Workgroup collaboration enhanced by the ability to link information across teams.

Example: Converting Documents to HTML

This chapter shows you the steps Ted took to convert documents to the plastics company's intranet. We'll show you how today's software can make this process easy—and inexpensive.

Converting the Newsletter

You'll recall that production managers at the plastics company wanted to implement a concept called best practices. They wanted employees at their plants to share ideas and learn from the experiences of other locations.

They tried to use a printed newsletter to accomplish this, but it was difficult to find the information they wanted from copies in multiple locations and from different months. One of Ted's goals for the intranet was to take the newsletters and turn them into an online goldmine of information.

Selecting the Conversion Software

The plant newsletters are written using Microsoft Word. Ted wanted to find software that would make the conversion from the native Word format easy. He also wanted a product that could be used by the newsletter authors at each location. He wanted the people who created the information to be able to do the conversion themselves.

Microsoft makes a free add-on product that converts Word documents to HTML-based web pages. This product is called Microsoft Word Internet Assistant . Ted experimented with the software and decided it could do the job. He liked the way the product became an integrated part of Word, providing a similar look and feel.

Converting Existing Newsletters

The first task for Ted was to convert the existing issues of the newsletter. Let's walk through the process.

> **TIP**
>
> The examples used throughout the book are for a fictitious company called KLP Industries. They are not the plastics company's real documents, but are representative of the real thing.

Figure 7-1 shows a newsletter in Microsoft Word before the conversion. This issue of the plant newsletter starts with a story about a problem that at least one facility is having with new equipment. This brief news item explains the basics of the problem and references other information.

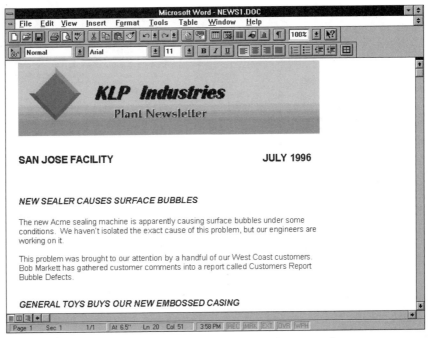

Figure 7-1: A newsletter in Microsoft Word before the conversion to an intranet document.

You can probably see the potential for at least one enhancement to the newsletter. When it's converted to the intranet, references to other information can be turned into a live hyperlink. This allows the reader to immediately follow up on the reference with a single mouseclick.

The first step in the conversion is to save the Word file as an HTML document. This is done by choosing a new option to the Save As dialog box that appears when Internet Assistant is added to Word. The dialog box is shown in Figure 7-2.

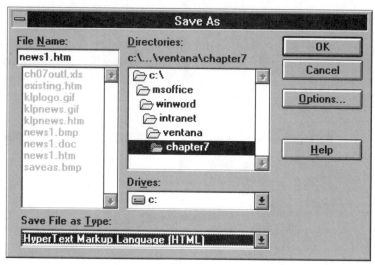

Figure 7-2: The Word File | Save menu now includes the ability to save to HTML.

When the newsletter is saved as an HTML document in this version of Internet Assistant, it loses some of its formatting— including the graphic. The converted file appears in Figure 7-3.

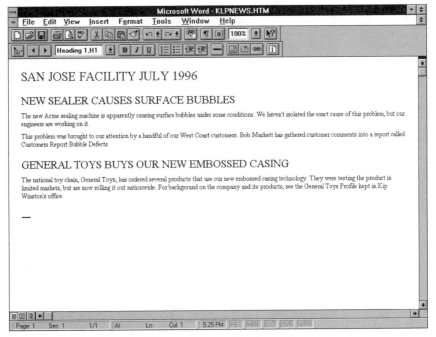

Figure 7-3: The converted file loses some of its formatting.

Note that the button bars at the top of the Word screen have changed. When you save a document as HTML, Word will automatically invoke Internet Assistant. The headings from the Word document are converted into HTML headings. One benefit of Internet Assistant is that you can tie HTML styles to Word styles. This makes the conversion process easier and allows you to do more formatting in Word.

In Figure 7-4, the graphic is brought back into Internet Assistant in order to add intranet enhancements to the document.

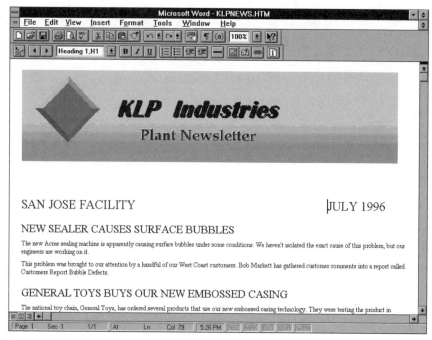

Figure 7-4: The document after the graphic image has been restored.

Adding Hyperlinks to the Newsletter

The newsletter also references a report on the customer complaints about the newly discovered defect. Let's create a hyperlink to the referenced information.

You want first to turn the name of the referenced report into the link. Drag the mouse over the text to highlight it, then click on the link symbol on the toolbar—it's at the right end of the lower bar. This brings up the HyperLink dialog box seen in Figure 7-5.

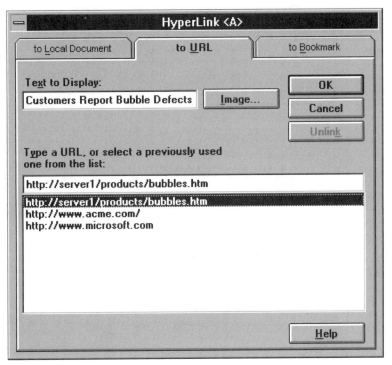

Figure 7-5: Creating a hyperlink in Internet Assistant.

Internet Assistant keeps track of the URLs you've used for previous hyperlinks. You can access the scrolling list to quickly pick a location.

Figure 7-6 shows the document in Internet Assistant after two hyperlinks have been set up. The second link points to the profile of a customer mentioned in the second news item.

Build an Intranet on a Shoestring

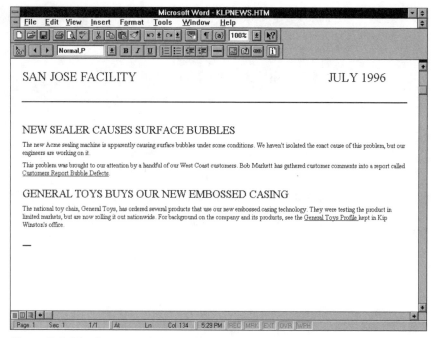

Figure 7-6: The document in Internet Assistant now has two hyperlinks.

Internet Assistant includes numerous features that simplify the placement of HTML codes. In Figure 7-7, we've added a bulleted list to our document. The List dialog box allows you to change the shape of the bullets—here they've been changed to diamonds.

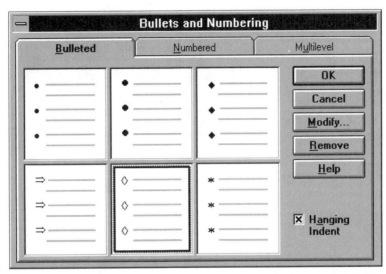

Figure 7-7: One of the Internet Assistant dialog boxes that simplify HTML coding.

Notice that the items in the list in Figure 7-7 are hyperlinks. You've now added five links to this document, each pointing to relevant and useful information. With a few mouseclicks, you've converted a static newsletter to a living document that can retrieve related information.

To get more information about Internet Assistant or to download a free copy of the product, visit Microsoft's Web site (http://www.microsoft.com/).

The Newsletter in a Browser

Figure 7-8 shows the converted newsletter as it appears in Netscape Navigator. This issue of the plant newsletter is now part of the company's online library of information.

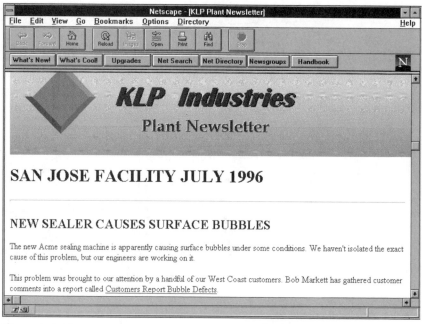

Figure 7-8: The converted newsletter as seen through Netscape Navigator.

Converting Company Policies

Ted knew that for many companies, some of the most ordinary intranet applications yielded the big paybacks. A lot of companies start by putting HR manuals on their internal webs. These documents get distributed to every employee, need to be updated at least partially several times a year, and are costly to print, distribute, and maintain.

With an intranet, you put one electronic copy online and let your employees access it when they want to. Some organizations have reported large dollar savings from this one application alone.

The plastics company has several hundred people who are involved with products in one way or another. Each of these employees gets a copy of the company's policy on product incident tracking. The policy is a long document containing information that requires frequent revision.

Ted wanted to convert company policies to the intranet wherever possible, and he decided to start with the product incident policy.

Selecting Software to Convert Policies

Ted and the intranet team were in charge of converting the company policies themselves. They wanted an HTML editor that offered more features than Internet Assistant. Ted brought in an evaluation copy of a product called HoTMetaL, from SoftQuad.

After evaluating HoTMetaL, the team decided it would be a good candidate for building the initial intranet content. The software lets you click to format web pages, but still shows you the coding behind your selection. This helps you learn how HTML works without having to code everything by hand.

The Product Incident Policy

Figure 7-9 shows the product incident policy before conversion. The document opens by explaining the purpose of the guidelines, then lists the sections of information available. One enhancement Ted wanted to add was the ability to jump right to a section within the same document—much like the capability Dr. Afrin added to the online version of the Hollings Cancer Institute's protocol documents.

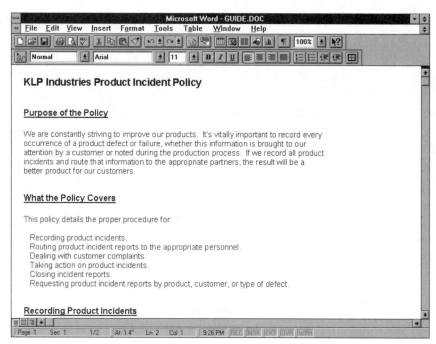

Figure 7-9: The product incident policy before the conversion.

The Policy in HoTMetaL

Ted copied the policy into HoTMetaL, where it was basically a long string of undocumented text. He used the software to add a few simple codes that split the text into paragraphs and converted the list of sections into an HTML list. The result is shown in Figure 7-10.

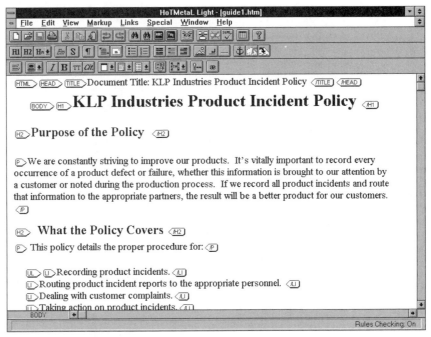

Figure 7-10: The policy in HoTMetaL with some simple coding.

You indicate the HTML formatting you want by highlighting text, then clicking on the appropriate icon. HoTMetaL displays the resulting HTML codes as graphical tags. You don't enter these codes manually, but you can still see what codes are used to carry out the formatting you want.

You can turn off the option to display the codes if you want.

Creating a Live Table of Contents

The next thing Ted wanted to do was enable the user to jump from the table of contents near the top of the document right to the referenced information. He did this by coding a link that references some location in the same file.

To accomplish this linking within the document, you highlight the destination and bring up the dialog box shown in Figure 7-11. This dialog box is invoked by clicking on the last icon in the middle toolbar. The icon shows an arrow linking two sections of a document.

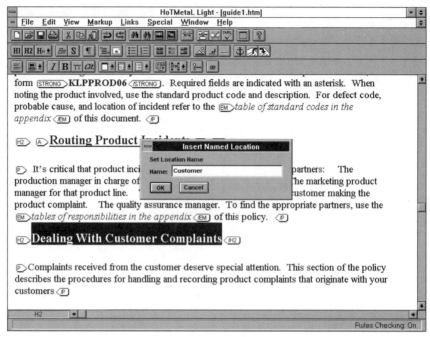

Figure 7-11: Creating a named location in a document using HoTMetaL.

To jump to a section of a document, you have to name the destination. The dialog box takes the first word from the highlighted text as the name by default, but you can enter a different name. In this case, "Customer" was entered as the name instead of "Dealing."

The next step is to highlight the text the user will click on to jump to the destination. You want each line of the table of contents to point to the named destination matching the content. In Figure 7-12, the table of contents has been converted to a list of hyperlinks, each pointing to a named location in the same file. HoTMetaL shows you the name that each link points to.

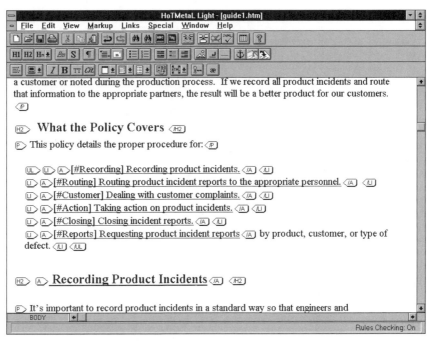

Figure 7-12: The table of contents is linked to the appropriate sections in the documents.

Let's take a look at how this works in the browser. Figure 7-13 shows the hyperlinked table of contents. Figure 7-14 shows what happens when you click on the Recording Product Incidents link. The browser takes you right to that section of the document.

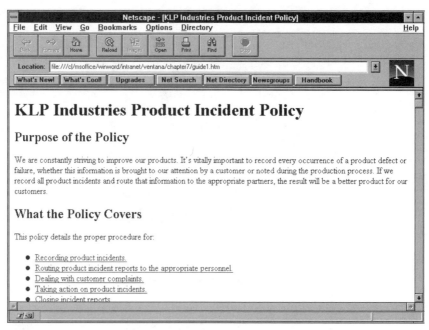

Figure 7-13: A hyperlinked table of contents.

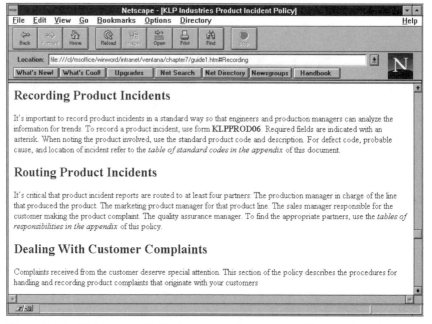

Figure 7-14: Clicking on a link takes you to the corresponding section of the document.

This simple technique allows you to take a long document and make it easy to read. Employees can jump directly to the appropriate information.

Linking to a Data Entry Form

The hard-copy policy guide refers the employee to a printed form by form number. The employee fills out the form manually, then sends it in to Quality Assurance, where someone keys the data from the form into a computer. When you implement an intranet, this double handling of the data is unnecessary. You use the intranet to automate this process.

We won't cover forms until Chapter 9, but we'll create the link now. To create the link to the form, you drag with the mouse to highlight the reference to the form, then click on the picture of an anchor. A hyperlink in a document is known as an anchor.

Figure 7-15 shows the Edit URL dialog box. You use a drop-down list to indicate the type of information you're linking to, which can be a local file, another web site, an FTP site, or other locations. During testing, you'll probably link to a local file. HoTMetaL has a Choose File button that lets you browse your hard disk to find the file.

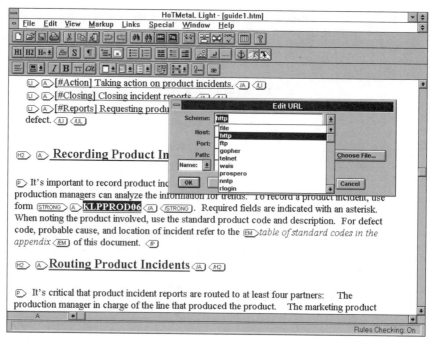

Figure 7-15: Creating a hyperlink in HoTMetaL.

Creating a Table

You'll notice that the italicized text in Figure 7-15 mentions a table of defect codes in the appendix of the document. HTML gives you the capability to create tables of text and numbers. HoTMetaL makes it easy to code.

To create the table to contain defect codes, move to the relevant spot in the document, then click on the picture of a table. A little dialog box pops up that asks how many rows and columns you want, then creates the table.

HoTMetaL offers a lot of ways to customize a table. Figure 7-16 shows some of the options. The table of defect codes is near the bottom of the screen. We've used the Markup menu to open several table formatting dialog boxes. Near the top of the screen is a dialog box that offers options to format a cell or a row or to change the whole table. To the right of the menu is the Edit Table dialog box and at the bottom is a dialog box that lets you align the text in the rows.

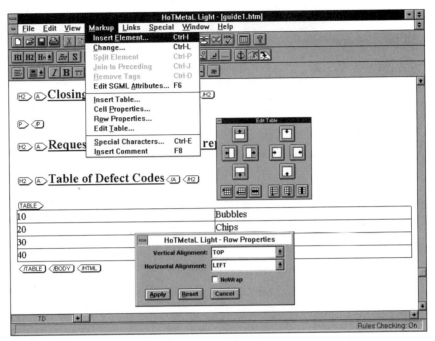

Figure 7-16: Table formatting options in HoTMetaL.

The table alignment options are HTML extensions. HoTMetaL lets you access HTML standards and Netscape extensions.

Coding HTML Extensions

Figure 7-17 shows the Insert Element dialog box. This screen lets you insert any HTML element, including HTML extensions like font size or blinking text.

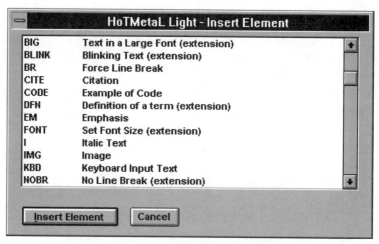

Figure 7-17: Inserting Netscape extensions using HoTMetaL.

Viewing the Extensions in Navigator

The browser screen in Figure 7-18 contains some of the HTML extensions we've coded into our policy document. We've changed the bullets of a list from the default circles to squares, added an enhanced horizontal line that's centered and wider than the default, and coded a table with a border and shading. We were able to use HoTMetaL to get some of the advanced features of HTML without having to code them by hand.

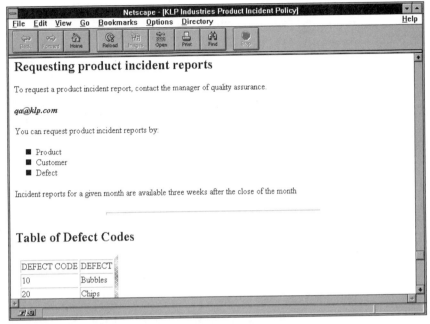

Figure 7-18: Viewing the HTML extensions in the browser.

Other HoTMetaL Features

HoTMetaL has a number of features that help an intranet developer. There's built-in spell checking, an outline view, macros, and an Undo button. There's a handy publish option, which lets you use local file references while you build and test documents, and then do a mass conversion of hyperlinks to a server name and directory when you want to store the document in production.

You can download the evaluation copy of HoTMetaL from SoftQuad's Web site (http://www.sq.com/). The current commercial version of HoTMetaL is $149. The Windows version of HoTMetaL has been available for some time, and at the time this was written, SoftQuad had just released the UNIX and Mac versions of the product.

Further Enhancements

In Chapter 8, we'll use web-page graphics to add navigation buttons to the product incident policy. We'll also use images to pretty it up a bit.

When we cover forms in Chapter 9, we'll add the ability to do the data entry for a product incident right in the intranet. At that point, we'll have taken the process a long way—from an expensive, manual process to an online point-and-click system.

HTML Tools of the Trade

When you build an intranet, you'll have to have some way of getting information into it. You could code everything from scratch, but typically it's a good idea to use conversion tools and HTML editors.

Conversion Tools

There's a product on the market for the Windows environment that can convert several documents into web pages at one time. The product is called HTML Transit, from a company called InfoAccess.

HTML Transit can convert files from many word-processor formats into HTML documents. It can convert a number of files at once in the background, and uses templates to determine how to translate files. You can set up the templates to insert navigation buttons, tables of contents, and indexes into the intranet pages it produces.

HTML Transit sells for $495. You can download an evaluation copy from the Web site (http://www.infoaccess.com).

HTML converters are available for all platforms. Most specialize in certain types of files. The World Wide Web is an excellent source for information on HTML converters.

Yahoo! has a category for HTML converters at its World Wide Web site. This Web page contains a list of 11 hyperlinks that point to other converter resources. Yahoo! also has links to over 10 commercial converters and over 30 shareware products in this category.

The National Center for Supercomputer Applications (NCSA) maintains a list of over 50 HTML converters. There is a brief description of each and a hyperlink pointing to the source Web site. NCSA also has a list of links to other converter resources.

The World Wide Web Consortium maintains perhaps the most comprehensive list of converters on the Web. There are easily over 100 freeware, shareware, or commercial products listed. The list includes converters for just about every conceivable word processor, and there are also converters for spreadsheets, plain text, and other formats.

To view this information, visit the following Web sites:

○ Yahoo! (http://www.yahoo.com/Computers_and_Internet/ Internet/World_Wide_Web/HTML_Converters/).

○ NCSA (http://union.ncsa.uiuc.edu/HyperNews/get/ www/html/converters.html).

○ The World Wide Web Consortium (http://www.w3.org/ pub/WWW/Tools/Filters.html).

Advanced HTML Editors

There are some advanced HTML editors on the market that display the HTML page exactly as it will appear in the browser and let you edit the display directly. Three of them are Netscape Navigator Gold, Microsoft FrontPage for Windows 95 and NT, and Adobe PageMill for Macintosh.

In Navigator Gold, the developer can add graphics to a web page. The onscreen display is formatted as it will appear in the browser. The developer can just type directly into the web-page window, and the software takes care of wrapping and aligning text and graphics.

You can download an evaluation copy of Navigator Gold from the Netscape Web site (http://www.netscape.com/). The licensed version costs $79.

Microsoft FrontPage also allows you to edit the web page directly. I watched an intranet developer use FrontPage to create an online newsletter for a client. As he typed the text into a section of the screen, it continually wrapped around the graphics on the page.

The capabilities of this product, and the others like it, are amazing compared to the days of typing HTML codes into a text editor.

The current list price for FrontPage is $149. You can get more information about the product at Microsoft's Web site (http://www.microsoft.com/frontpage/).

Adobe PageMill is a WYSIWYG editor for the Macintosh. It's one of the HTML editors that was used to develop the intranet and Internet web pages for Silicon Graphics.

You can get more information about Adobe PageMill at Adobe's Web site (http://www.adobe.com/).

There are a number of HTML editors for the various platforms. Yahoo! lists over 70 products: over 40 for Windows, over 20 for the Mac, and 9 for UNIX X Windows.

You can access the Yahoo! index of HTML editors at the Yahoo! site (http://www.yahoo.com/Computers_and_Internet/Internet/World_Wide_Web/HTML_Editors/).

Moving On

This chapter showed you how to convert existing company information into live, clickable intranet documents. You can use this information to start reaping the benefits of an internal web.

In the next chapter, we'll explore web-page graphics. You'll learn how to use graphic images to provide navigation and more attractive intranet documents.

Add Graphics to Your Web Pages

We've moved some corporate information into intranet documents. Now we'll enhance those documents by adding graphics.

You add graphic images to your intranet documents to:

○ make your documents more appealing.

○ draw attention to important information.

○ provide easy navigation.

○ add content; sometimes images are the information.

In this chapter we'll take the two intranet documents we've already started, the newsletter and the product incident page, and enhance them with graphics. I'll also show you how to take a report and turn it into a live document that lets your users drill down for more information.

You'll learn how to work with web-page graphics and pick up a couple of tricks that will make things easier.

Overview of Web-Page Graphics

There are two dominant graphic formats on the Web, Graphics Interchange Format (GIF) and Joint Photographic Experts Group (JPEG). An overwhelming majority of images on your internal web pages will be one of these two formats.

GIF Images

GIF files are stored in a compressed format so they take less time to transmit across phone lines. The GIF format was the graphic standard in the early days of the Web, so some browsers are capable of viewing only GIF images.

Two very useful enhancements were added to the GIF format: *interlacing* and *image transparency*. Interlacing is the ability to display the graphic in progressive stages, showing more detail with each pass. This allows the browser to display a rough sketch of the image, then immediately begin displaying text. The user doesn't have to wait for the entire image to be displayed before being able to scroll through the document.

All images are inserted into web pages within rectangular frames. The image transparency feature lets you hide all but the image itself—a round bullet point for example—so the surrounding rectangle doesn't appear on the document.

JPEG Images

JPEG was designed to provide a higher quality picture than GIF, but can also be compressed to a smaller file than even the GIF compression allows.

Although JPEG images allow a higher resolution image and can be compressed to smaller file sizes, they aren't as widely used as GIF graphics. The GIF format is more common because of its ability to interlace the image and to make part of the image transparent.

Netscape recently added the ability to progressively load JPEG images, but this ability hasn't been on the market very long.

All the images used in this chapter were printed from GIF files.

Inline Graphics

When you design an intranet document that includes a graphic image, you don't put the image itself in the HTML file. You code a reference to the image in the HTML, and the browser adds the image to the document on the client. The resulting document makes it look as if the graphic images were there all the time.

Let's start using graphics to enhance the intranet documents we built in the last chapter.

Adding Images to Documents

You'll remember that the KLP plant newsletter includes a logo. Figure 8-1 shows the newsletter in the web browser.

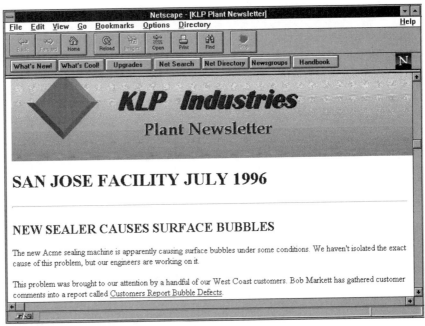

Figure 8-1: The KLP newsletter includes a logo.

Our product incident policy document looks kind of drab without a logo (Figure 8-2). Let's spruce it up by adding the KLP Industries logo to the top of the document.

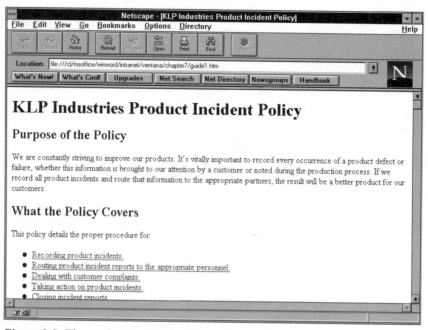

Figure 8-2: The product incident policy without a logo.

Creating Your Own Image

The first thing you need to do is create the image and save it as a GIF file. Right now you're probably thinking that you're not an artist. How can you possibly create a logo for your intranet documents?

I'm not an artist either. I'm going to show you a trick to get around your lack of artistic ability.

You can build the logo by using a shareware graphics program to capture part of a screen from a common presentation software package. Then you're going to use the shareware software to save that image as a GIF file.

First let's build the logo. I'll let you in on a secret. I didn't draw the KLP logo. I just used a template in Microsoft's PowerPoint, added some text, and did a screen capture.

Figure 8-3 shows one of the templates in PowerPoint with the text you'll use for your logo. I used the diamonds template, changed the background color, and added the text.

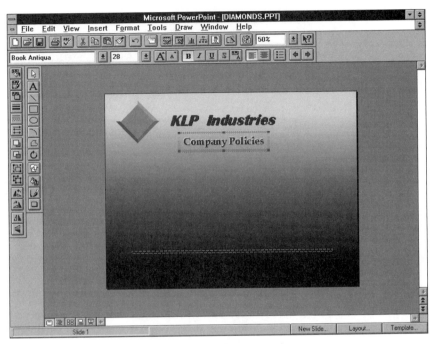

Figure 8-3: Building the logo in Microsoft PowerPoint.

Capturing & Converting the Image

Now that you have the logo designed, you have to convert it from the PowerPoint presentation to a GIF file. Let's use Paint Shop Pro from JASC, Inc., first to capture and then to convert the image.

Ted also selected Paint Shop Pro for the plastics company's intranet. The software converts graphics from many formats to GIF and JPEG files. It also has several features that let you create and edit images. Ted used the software to create graphics for his intranet.

Paint Shop Pro is included on the Companion CD-ROM. You can find the latest version at JASC's Web site (http://www.jasc.com). You can download an evaluation version of the software. The registration fee is $69.

To convert the PowerPoint screen in Figure 8-3 to a GIF file, use Paint Shop Pro's screen capture function. You can capture the entire screen, only the active window, or an area of the screen. You set up the hotkeys before doing a screen capture.

To capture the image, toggle to the PowerPoint screen and press the hotkeys for Area—in my case Ctrl+Shift+F5. This puts a pointer on the screen. Use the mouse to stretch this pointer into a rectangle, outlining the area you want to capture. When you release the mouse button, the image appears in Paint Shop Pro as shown in Figure 8-4.

Figure 8-4: The captured image in Paint Shop Pro.

The screen capture process automatically puts the file in the bitmap (BMP) format. You want a GIF file, so use the File I Save As command to save the file as a GIF.

Now you've got the logo in a GIF file that can be displayed in an intranet document.

Putting the Image in the Document

Let's use HoTMetaL to put the logo into the product incident policy document. Bring the document up in HoTMetaL, as shown in Figure 8-5, and insert a reference to the GIF file near the top of the file.

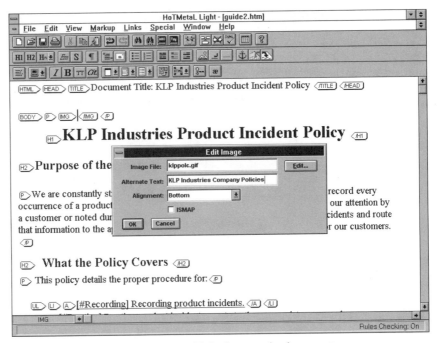

Figure 8-5: Using HoTMetaL to add the logo to the document.

Position the cursor in the document and click on the image icon. This brings up the dialog box seen in Figure 8-5. Here you enter the name of the graphics file, alternate text that's displayed by browsers that can't handle graphics, and the alignment of any text that appears next to the image.

Adding Graphic Separators to the Document

Now we'll add a little more pizzazz to the product incident page by putting a colorful separator under the document title. There are a number of sources for web-page graphic files. I've included some of them on the Companion CD-ROM for you to use in your intranet documents.

Figure 8-6 shows examples of the kinds of bars you can use as separators in your documents. Let's use the bar called marble.gif in the product incident page.

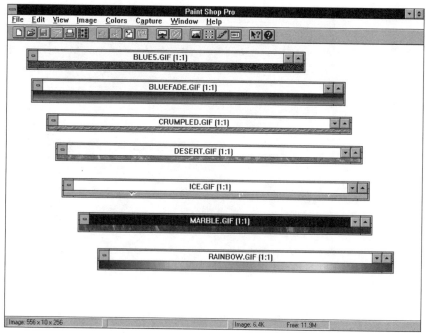

Figure 8-6: An example of bar images that you can use as separators in your intranet documents.

To include the bar in the product incident document, follow the same method you used in HoTMetaL to add the logo. The resulting document is shown in Figure 8-7.

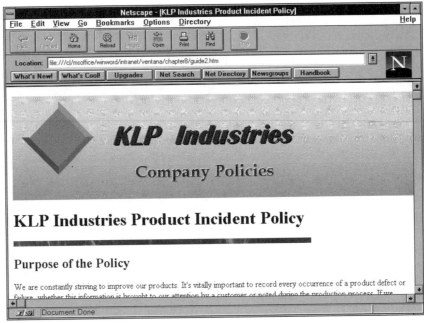

Figure 8-7: The product incident policy guide with a logo and a bar image.

Compare the screen in Figure 8-7 to the original in Figure 8-2. A little bit of graphics goes a long way in improving the appearance of your intranet documents.

Add Hyperlinked Graphics to Documents

You can use graphic images as hyperlinks so that your users can navigate by clicking on images. Using this capability in your intranet screens provides intuitive navigation.

The product incident policy document contains a section that tells the employee how to get product incident reports by product, customer, and type of defect. In the printed guide, this was just a bulleted list that told employees what types of information were available. To get the reports, they had to call the quality assurance manager.

Ted wanted to automate the process using the intranet. He decided to have hyperlinks to other web pages containing the reports themselves. Instead of having to call around to get the information, employees could merely click in a document and the intranet would retrieve it for them instantly.

Let's add this capability to the KLP Industries product incident guide. We'll turn the list of report categories into hyperlinks and precede them with graphical bullets. We'll set this up so the user can click on either the text or the bullet that precedes it to jump to the desired information.

Adding Hyperlinked Graphics

Let's use HoTMetaL to add the hyperlinked, graphical bullets to the product incident policy document. Figure 8-8 shows this.

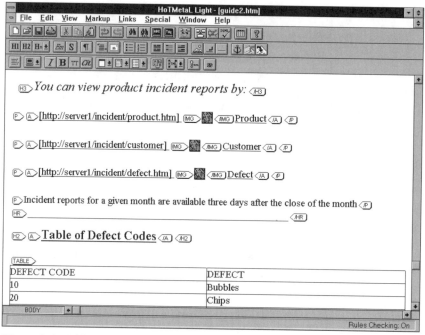

Figure 8-8: Adding hyperlinked graphics to the policy document.

To create the clickable bullets, you first add a hyperlink for the text. Then you move the cursor inside of the hyperlink in HoTMetaL and use the image icon to insert an image. In this case, I pointed to a GIF image of a square bullet. The image takes on the same hyperlink as the accompanying text.

Figure 8-9 shows how this appears in a web browser. Both the text and the bullet are highlighted in blue, indicating a hyperlink. The user can click either the bullet or the text to retrieve the next document.

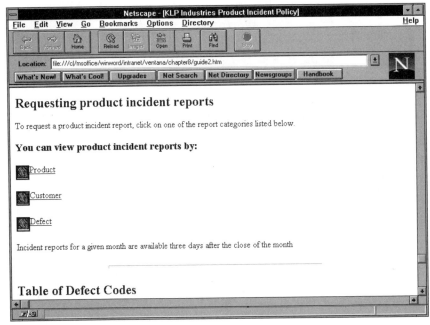

Figure 8-9: Hyperlinked bullets in the policy document.

Adding Navigation Bars to Documents

One of the most powerful forms of graphic-based hyperlinks is the ability to create a navigation bar. You can create a row of buttons or icons for users to easily navigate around the intranet. You can put this navigation bar on most intranet documents so that users are never more than a mouse click away from the key sections of your internal web.

You can tailor the navigation bar for each section of the intranet. The intranet home page and department home pages will typically have navigation bars that jump to other sections of the intranet. Navigation bars on documents themselves can have navigation bars that point users to information or functions that are related to the information contained on the document they're working with.

The plastics company wanted to use the intranet to implement a best practices application using the plant newsletters. Ted had converted the newsletters to HTML documents, but wanted to provide a way to search and navigate through all the issues of the newsletter from all locations. To do this, he added a navigation bar to the newsletter documents.

Let's do the same thing for our KLP Industries newsletter.

Creating the Image

You'll start by finding a GIF image containing a row of blank buttons. Figure 8-10 shows this GIF in Paint Shop Pro, and it's also included on the Companion CD-ROM.

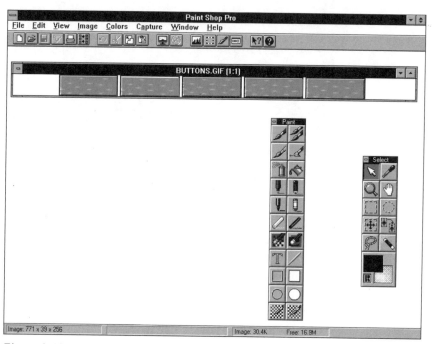

Figure 8-10: A GIF containing a row of blank buttons.

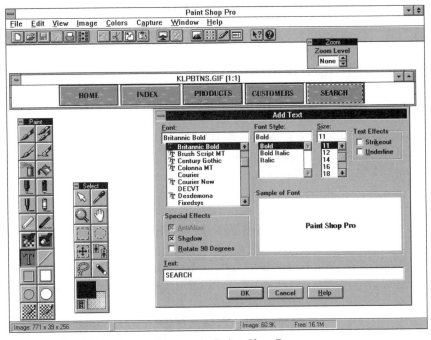

Figure 8-11: Adding text to buttons in Paint Shop Pro.

The next step is to use the Paint Shop Pro Text icon to add the button text. Figure 8-11 shows this procedure in action.

Invoke the Add Text dialog box by clicking on the T in the Paint toolbar. You can use the dialog box to select the font size and type, then enter in the text. Also, check the box for the shadow effect. This gives a 3D look to the text.

Label the buttons Home, Index, Products, Customers, and Search. The Home button returns to the intranet home page. Index brings up a table of contents for all issues of the newsletter.

The Products button lets an employee jump to a screen containing information on the company's products. Someone who reads about a product in a newsletter can find out more about it. The Customers button serves a similar function for customer information.

The Search button brings up a screen that lets the employee search all issues of a newsletter by keyword. I'll show you how to add search capability to your intranet in Chapter 11.

Creating an Image Map

Although there are five buttons in the image we created, it is stored as one GIF file. We can't simply make this a hyperlinked image because we need to jump to five places, not one. We're going to use a feature called an *image map*.

An image map lets you create hyperlinks out of individual sections of a single image. We need to create separate hyperlinks for each button in the one image.

To create our image map, let's use a piece of software called Mapedit. Mapedit is a shareware program developed by Thomas Boutell. The program is included on the Companion CD-ROM. You can download the most recent version from his Web site (http://www.boutell.com/mapedit/). Registration is $25.

Figure 8-12 shows our button image in Mapedit. The Tools menu lets you select a shape to use to outline each section of the image map. I'll use a rectangle shape to outline each of the buttons.

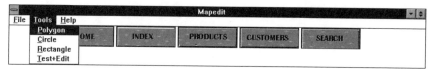

Figure 8-12: The button bar in Mapedit, an image map editor.

After you outline each section that will become a separate hyperlink, you click on the right mouse button. This brings up the dialog box shown in Figure 8-13.

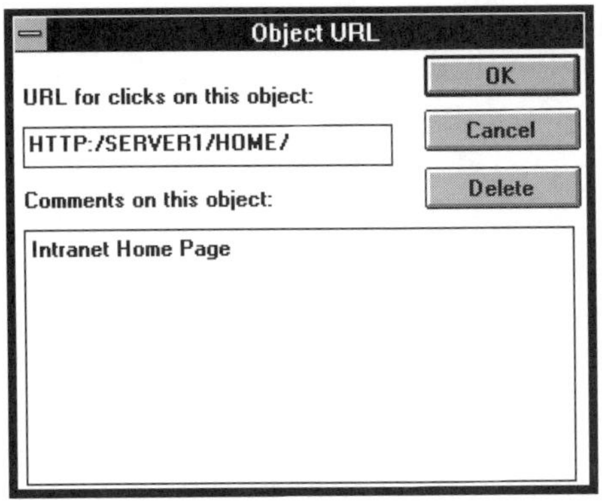

Figure 8-13: Assigning a URL to a section of the image.

You use the Object URL dialog box to indicate what document the intranet should retrieve when a user clicks on this section of the image map. You can also enter a comment that will appear in the image map file but won't appear in the intranet document.

The completed image map is a text file (shown in Figure 8-14). The file contains a line for each section of the image map. The beginning of each line is the code "rect," which tells the server to expect a rectangle. Following that is the URL, which specifies the document to be retrieved. At the end of each line are the coordinates for the area of the image that defines the hyperlink.

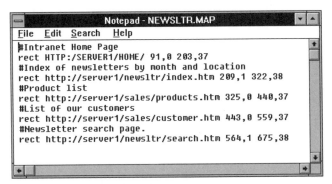

Figure 8-14: The final image map file.

The file is stored on the server. When the user clicks in the image in the document, the server looks in the image map file and finds which URL matches the area where the user clicked. Then the server uses the URL to retrieve the document that matches that section of the image map and returns it to the browser.

Putting an Image Map in a Document

To use an image map in a document, you need to use codes that tell the browser two things: that an image on the web page is to be used as an image map, and the location of the map file that contains the coordinates and the associated actions for each coordinate.

The HTML that associates a server map file with an image might look something like this:

```
<A HREF="button.map"><IMG SRC="buttons.gif" ISMAP><A/>
```

This code tells the browser to load an image called buttons.gif into the web page, then when the user clicks on this image, it sends the coordinates of the click to the map called button.map.

Figure 8-15 shows how you could put the button bar as an image map in our newsletter documents by creating a hyperlink that points to the location of the image map file. In this case it's http://server1/cgi-bin/imagemap/newsbtns.map. Then you insert the image and change the attributes to identify it as a type ISMAP.

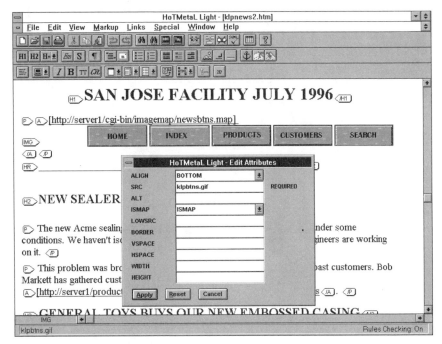

Figure 8-15: Using HoTMetaL to include an image map in a document.

Figure 8-16 shows how this turns out in the browser. We now have clickable buttons for employees to use to navigate through intranet information.

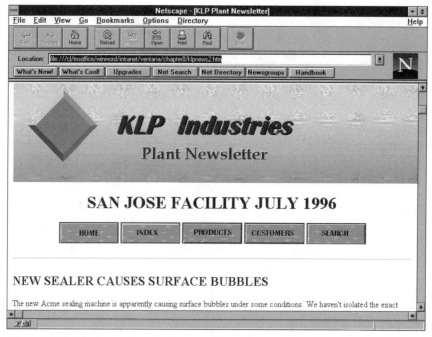

Figure 8-16: The button bar in the newsletter document.

This is a powerful feature. You can use image maps to create clickable buttons; you can even use them to allow navigation from some more complex image—such as a U.S. map or a globe.

We've now used graphics to spruce up KLP's intranet documents and to provide intuitive navigation. Let's look at one more trick you can use to turn a report into a live document employees can use to drill down into the details.

Creating a Drill-Down Report

At the end of Chapter 2 we said Ted wanted to use the intranet to let employees click on some area of a report to reveal the details behind each report. The action of clicking on summary information to reveal the details behind it is frequently referred to as "drilling down into the details." Figure 8-17 shows an example drill-down report. The expense categories and the pie chart are clickable hyperlinks. Clicking on a category reveals the details behind each element.

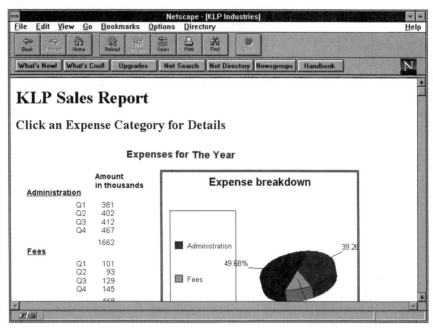

Figure 8-17: A live, clickable drill-down report.

When you saw this report in Chapter 2, you probably thought this must be difficult to do, right? How can you give your users the ability to drill down into the details behind a report without a lot of programming?

It's easy, and it doesn't require a single line of programming code.

By now you've probably guessed how you would provide the drill-down feature. You just create an image map that highlights areas of the report and link the areas to intranet documents that contain the appropriate detail. Piece of cake.

But what about the report itself? How are you going to get that into a web page?

As complicated as this looks, I have to let you in on another secret. It's easy. To put the report in the web page, just bring it up in the report generator software—in my case I used Powersoft's PowerViewer—and use Paint Shop Pro to capture the image to a GIF file.

Figure 8-18 shows the report in PowerViewer. When I designed the report, I made the expense categories blue and underlined them so they would look like the usual hyperlink. I also added the phrase that says, "Click on a category for more details." The only thing left is to capture the screen using Paint Shop Pro and code the image map using Mapedit.

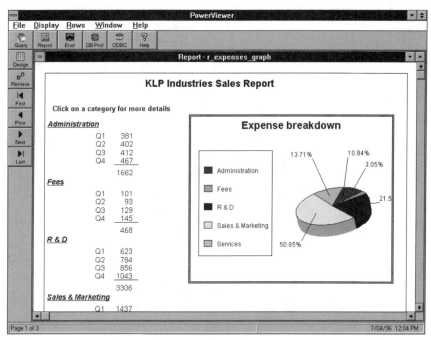

Figure 8-18: A report generator can be used as the source of a GIF for a drill-down report.

Web-Page Graphics Resources

Here are some places to go on the World Wide Web to find more information about graphics software and to find web-page graphics that you can download and use in your intranet.

Graphics-Manipulation Software

Paint Shop Pro is one of several software packages on the market that can prepare images for web pages. Here are some more:

○ Image Alchemy, from Handmade Software, Inc., is a graphics tool that can convert images between formats. It is available for the PC, Mac, and UNIX platforms. For more information, visit the Web site (http://www.handmadesw.com/hsi/products.html).

○ Graphics Tools, from DeltaPoint, is a screen capture and image-processing product for Windows systems and Macs. It sells for $169. You can download an evaluation copy from their Web site (http://www.deltapoint.com).

○ Graphics Converter Gold, from IMSI, is an image capture and conversion package available for Windows. It sells for $39.95. For more information, visit the Web site (http://www.imsisoft.com/).

○ ImageMagick for UNIX is a freeware image-conversion program. For information and to download the product, visit their Web site (http://www.wizards.dupont.com/cristy/ImageMagick.html).

○ Joseph Walker maintains an extensive list of graphics software for various platforms. You can visit the site that contains the list (http://www2.bae.ncsu.edu/bae/people/faculty/walker/hotlist/graphics.html).

○ Brian Stark maintains a list of graphics software (http://www.public.iastate.edu/~stark/gutil_sv.html). The list indicates whether software is freeware, shareware, or commercial. There are links to FTP sites where you can download the latest version of the products.

Image Map Software

We used Mapedit from Thomas Boutell in this book. Mapedit runs on Windows and UNIX platforms. You can download the latest version (http://www.boutell.com/mapedit/). The registration fee is $25.

Mac-ImageMap is a freeware image-map editor for the Macintosh. You can download a copy from their site (http://weyl.zib-berlin.de/imagemap/Mac-ImageMap.html).

Yahoo! has links to image-map software for all platforms (http://www.yahoo.com/Computers_and_Internet/Internet/World_Wide_Web/Programming/Imagemaps/).

Web-Page Graphics

There are numerous places on the World Wide Web that maintain archives of web-page graphics. These collections include buttons, bars, banners, backgrounds, and pictures.

Some of the Web sites offer graphics for noncommercial use only. Others make their collection freely available to anyone. Please respect the webmasters' wishes about noncommercial use and only download graphics from the nonrestricted sites.

Yahoo! maintains links to over 80 graphics collections (http://www.yahoo.com/Computers/World_wide_Web/Programming/Icons).

To transfer an image from a Web site to your desktop using Netscape Navigator, you right-click on the image, highlight Save As, and release the mouse button. This brings up a dialog box that lets you indicate where to save the file.

Moving On

You can use simple, inexpensive software to create graphics for your intranet. You can capture images of logos, reports, and other data from common office software and use these images to create professional-looking, clickable documents. You can also use clip art that you obtain from the World Wide Web to add pizzazz to your information. When users ooh and aah over your designs, don't tell them how easy it was.

Web technology also lets you embed data entry forms in your documents. In the next chapter, you'll learn how to use web-page forms to automate some of your company's work processes.

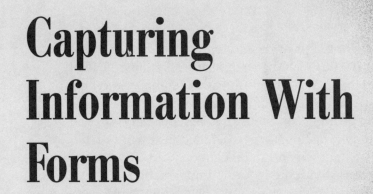

Capturing Information With Forms

The web pages we've built so far move information in one direction only. Employees request data through their web browsers, and the server delivers it. The intranet is also capable of taking information the other way—web pages can contain data entry forms that capture data from users and send it to the server for processing. This capability lets you use your intranet to automate company work processes.

Let's start with an example of how a real-life company uses forms to automate work tasks. Then we'll look at how we would use an intranet form to replace the paper version used for KLP Industries' product incident tracking system.

Automating Work Tasks

HTML includes the ability to embed a form in a web page. You can use this form to capture data from the user and send it to the server for processing. Web page forms allow you to use the intranet to automate work tasks that require phone calls, paper forms, and other manual procedures.

A&a Printers is a printing and digital graphics company in Menlo Park, California. Their work processes involve the typical things printers do, including filling out estimates and helping customers plan the details of their projects.

For many printing companies, these types of tasks are done over the phone. Customers give detailed information, the company takes it all down and puts them on hold, and finally the company returns with the requested information.

A&a Printers thought there must be a better way to serve their customers. Why should customers have to call in and be put on hold while someone writes down all the details needed for an estimate? Why not automate the process and let customers do their own estimates and planning on a computer?

A&a Printers designed a system that lets customers put down their telephones and fire up their web browsers. A&a Printers used web-page forms to automate customer work processes and made the system available on the World Wide Web.

Figure 9-1 shows the A&a home page on the World Wide Web. From this page, customers can access project estimating and planning processes, see a list of available specialists, or download software and graphics.

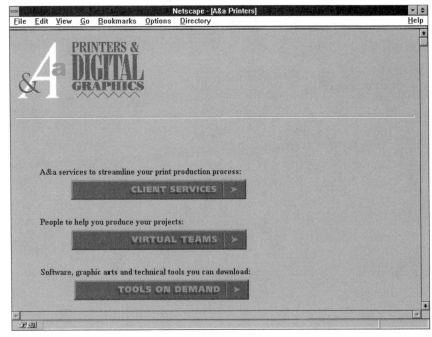

Figure 9-1: The A&a Printers home page lets customers access automated work processes.

Customers point their browsers to this home page and access customer service functions with mouse clicks.

From the home page, customers can access the client-services menu shown in Figure 9-2. This page links to a project estimate form and project-planning tools. Customers can also check the current production schedule to see when there might be available time for a new project.

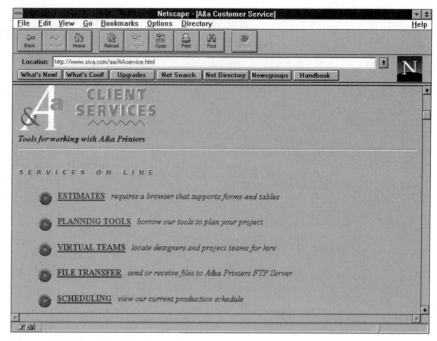

Figure 9-2: The A&a client-services page.

Example: Estimating a Project

If a customer clicks on the Estimates link in the client-services page,
the form shown in Figure 9-3 appears. This part of the form has
input areas for customer contact information, a drop-down list of
sales reps, and radio buttons to indicate the priority of the project.

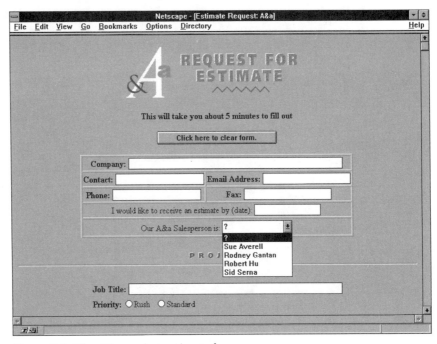

Figure 9-3: The A&a project estimate form.

Figure 9-4 shows another section of the form. There are radio buttons for mutually exclusive options, check boxes for options with multiple possibilities, and a scrolling text area for comments. The form probably resembles something that customer service reps at the printing company used to fill out while the customer waited on the phone. Now customers can fill this out directly, by clicking with a mouse.

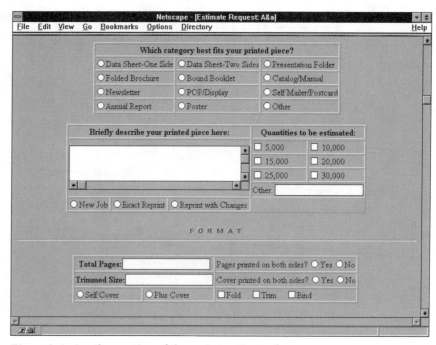

Figure 9-4: Another section of the project estimate form.

This online form is available 24 hours a day. Customers don't have to call in to request an estimate; they can use the form from their business or from home—at their convenience. They can see all the options that are available, and they don't have to rely on someone else asking the questions. The online form is quick and complete.

The automated form brings benefits to A&a as well. They don't have the usual problems of paper-based systems. The data is captured electronically.

Example: Planning a Project

If a customer chooses Planning Tools from the client-services screen, he or she sees the choices in Figure 9-5. This screen links to a form that the customer can use to calculate shipping weight, and another that calculates the thickness of the printed document's spine.

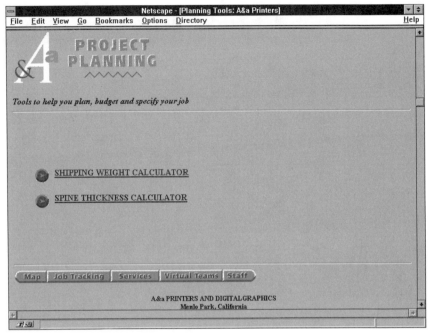

Figure 9-5: The planning tools available at the A&a Web site.

Figure 9-6 shows the shipping weight calculator. There are drop-down lists for the body and cover stock and input areas for the other data. When the customer fills out the form and clicks on Enter, the results are calculated and returned to the browser (see Figure 9-7).

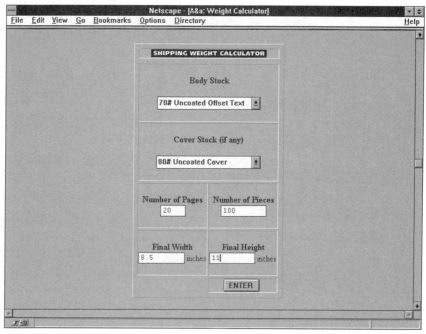

Figure 9-6: The A&a shipping weight calculator.

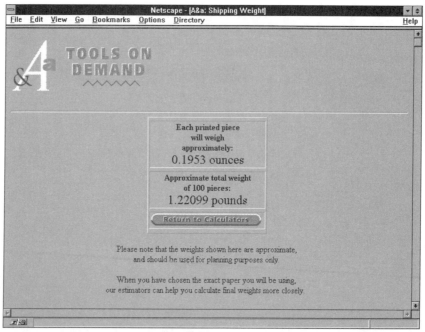

Figure 9-7: The shipping weight is calculated and returned to the customer's web browser.

Web Automation Advice

Robert Hu is president and CEO of A&a Printers. He had some advice for intranet developers who want to use the technology to automate company work tasks: "As in any new technology, it is important to design the process first before deploying the system."

Hu believes web technology gives companies the chance to change their work processes as they automate them. "I prefer not to think of it as automation but as process reengineering," he said. "The real challenge is to design a better work flow using technology to leverage human intelligence."

How do you know which processes to automate? Hu said he picks processes that use the strengths of the computer. "Computers are wonderful at repetitive and ordered worlds; human beings excel in analysis and problem solving. We try to keep that in mind as we design tools and services we offer over our Web."

Creating a Form

In the last two chapters we built an online version of KLP Industries' product incident policy. Part of this policy refers the employee to a paper form they fill out to record a problem with a product.

Why continue to use a paper form? We've put the procedure guide online. Why not link it to an electronic version of the product incident tracking (PIT) form?

Let's see how we would use an intranet form to automate this process.

Example: the PIT Form

Figure 9-8 shows the upper half of a web-based product incident tracking form. The employee enters the product ID and description, then uses a drop-down list to indicate the type of defect.

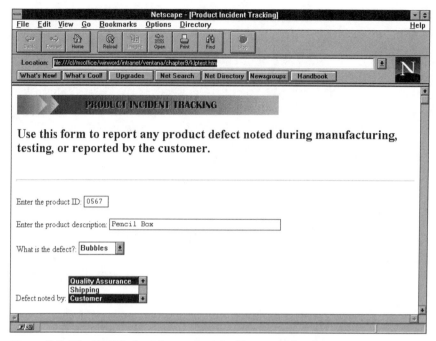

Figure 9-8: The KLP Industries product incident tracking form.

Then, he or she records how the defect was discovered by using a scrolling multiple-selection list. This list lets the employee pick more than one option by holding down the Ctrl key and clicking in the list. A defect might have been discovered in more than one location.

The rest of the example form appears in Figure 9-9. Check boxes are used to indicate the probable cause of the defect, since there can be more than one factor causing the problem. Radio buttons are used to enter the amount of damage. There can be only one choice in this category.

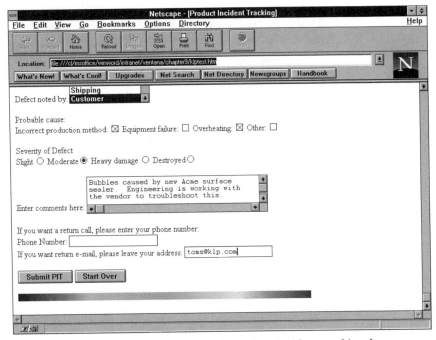

Figure 9-9: The remainder of the example product incident tracking form.

A scrolling text area is used to record comments. The employee might want to be contacted about this incident. There are input areas for a phone number and e-mail address.

There are two buttons on the form. The Submit button sends the data to the server. The Start Over button clears the form.

Creating the Form in HoTMetaL

How do you build this form? It's just a series of HTML codes, like any other part of an intranet document. Figure 9-10 shows the form in the HoTMetaL HTML editor.

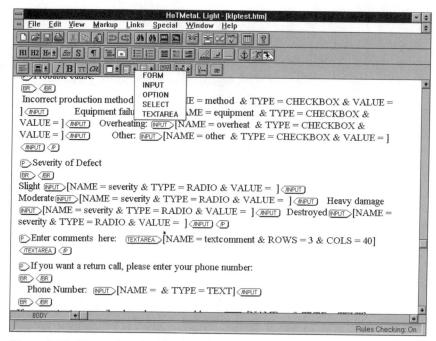

Figure 9-10: The product incident tracking form in the HoTMetaL HTML editor.

HoTMetaL has an icon for building a form. When you click on it and hold the mouse button down, you get the menu shown on the menu bar in Figure 9-10. Each menu item performs specific functions:

- ○ Form is used to indicate the beginning of a form.

- ○ Input creates single line input areas, check boxes, radio buttons, and command buttons.

- ○ Option defines each choice in the lists.

- ○ Select is used for scrolling lists.

- ○ Text area defines a multiline entry box, such as the one used for comments in the PIT form.

The form is built by repeatedly selecting elements from this menu. In the middle of the screen you can see the code for the Severity of Defect radio buttons. Forms contain what are called name/value pairs. When the user clicks one of these radio buttons, the browser creates a variable named severity and one of four values: slight, moderate, heavy damage, or destroyed.

The name/value pair is what gets sent to the server. It's up to the server to figure out what they mean and take appropriate action. This is covered later in the chapter, in the section called "Processing Behind Forms."

You'll notice that there are more types of form elements than menu choices in Figure 9-10. You specify the type of element—check box, radio button, and so on—by editing the attributes of the current portion of code. Figure 9-11 shows this process in action.

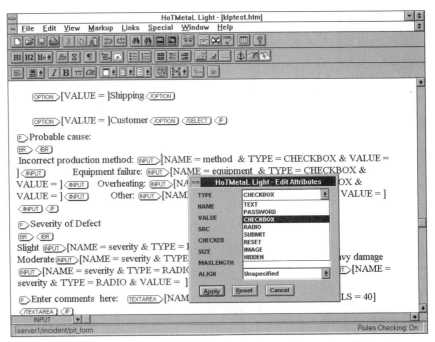

Figure 9-11: HoTMetaL lets you determine the form element by editing the attributes of an area of code.

Using a Text Editor to Create Forms

If you're used to designing data entry forms in a GUI programming environment like PowerBuilder, Visual Basic, or Delphi, you'll be disappointed with HTML form design in most HTML editors. Many HTML editors provide some way of clicking on an icon or menu to select a form element, but you're placing the elements line by line in text mode.

This process of designing a form can become tedious in a hurry. With a program like HoTMetaL, you find yourself constantly clicking on an icon to enter the next line of code—one line at a time.

A shortcut for designing forms is to use a plain text editor to enter the form codes. For repeated coding, such as a drop-down list, you can use copy and paste to speed things up.

Netscape Navigator Gold, Microsoft FrontPage, and Adobe PageMill are examples of HTML editors that allow you to layout forms in a more graphical environment than HoTMetaL.

Another shortcut for building forms quickly is to copy an existing HTML file containing a form to a new name. Then edit the existing HTML code with a text editor, using the editor functions to copy or delete form code and changing the text to match the form you want to create.

Figure 9-12 shows the product incident tracking form HTML code in Windows's notepad. You can see that it would be easy to add elements to a list of radio buttons or check boxes using copy and paste.

```
Notepad - KLPTEST.HTM
File  Edit  Search  Help
<!DOCTYPE HTML PUBLIC "-//Netscape Comm. Corp.//DTD HTML//EN" "html-net.dtd">
<HTML><HEAD><TITLE>Product Incident Tracking</TITLE></HEAD>
<BODY><IMG SRC="pitbnr.gif" ALT="Product Incident Tracking" ALIGN="BOTTOM">
<H2>Use this form to report any product defect noted during manufacturing,
testing, or reported by the customer.</H2>
<P><BR></P>
<HR>
<FORM ACTION="server1/incident/pit_form" METHOD="POST">
<P> Enter the product ID:
<INPUT NAME="prod_id" SIZE="5" MAXLENGTH="5"></P>
<P> Enter the product description:
<INPUT NAME="prod_desc" SIZE="40" MAXLENGTH="40"></P>
<P>What is the defect?:  <SELECT NAME="defect" SIZE="0">

<OPTION VALUE="1">Bubbles</OPTION>
<OPTION VALUE="2">Chipped</OPTION>
<OPTION VALUE="3">Cracked</OPTION>
<OPTION VALUE="4">Dented</OPTION>
<OPTION VALUE="5">Stained</OPTION>
<OPTION VALUE="6">Other</OPTION></SELECT></P>
<P><BR>Defect noted by:
<SELECT NAME="noted_by" SIZE="3" MULTIPLE="MULTIPLE">
<OPTION>Manufacturing</OPTION>
<OPTION>Quality Assurance</OPTION>
<OPTION>Shipping</OPTION>
<OPTION>Customer</OPTION></SELECT></P>
<P>Probable cause:  <BR> Incorrect production method:
<INPUT TYPE="CHECKBOX" NAME="method">          Equipment failure:
<INPUT TYPE="CHECKBOX" NAME="equipment">    Overheating:
<INPUT TYPE="CHECKBOX" NAME="overheat">        Other:
<INPUT TYPE="CHECKBOX" NAME="other"></P>
<P>Severity of Defect <BR>Slight <INPUT TYPE="RADIO" NAME="severity">
Moderate<INPUT TYPE="RADIO" NAME="severity">   Heavy damage
<INPUT TYPE="RADIO" NAME="severity">  Destroyed<INPUT
TYPE="RADIO" NAME="severity"></P>
<P>Enter comments  here:
```

Figure 9-12: The PIT form HTML in a text editor.

The Future of Form Creation

The way developers create forms hasn't changed much since forms were added to HTML a couple of years ago. But it's bound to change soon. Adobe Software's PageMill HTML editor allows GUI drag-and-drop forms editing. The product started out as Mac-only software but should be available for Windows by the time you read this.

As HTML-editing software matures, you'll see more products that offer the drag-and-drop forms creation capability similar to that offered in traditional client/server software.

Adding the Processing Behind Forms

You've seen how to build a form, but how do you program the processing behind it?

The form tag in the HTML code contains a URL that references a program on the server. When you click on the Submit button, data is sent from the browser to the server and from the server to the executable program through something called a Common Gateway Interface (CGI).

The CGI programs that process web form data are usually written in C or Perl on UNIX systems. Some Windows web servers allow CGI programs to be written in BASIC.

CGI programming is beyond the scope of this book. There are entire, thick books on the art of CGI programming.

You'll have to create some kind of program to process form data. How do you learn how to do this?

Using CGI Programming Templates

Ted wanted to automate some of the plastics company's work processes using the intranet. He had never worked with Perl and was only vaguely familiar with C. Ted bought a book on Perl that included a CD with a number of examples. The examples included matching forms and programs that register a user, order a product, or process an online catalog.

Ted used the forms and programs as templates for his intranet. He modified the forms to match some process that he wanted to automate, then he edited the programs to match the form modifications. This let him get started right away without having to learn how to code the CGI programs from scratch.

You can use the same shortcut for your intranet. There are a number of HTML books on the market that cover CGI programming and include form and code samples. You can use these books to build a library of program templates.

Using PolyForm by O'Reilly Software

Sometimes you just want to use a form to capture data that will be processed later. Other times you want to take data from a form and send it in an e-mail message. Why learn a complicated language to accomplish these simple tasks?

Ted downloaded an evaluation copy of O'Reilly Software's PolyForm. PolyForm simplifies the process of capturing data from an intranet form. You can download an evaluation copy of PolyForm from O'Reilly Software's Web site (http://www.ora.com).

Let's take a look at PolyForm in action. Figure 9-13 shows PolyForm's Control Panel. The developer uses this screen to indicate the name of the form's HTML file and to give the form a title. You use the menu options to start building the form and to indicate what you want the program to do with the data.

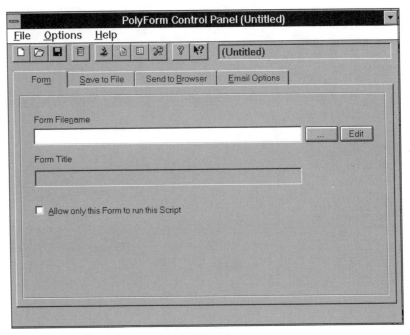

Figure 9-13: The PolyForm Control Panel.

Build an Intranet on a Shoestring

Clicking on the Wizard icon (the fifth button from the left) brings up the PolyForm Script Wizard, shown in Figure 9-14. Your first step is to choose either a blank form or one of the prebuilt form templates that come with the software. Figure 9-15 shows the Timesheet form template in a web browser.

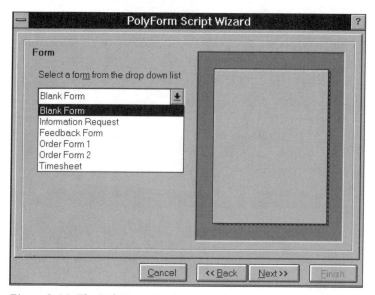

Figure 9-14: The PolyForm Script Wizard. Your first step is to select a form template.

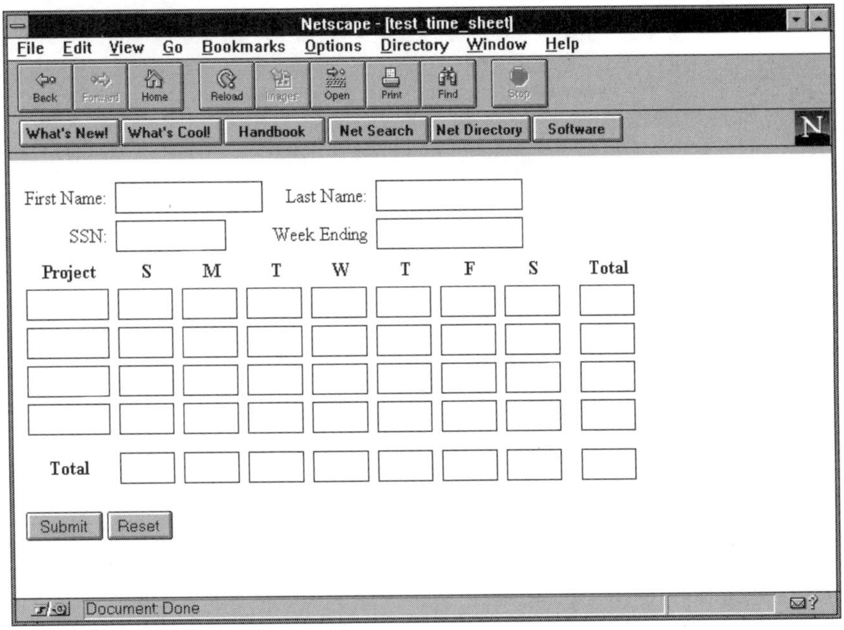

Figure 9-15: The PolyForm Timesheet template.

The next step in the Script Wizard is to tell PolyForm what you want to do with the data. This screen is shown in Figure 9-16. You can save the form's data in a simple text file with name/value pairs. You can also choose to save the data to a comma-delimited file for importing into a database or other software. Or you can choose to have the data sent in an e-mail message without saving it.

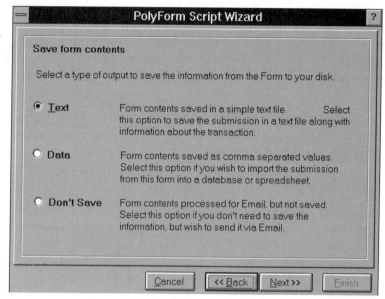

Figure 9-16: PolyForm gives you three options for saving the form data.

PolyForm assumes you're not going to process the form data immediately, but will either collect the data for later processing or send it in an e-mail message. If this is the case, PolyForm greatly simplifies form processing and eliminates the need to code a CGI program.

PolyForm sells for $149. You can get more information or download an evaluation copy of PolyForm from O'Reilly's Web site (http://www.ora.com).

Novell's Netware Web Server

Ted used the Netscape Communications Server for the plastics company's intranet, but he brought in an evaluation copy of Novell's Netware Web Server. One feature he was interested in was the ability to do CGI programming in BASIC.

Netware Web Server comes with demos that show how to process form data in BASIC. Figure 9-17 contains one of these examples—an order entry application.

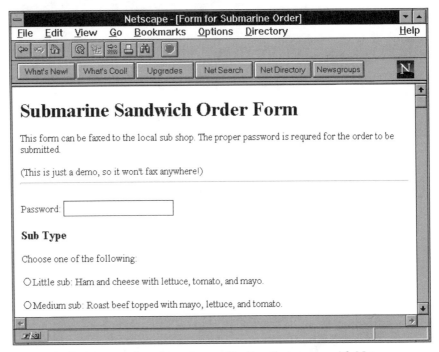

Figure 9-17: An example order entry application that comes with Netware Web Server.

The code that creates and processes this form is shown in Figure 9-18. The BASIC code uses simple print statements to construct the form. The second line of the program checks to see if the user has already entered data into the form. If so, the program branches to BASIC code that processes the data from the browser.

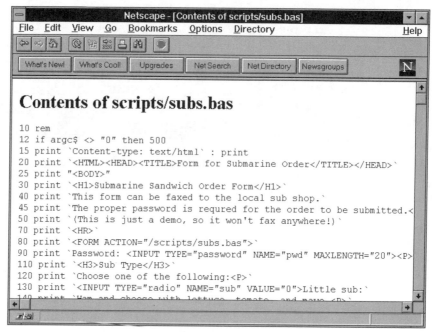

Figure 9-18: BASIC code used to create the form shown in Figure 9-17 and to process the data sent from this form.

Ted had programmed extensively in BASIC. He thought about bringing the Netware Web Server in as a second server and using it to handle the more complex form-processing tasks.

You can find more information about Novell's Netware Web Server at their Web site (http://www.novell.com).

> ## *The Future of Web-Form Programming*
> Like form design, web-server programming is due for improvements. In the early days of the World Wide Web, most web servers were in UNIX and programmed by developers familiar with UNIX scripting languages like Perl.
>
> Today a growing percentage of web servers are running in Windows and Macintosh platforms. Developers in these environments often have no experience with UNIX scripting languages. You're bound to see a number of products appear on the market that simplify the process of coding the programming behind web forms.

Creating an Interactive Intranet

Web-based forms allow you to expand your intranet from passive documents to interactive processing. You can use intranet forms to give employees on-demand tools they can use in their daily work processes.

Karilee Wirthlin is a consultant working on intranets at Silicon Graphics and a company called Portal Information Network. She feels that web forms play a vital role in the success of an intranet.

"I think that any web site, but especially an intranet web site, needs to be tool-based to be effective," she says. "You can certainly post pages and pages of information, but people most likely will not revisit static information. Applications like our (Silicon Graphics's) online conference scheduler or software install tools are easy to use and always available at your fingertips."

Companies use forms in their intranets to:

- order supplies.
- reserve conference rooms and equipment.
- sign up for seminars.
- manage company property.
- function as work-process tools specific to the industry (like the A&a Printers weight calculator).

○ facilitate employee feedback surveys.

○ report and track help desk problems.

○ give price estimates.

○ report customer calls.

Use forms in your intranet to bring the benefits of point-and-click interaction to your organization.

Moving On

Now you've seen how to add text, graphics, and interactive forms to your intranet documents. So far we've built our web pages from scratch. In the next chapter you'll learn how to use web-page templates to speed up intranet development.

Intranet documents are text files containing simple HTML coding. It's easy to put together a library of these files to clone as you add content to your internal web. I'll show you how to simplify web-page design significantly by using preexisting templates in the development process.

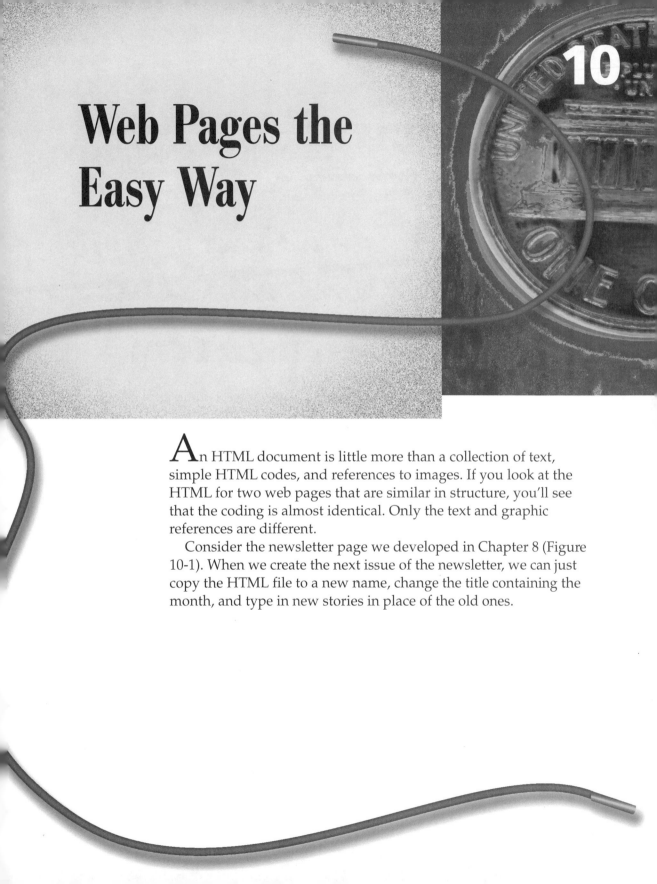

Web Pages the Easy Way

10

An HTML document is little more than a collection of text, simple HTML codes, and references to images. If you look at the HTML for two web pages that are similar in structure, you'll see that the coding is almost identical. Only the text and graphic references are different.

Consider the newsletter page we developed in Chapter 8 (Figure 10-1). When we create the next issue of the newsletter, we can just copy the HTML file to a new name, change the title containing the month, and type in new stories in place of the old ones.

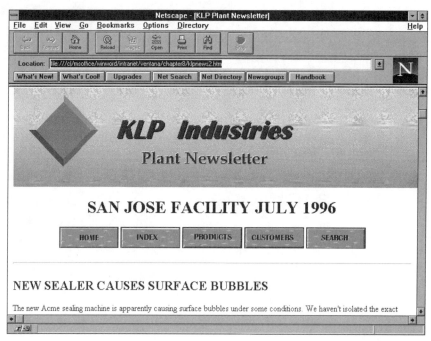

Figure 10-1: The plant newsletter web page can act as a template for future issues.

What does this buy us? We retain the HTML that points to any logos, bars, and buttons. We keep the same image map for the navigation bar. We retain the heading styles used in the document and just have to type the new headings over the old. If we had any special formatting, such as text that wrapped around a graphic, we could copy that to other places in the newsletter as needed.

In short, we save time and effort. And get the next intranet document up and running that much quicker. We also start to spread a common look and feel throughout our internal web.

Using Web-Page Templates

Web documents that can be used as a starter for other pages are called templates. There's nothing special about them. They're regular, working HTML files, but they have a design that we want to repeat with future documents.

You can use web-page templates to speed up the development of your intranet content.

How to Use a Template

You can create a new document out of an existing template in a few easy steps:

1. Copy the template to a new name.

2. Change image references for elements like logos and bars to different images if necessary.

3. Delete the elements that aren't needed.

4. Move web-page elements around to match the structure you want for the new document.

5. Type in the new text (or better yet, cut and paste in the new text).

6. Add new HTML elements for appearance and navigation.

Navigation Elements in Web Page Templates

You have to be careful when you use navigation elements like buttons or icons in a web page template. Web pages have different navigation needs. A home page might have buttons linked to the major sections of the intranet. An interior document, like a newsletter, might have an entirely different set of buttons. You couldn't use the same template for both web pages or the navigation bar would be inappropriate for one or the other.

There are a couple of ways to handle this. One method is to have enough different templates that this doesn't become a problem. You might have a department home page template, a newsletter template, and so on. Another way to deal with this is to not hardcode buttons or icons in the templates at all. You might want to put some text where the navigation bar would appear to remind users to add navigation to their web pages. Something like "Put Navigation Bar Here" across the top of the page reminds them to include navigation controls in their web pages.

As you start to build your collection of web-page templates, you'll find yourself building new intranet documents by adding the bare minimum to an existing template.

Ideal Templates

You can use any existing web page as a template for future designs, but the ideal template has certain features:

○ **A minimum of text.** You don't want too much to delete. A good template is a skeleton with just enough text for you to get the idea of how the final document will appear.

○ **A couple of different kinds of images.** A useful generic template might have graphic elements like a logo, a banner, bars, an image with text wrapped around it, and a bulleted list using graphics. You can move the elements around or delete them if you don't need them. You can do cut and paste operations on this kind of template to quickly pull together the design you need.

○ **A design appropriate to a broad class of documents.** You'll want to put together a library of web-page templates, each serving a distinct purpose. You might have a newsletter page, a catalog page, a generic survey form, and other types of template documents. Each is suited for a certain kind of intranet document. If you have a broad library of templates, you'll cut down on the amount of customization you have to do for each new page you create.

○ **Standard company elements.** The company logo is an obvious choice here. If divisions of the company have certain symbols, you'll want to include those on at least some of your generic templates.

○ **Consistent navigation designs.** A good element to include on every page is a navigation bar. You may find yourself customizing it for different parts of the intranet—marketing may have different navigation needs than manufacturing, for example—but certain buttons will be constant throughout. You might have a Home button on every page, and a Search button on most pages. (See the sidebar on using navigation bars in templates for a warning about including navigation buttons or icons in templates.)

If you use icons, make sure you and other developers use consistent images for common functions. Intranet users will soon use icons without a second thought if you use consistent symbols throughout.

Where to Get Web-Page Templates

After you've added a number of documents to your intranet, you'll have some samples you can use as templates. But what do you do when you first start building your intranet? How do you start building your template library?

Ted found two good sources for web-page templates: web-page development software and web-page books.

Templates With Software

Some software packages come with web-page templates. Many HTML editors include at least a handful of generic, starter web pages. Here are some products that include templates.

HoTMetaL

Ted discovered that HoTMetaL comes with a set of web-page templates. The templates are rather simple, but they're enough to get started.

Figure 10-2 shows one of the HoTMetaL templates as it appears in a Netscape browser. This page contains a logo, a bar, and some hyperlinks. It could be a starter page for your home page or departmental home pages on the intranet.

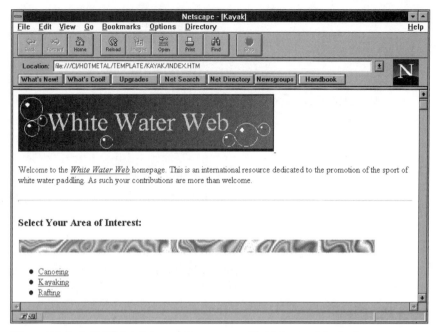

Figure 10-2: A HoTMetaL template as seen with Netscape Navigator.

Figure 10-3 is the same template as viewed from within HoTMetaL. You could quickly convert this to a starter page for your intranet by changing the logo to your logo and substituting a different bar image, if desired.

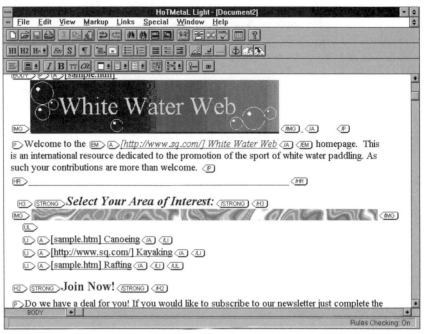

Figure 10-3: A template in HoTMetaL.

You'll want to have a couple of templates that have some features like hyperlinked graphics or a form.

Netscape Navigator Gold

Netscape has assembled a group of web-page templates for use with Navigator Gold. You can see them at Netscape's Web site (http://www.netscape.com/).

Figure 10-4 shows one of the templates, a newsletter page. The page has a logo, horizontal rules as dividers, and text wrapped around an image that's aligned to the right of the page.

Figure 10-4: A Netscape Navigator Gold web-page template.

The Netscape template in Figure 10-5 uses some more alignment tricks. Text is wrapped along the left side of one image and
along the right side of another. This could be a starter document
for an information page about products or customers.

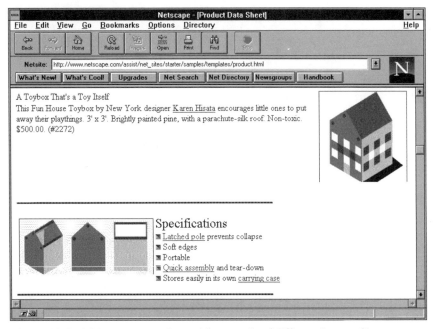

Figure 10-5: A Netscape template with a couple of different image alignment arrangements.

Have you ever visited a Web site and wondered how they pulled off some neat feature on the page? If you use one of the browsers that can display the HTML source, you can find out. This is a good way to learn some HTML tricks.

Figure 10-6 shows the template from Figure 10-5 with the View Source option on in Netscape's browser. This reveals the coding used to size and align some of the images in the page.

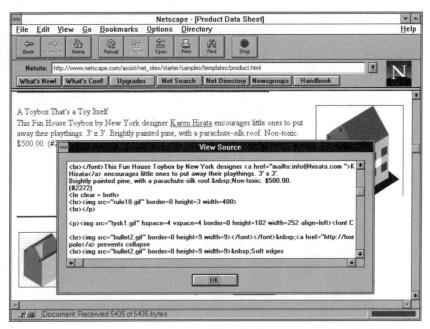

Figure 10-6: Use View Source command in Navigator to see the code behind some interesting features.

Microsoft FrontPage

Microsoft's FrontPage also comes with web page templates, including a corporate home page, a customer support page, a project status document, and a personal home page. The corporate home page has a navigation button bar. The project status document has text-based navigation hyperlinks across the top. It's easy to turn these templates into working pages.

Templates With Books

Ted picked up an HTML tutorial. The book contained a CD with a number of web-page templates. Ted was able to quickly convert a couple of these templates to working intranet pages. The accompanying text told how to modify the templates using images and HTML coding.

Most of the HTML how-to books contain templates. Ventana's

HTML Publishing on the Internet is a good example. It contains templates that illustrate various points in the text. These same web-page templates can be used as starter documents for your intranet.

A Library of Templates

As you build your template collection and modify the templates with corporate standard logo and navigation bars, you'll find yourself with a very useful set of starter pages. From that point, you'll spend little time coding the basic structure of your intranet documents and instead will concentrate on the unique content of each document.

Ted put together templates to use for the newsletter, policy manuals, and department home pages. This will help other developers and users quickly design content.

Start building your library of templates as early as possible in the intranet development process. This will not only save you time, it will start to evolve into a standard look and feel for your internal web.

Moving On

This section of the book showed you how to build intranet content. You learned how to enhance your intranet documents and how to use templates to speed up the process. Now we're going to turn our attention to adding functionality to the content of your intranet.

The next section of the book focuses on ways that you can add value to your internal web. The next chapter covers adding search software that will increase the value of your intranet as a repository for corporate information.

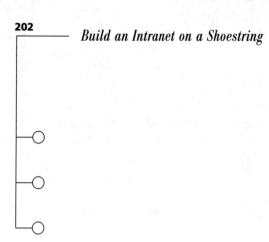

SECTION 4

Adding Value to Your Intranet

You've seen how to build an intranet and add information to it. Now you'll learn how to add software that will increase the value of your intranet significantly.

11

Finding Intranet Information Fast

One big advantage you can give your users from the start of your intranet is the ability to search through your company's information. You can use search software to tap into the gold hidden in your organization's documents.

This chapter shows you the features that search engines offer and how to pick a product that will enhance the value of your intranet.

The Value of Intranet Searching

An intranet and a full-featured search engine are a powerful combination. You can give your users the ability to find information that was previously hidden in the corners of your organization. Here are some of the ways you can use a search engine to increase the value of your intranet:

○ **Find related information.** An intranet search can reveal insights that just weren't possible when information was scattered in hard copy format throughout the company.

Entering the name of a customer or product may bring up a wealth of information on a topic from several departments in the corporation.

Employees will suddenly find sources of information that they didn't know existed. The intranet, coupled with search software, will uncover treasure that has been hidden because no one knew how or who to ask.

○ **Tap into libraries of information.** Many companies have realized significant benefits by putting libraries of technical documents and other reference information on an intranet, then letting employees search those libraries to quickly find the information they need. This unleashes the benefits of the information resources the company has collected.

○ **Share the news.** Almost every company has some way to disseminate news. Some distribute printed newsletters. Others post information on glass-covered bulletin boards. Some companies hold frequent meetings to pass along company news items.

These are all *push* methods of distributing information. You push information at employees and hope they remember it if they should need the information later.

An intranet with a search engine lets employees *pull* information. They only go after what they need, when they need it. Company news retains it value when you can find it when you most need it.

○ **Skip the phone call.** When you post company policies, guidelines, and related information on the intranet, you cut down on the number of times people have to call around to find some piece of data. If it's out there, they can use search software to find it.

How Does Search Software Work?

The best way to see how search software works is to look at examples. Let's compare two of the search engines on the World Wide Web—two products that are also available to you for your internal web.

AltaVista

Digital Equipment Corporation makes AltaVista, one of the most popular search engines for the World Wide Web. The company has just announced their intention to make the software available for intranets.

Figure 11-1 shows the opening screen of the AltaVista search engine on the World Wide Web. You can access this screen at the Alta Vista site (http://www.altavista.digital.com/).

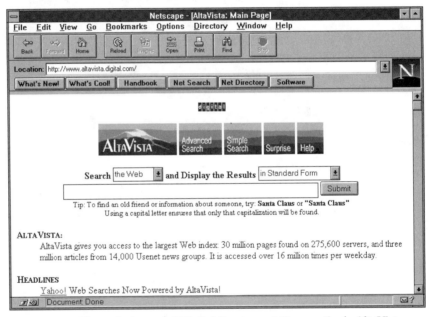

Figure 11-1: The main screen of Digital Equipment Corporation's AltaVista search engine.

From the screen shown in Figure 11-1, you type in a word or phrase, then click on Submit. The search engine combs through the indexes it has built of Internet documents, then returns a list of hyperlinks to documents matching your search parameters.

Let's see what happens if you search for information about search engines.

Figure 11-2 shows the list returned if you enter the phrase "search engines" into the input area of the AltaVista search screen. The search turned up around 200,000 references to this query.

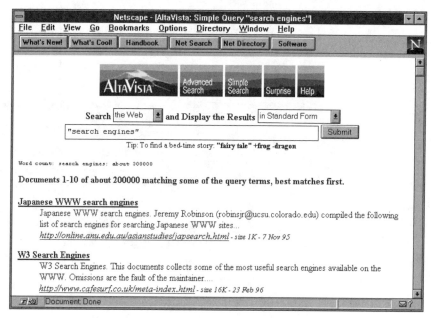

Figure 11-2: AltaVista returned around 200,000 documents matching a search for the phrase "search engine."

How AltaVista Shows Search Results

The results screen in Figure 11-2 lists the results as hyperlinks to the documents, followed by a brief explanation of what the documents contain. AltaVista follows each reference with the URL of the document (hyperlinked), which helps you determine the source of the information at a glance. The last part of the document reference shows the document size and date.

Search engines return search results as a list of hyperlinks pointing to the documents matching the search criteria. The hyperlinks are usually sorted from the most to the least relevant. Each search engine determines relevancy a little differently. Most count the number of times the keywords appear in a document.

Some give more weight if the search terms are found in the title or near the top of the document.

One measure of a search engine's effectiveness is how good it does at ranking the relevancy of the search results. This determines how easy it is to decide which links to investigate further.

Obviously this search was too broad. There's no way you're going to wade through 200,000 hyperlinks to find the information you want. You'll have to use the advanced features of AltaVista to narrow your search.

Narrowing the Search in AltaVista

A good search engine gives you advanced search syntax that you can use to narrow in on the precise information you're looking for. AltaVista is popular because it gives you more syntax options than most other search software.

The AltaVista syntax offers several options for structuring a precise search. Some of the features are:

- ◯ The ability to list words that must be found on a document.
- ◯ The ability to list words that cannot appear in the document.
- ◯ The wildcard character (*). This is useful when a word might be singular or plural.
- ◯ Logical operators AND, OR, and NOT to construct complex queries.
- ◯ The NEAR operator to specify words that must appear within ten words of each other in a document.
- ◯ The ability to limit the search to document titles, hyperlink references, image names, or other parts of HTML files.

The more options your intranet search software has, the easier it will be for employees to find precisely the data they are looking for.

You can reduce the results to a smaller number by going after comparisons of search engines. You'll want to find the phrases "comparison of search engines" and "search engine comparison," so you need to bring up the advanced search screen and use two AltaVista options: the keyword NEAR and a wildcard. This search appears in Figure 11-3.

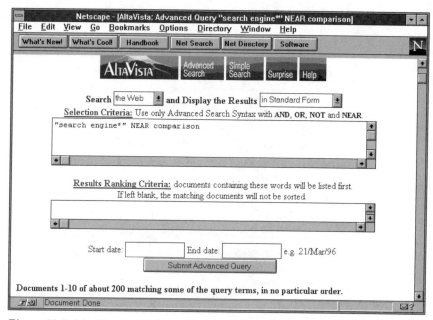

Figure 11-3: Limiting a search in AltaVista by using optional syntax.

The revised search query returns only 200 matching documents, a significant reduction from the 200,000 previously returned. The documents found by the revised search are probably more appropriate to your intended use.

Excite for Web Servers

Excite, Inc. (formerly Architext) also has a search engine available on the World Wide Web and for intranet use. Let's see how Excite handles our search on "search engines."

Figure 11-4 shows the screen you'll see if you visit Excite's advance search screen (http://www.excite.com/advanced.query.html). This page gives tips for searching along with the search entry areas.

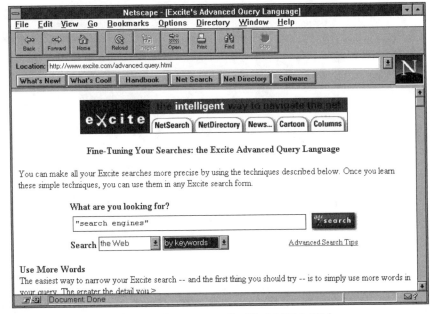

Figure 11-4: The Excite search screen on the World Wide Web.

The results of this search are shown in Figure 11-5. Excite returned over 200,000 document references—similar to the number returned by AltaVista.

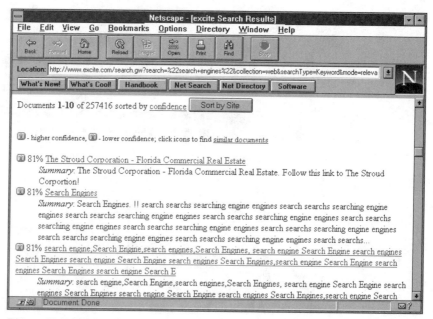

Figure 11-5: Excite also returned over 200,000 documents matching the phrase "search engines."

How Excite Shows Search Results

You'll notice that Excite formats the search results page a little differently than AltaVista does. It gives a hyperlinked title, followed by a summary, which *is* similar to AltaVista. But it also gives a confidence factor, which AltaVista did not. The confidence factor is a calculation of the relevance of each document.

AltaVista does a relevance calculation and uses it to rank the results, but doesn't display the number. The confidence factor Excite displays is useful information. Excite might return 10 documents; 3 of these might be highly relevant to the search and the remaining 7 might be stretching the connection. The confidence factor gives you an idea of how relevant the software thinks each document is. The color of the icon next to each factor changes from red to black as the confidence falls below a certain threshold.

The icon next to each reference can also be used as a query by example. You can click on the icon, and Excite will do another search using the referenced document as a guide for the search parameters. This can also be a useful feature.

Excite does not offer the URL of the sites found, which on an intranet might be an inconvenience since it's nice to know whether a document is in the Marketing or HR directory.

Limiting the Search Using Excite

You'll want to limit the Excite search, just like you did with AltaVista. Excite doesn't have nearly as many options as AltaVista has, but it does have some syntax for refining a search.

Figure 11-6 shows the syntax you can use to find documents comparing search engines. Since you want to limit the results to documents that compare search engines, you surround the phrase "search engines" with quotes indicating the words must appear next to each other, then precede the word "comparison" with a plus sign to indicate that it must appear somewhere in the same document.

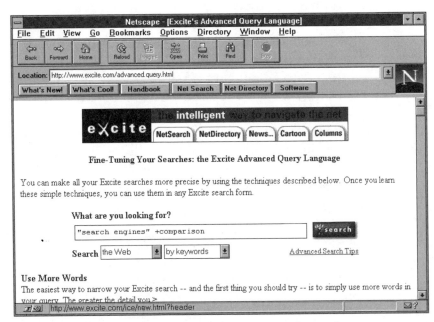

Figure 11-6: Using the plus sign in Excite to narrow the search.

Here are the search options in Excite:

○ Precede a word with a plus to indicate that it must appear in the document.

○ Precede a word with a minus to signify that the word must *not* appear in the document.

○ Use AND to specify multiple words that must appear some-where in the document.

○ Use OR to cause documents to match the criteria if any of the listed words are in the document.

You can find detailed instructions on the syntax for each search engine by reading that product's online help. For AltaVista, you would click on the Help icon shown at the top of Figure 11-3. For Excite, there is a hyperlink called Advanced Search Tips, as shown in Figure 11-6. The help screens for search syntax usually give examples to help you understand how you would use the various options to narrow your search for information.

The results of the advanced search are shown in Figure 11-7. The plus sign doesn't give you as much control as AltaVista's NEAR keyword. The Excite search has returned almost 7,000 references compared to the 200 that AltaVista returned. The references at the top of the list are more relevant than in the unqualified Excite search, however. You can tell from the descrip-tions of the documents that most of these definitely cover search engine comparisons. Compare this to the results list shown in Figure 11-5, where the first document on the list is from a Florida real estate company.

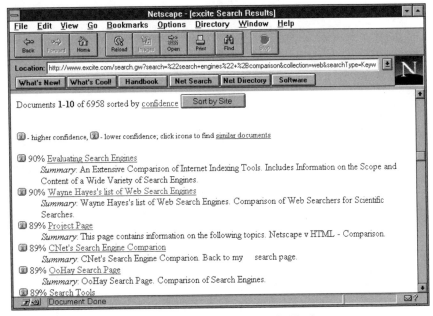

Figure 11-7: The results of using advanced syntax in Excite.

Search Engine Selection Criteria

When you select search software for your intranet, you want a product that will make it easy for your users to find information quickly. Fortunately, you and your users can test-drive these products. Just go to the company's site on the World Wide Web and use the software to look for information.

In addition to the criteria we saw in AltaVista and Excite (search syntax and displaying search results), you also want to look at installation, configuration, support, and indexing.

Search Syntax

There is nothing more frustrating than trying to find one particular bit of data and getting a list of thousands of documents back from a search engine because it doesn't have features to limit the search. You want to give your users as much search flexibility as possible.

Both Excite and AltaVista have syntax that will help narrow a search. With some of the older search engines, advanced search syntax may be limited.

One handy feature is the ability to include or exclude words or phrases from the search. Another useful feature is the ability to specify words that must be close to each other. AltaVista does this with the NEAR keyword.

AltaVista also lets you use wildcards. This is extremely helpful when a document might contain more than one form of the word you're using for a search.

Test search software to see how easy it is to narrow in on data.

Search Results List

How does the search engine format the list of hyperlinks to the documents matching the search? A few extra features can make it easier for users to decide which documents they want to explore.

AltaVista includes the full URL of the document in the results list. This can help employees see where the information is coming from. Excite displays a relevancy percentage to help people see at a glance which documents may not be as useful.

When you're trying various products, pay attention to how the results list helps you decide which documents are worth a look.

Installation, Configuration & Support

How easy will it be to set the software up to search your company's network for information? The only way you can tell is to install an evaluation copy at your site.

Some older UNIX search engines may require tinkering with system files and parameters. Other products can be maintained by clicking in web-page documents that come with the software.

The success of your intranet may hinge on how easy it is to find information. Don't rely on search software that has questionable support. You'll want to know that help is available if you need it.

You'll be using the search software a lot. Make sure you're comfortable with it.

Document Indexing Options

Search engines prepare your intranet for searches by noting which words appear in which documents. The software creates an index that relates each word to the documents where it appears. This allows the search engine to very rapidly return a list of all documents that meet your search criteria.

You'll want to give your users the option of searching subsets of the intranet. The plastics company wanted to give employees the ability to search through newsletters. They needed to index documents as a collection, instead of scattering them among other information.

You'll want to choose software that makes it easy for you to search the whole intranet or some related subsection of information.

Ted's Search Engine Selection

Ted selected Excite to provide the search capability for the plastics company's intranet. Excite is available free, although support costs $995 per year. Excite runs on the Netscape Communications Server that the plastics company uses, and has some options for limiting searches.

Excite, Inc.'s product literature promises that you'll have the product up and searching your intranet within thirty minutes. Ted found that this was true.

Let's take a look at how you work with Excite.

Setting Up Searching on a Subset of Information

Ted wanted to see how easy it was to configure Excite for searching only a subset of information. He wanted to let users search through the plant newsletters without seeing search results from unrelated data.

Excite is managed through web pages. Figure 11-8 shows the web page you use to set up a document collection. Excite uses the term "collection" to refer to a subset of documents that you want to search.

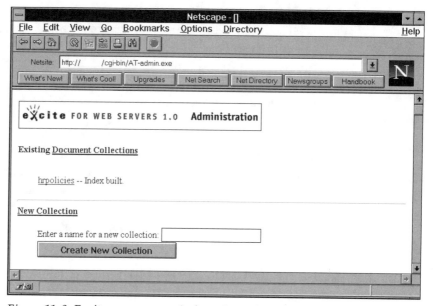

Figure 11-8: Excite management is done through web pages. Here you supply a name for a subset of intranet documents.

You tell Excite which documents belong in a collection by setting up index rules. Figure 11-9 shows the screen you use to do this. Name the directories containing the files in this collection, then give the file specification—which can include wildcards. This allows you to index only a subset of a directory's files based on some naming convention.

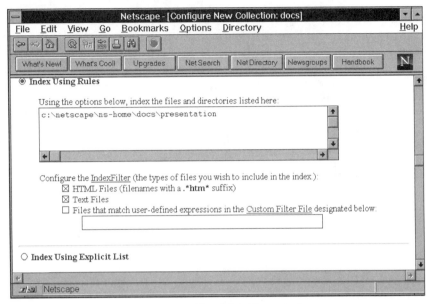

Figure 11-9: Use this screen to specify which files to index.

Indexing the Documents

Once you have specified a document collection, click on a button and Excite indexes all the words in each document in the collection. Figure 11-10 shows the screen Excite displays when the indexing is complete. The product tells you the size in bytes of the documents that have been indexed.

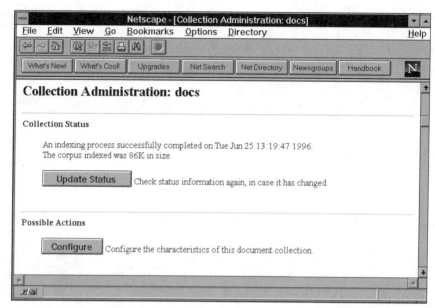

Figure 11-10: Excite displays this screen to confirm that the documents have been indexed.

Setting Up the Search Page

After Ted indexed the information, he had to give users a way to kick off a search. Excite makes this easy. Figure 11-11 shows the screen used to generate the search page. This screen lets you specify a banner to appear above the search area, then lets you enter the text that will describe the documents to be searched. With a few mouse clicks, you can generate a search page for the intranet.

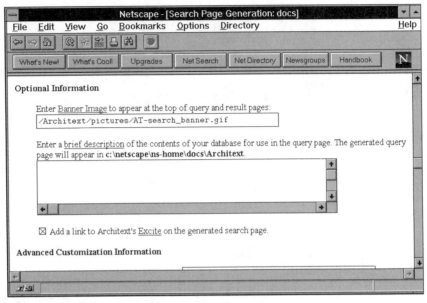

Figure 11-11: Generating a search page in Excite.

To see what the completed search page looks like, let's look at an example for KLP Industries. Figure 11-12 shows a search page that lets employees of the fictional KLP Industries search through a collection of customer call reports. To create this page, you tell Excite what image to use for the banner and what text you want to use for the names of the documents. Excite generates the HTML for you, including the call to the search engine that's associated with the Search button.

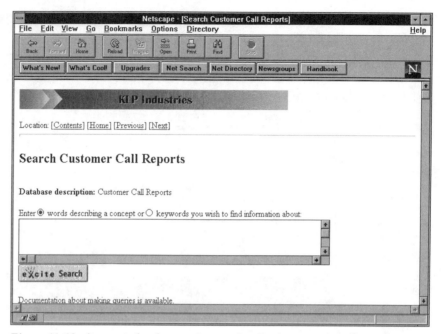

Figure 11-12: An example of a search page that Excite automatically generates.

You can modify the HTML that Excite generates—for example, you might want to substitute your own Search button for the one that Excite includes.

Setting Up the Results Page

You use a screen similar to the one in Figure 11-11 to specify how you want Excite to return the results. Just as with the search page, you can specify a banner and some text that should appear on the list of hyperlinks that Excite displays to users in response to a search.

Sometimes you don't want Excite to generate the search or results pages. You might want to have more control over their appearance, structuring them to match other intranet documents.

Excite lets you customize the search and/or results pages by using templates. Figure 11-13 shows the screen that lets you specify which templates to use.

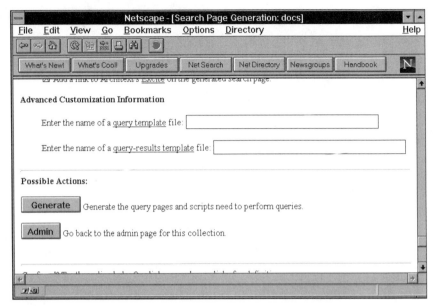

Figure 11-13: You can customize the Excite search or results pages by using templates.

To customize a results page, for example, you code an HTML document the way you want it to appear. Then you embed a special code at the spot in the document where you want Excite to start displaying search results. When a user initiates a search, the document appears with search results seamlessly embedded.

This gives you a lot of control over how users see search pages and search result pages. You can make these documents look like the standard document on your intranet.

Finding Search Software for Your Intranet

There are a number of search engines for all platforms. One site on the World Wide Web lists over 40 products. Fortunately, search engines are one product that you can definitely try before you buy. Because they are available for use on the World Wide Web, it's easy for you to compare the features of different search engines.

Here are some examples of search engine products and the platforms they run on:

○ **AltaVista Search Private Extensions** was just being finalized as this was written. It will initially be available for Windows NT and the DEC Alpha UNIX platforms. Pricing had not yet been determined. You can test the product and get more information at DEC's Web site (http://www.digital.com).

○ **Excite for Web Servers** runs on Windows NT and various UNIX platforms. The product is free. Support costs $995 per year. You test-drive the product and download a copy from the company's Web site (http://www.excite.com/).

○ **Apple e.g.** is a freeware product from Apple for the Macintosh. You can download a copy from Apple's Web site (http://www.cybertech.apple.com/appleeg.html).

○ **SearchServer** from Fulcrum Technologies is available for the Windows, Mac, OS/2, and UNIX platforms. For more information, visit Fulcrum's Web site (http://www.fulcrum.com/).

Search Engine Resources

Here are some resources for finding out more about search engines, including hyperlinks to the products themselves:

○ **Matrix of Search Engines.** The University of Michigan maintains a matrix of search engines (http://www.si.umich.edu/~fprefect/matrix/matrix.shtml). Figure 11-14 shows a section of the list. The matrix links to information and brief evaluations for each product, and also to the software itself.

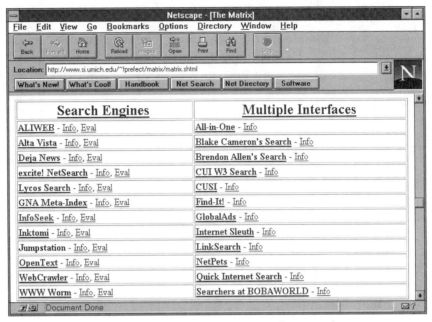

Figure 11-14: A matrix of information on search engines maintained by the University of Michigan.

○ **C I Net Search Engine Reviews.** C I Net has reviews of and links to 19 search engines at their Web site (http:// www.cnet.com/Content/Reviews/Compare/Search/).

○ **The Search Page.** This Web site is maintained by J. Marcus Zeigler. It is an extensive collection of hyperlinks to information about searching the World Wide Web, including links to reviews and tutorials about search engines. Definitely worth a visit (http://www.accesscom.com/~ziegler/search.html).

Moving On

You can enhance your intranet by giving users a way to easily find the information stored on it. Search engines extract value from your company's information in ways that were never possible before.

Discussion group or forum software also adds to the value of your internal web. This type of product makes it easy for employees across functions, divisions, and geography to share information and ideas. The next chapter shows you how to add this capability to your intranet.

Sharing Ideas on an Intranet

12

Many companies are using an intranet for an application called "best practices." The concept of best practices means the whole company benefits from the best ideas of employees from anywhere in the organization. To implement this application, you set up an environment that makes it easy for people to share ideas. Employees are exposed to ideas and procedures from around the company, and the best practices spread throughout the corporation.

You can provide a huge benefit to your company if you can use your intranet to establish an environment that makes it easy for employees to collaborate. Your company will reap the benefits of sharing the best ideas of employees across the organization.

One type of software you can use to help employees share ideas and practices is called discussion group software. This software is also called groupware or workgroup software.

This chapter shows you how to add value to your intranet by installing discussion group software.

Take the West Coast plastics company, for example. The company wanted the production facilities to share the best practices across locations. They put the plant newsletters on the intranet and let employees use search software to find all newsletter articles on a given topic. This was a good start of a best practices application, but it wasn't enough.

The newsletters contain one-way information. Someone writes an article and other employees read it. In earlier chapters, you saw a newsletter article about a product defect: surface bubbles in some of the products. This article provides useful information to all production facilities, but it doesn't provide the two-way communication that's necessary to solve the problem.

The plastics company needed some way to both collect ideas from employees on how to solve the problem and to let other employees learn from and respond to those ideas.

That's what discussion group software is for.

What Is Discussion Group Software?

Discussion group software allows employees to post messages that can be read by other employees across the company. You can respond to someone else's message; your response is appended to the original message.

Figure 12-1 shows how this works. This screen, from a demo of O'Reilly & Associates's WebBoard, shows a note and the options you have for working with that note. You can either post a new note or add a reply to the current note.

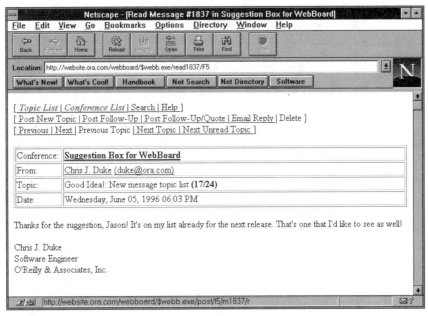

Figure 12-1: Using O'Reilly's WebBoard to view and respond to a note.

If someone responds to your reply to the original note, their response is appended to yours. Now you have a chain of three messages. As more employees post responses, the chain grows.

The chain of messages and responses is called a *thread*. A thread displays the original message and all responses in chronological order. Some discussion group products use indentation to visually display the order of the notes and replies.

Figure 12-2 shows an example of threaded discussions in O'Reilly's WebBoard. This screen shows the discussions posted on the topic of image maps. Notice that the software indents replies to a note to make it easier to tell which are original notes and which are responses.

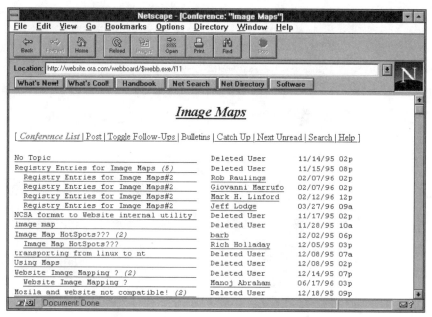

Figure 12-2: An example of threaded discussions in O'Reilly & Associates's WebBoard.

An employee at one of the plastics company's production facilities could post a note asking if anyone else has encountered bubble defects in products. Other employees could reply to the question, starting a thread on this topic. Employees at all facilities could learn from this exchange of ideas.

Organizing Ideas

Discussion group software provides another useful service; it organizes notes into collections of related ideas.

Many of the discussion group products use the terms *conference* and *topics*. A conference is a broad theme that's used to provide structure to employees' notes. Topics are like subcategories. They organize notes into narrow areas so you can see at a glance what subject is covered by a group of notes.

The screen in Figure 12-2 contains examples of both conference and topics. The conference is image maps. Each new note posted starts a topic, and replies to that note become part of that topic.

One of the topics in Figure 12-2 is image map hot spots. This topic contains the original note and one reply.

Figure 12-3 shows a list of conferences maintained at the WebBoard demo site (http://website.ora.com/webboard/$webb.exe). This list lets you see at a glance which subject areas are available. WebBoard also lists the number of messages in each conference, which gives you an idea of the activity in each conference.

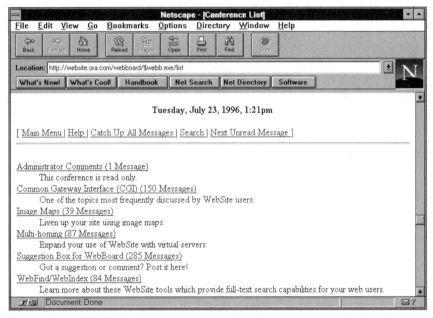

Figure 12-3: O'Reilly's WebBoard shows a list of conferences, including the number of messages in each conference.

Discussion group software groups notes into conferences and topics to make it easier to extract value from the ideas posted by employees.

The plastics company could start a conference on product defects. An employee could post a message in this conference about the bubble defect, which would start a topic on bubble defects. This structure makes it more likely that someone with the information you need will find the note and post a reply.

Advantages Over E-Mail

Why not use e-mail instead of discussion groups? Couldn't employees just exchange messages using existing e-mail software instead of using discussion groups?

One major limitation of e-mail is that you only see a note if someone sends it to you. Discussion group software lets you post information for anyone to see—you don't have to send each person a note.

Also, it may be difficult to keep a thread of ideas intact using e-mail. Let's look at an example.

If you're a production supervisor at the plastics company and you want to gather input on the bubble defect using regular e-mail, you have to go through some awkward procedures.

You'll probably start by sending a note to production supervisors at the other facilities. You'll ask them to pass the note along to anyone who can help with the problem. Now the fun starts. Before long, this note has been forwarded to 20 or 30 people. Input starts coming back from a number of employees. How do you make sure everyone sees the ideas from their colleagues?

E-mail is not a good solution for this situation. You could go through the tedious effort of forwarding replies back to a large list of people, but you're probably going to miss some key contacts. And what about the people who didn't get this note from you or the other supervisors?

Discussion group software solves these problems by acting as a public forum that records the back-and-forth exchange of ideas in chronological order. The software also organizes the notes into a topical hierarchy, making it easy to find the appropriate discussions.

Web Enhancements to Discussion Group Software

Discussion group software existed before the World Wide Web, but the Web brings enhancements to this category of products. You can enjoy the same enhancements on your intranet.

Web Browser Client

Before the Web, each discussion group product had its own proprietary client. The software had to be installed on every workstation, was often limited to one platform, and each product had a different interface.

The Web changes that. Web-enabled discussion group software uses a standard web browser as its client. This means the client software is platform independent and provides a consistent interface. You don't have to install any special client software to allow intranet users access to these products. Employees use their web browsers to share ideas.

It's easier than ever to make discussion groups available throughout your organization.

Hyperlinks to Discussion Groups

It's easy to link web-based discussion groups into your intranet. You just create hyperlinks that point to the software. Employees reading a document about some topic can jump right to the appropriate discussion group and share ideas.

The plastics company could put a hyperlink in the newsletter issue that covered the bubble defect. This link could point to a conference about the topic. An employee might read about the bubbles, jump to the conference, post a suggestion, then return to the newsletter. Your company would immediately capture employee ideas, and this would speed the response to the problem.

Hyperlinks in Discussion Group Messages

Many discussion group products allow you to put hyperlinks right in the body of a message. This is a powerful feature. You could post a message about some document on the intranet, say a corporate policy, then code a hyperlink pointing to that document. Anyone reading the message could click on the hyperlink and jump directly to the document itself before responding to your note. This feature saves time and extracts the value from intranet documents.

If you were posting a message about the bubble defect, you could add appropriate hyperlinks: one that points to a photo of the damaged product, another that links to customer comments, and a third that references a document from a vendor.

There are many uses for hyperlinks in discussion group messages. Someone in marketing could ask for feedback on a new product design and code links pointing to photos of the product. Someone in human resources could respond to a question by coding a link to some corporate policy document.

Ted's Discussion Group Software Selection

Let's use the plastics company's intranet to walk through how you would install discussion group software on your intranet.

Ted, the project leader for the plastics company's intranet, downloaded an evaluation of a discussion group product from Digital Corporation. When he downloaded the product, it was called Workgroup Web Forum. Digital has since changed the name to AltaVista Forum. I'll refer to the old name in this section, since that's the product Ted worked with.

The plastics company planned to use discussion software to share best practices across the corporation. They also planned to use it for online computer support and to allow various departments to gather feedback on projects and procedures.

Installation

Ted found that installing Workgroup Web Forum was easy. He started the installation by copying the downloaded software to a working directory on the Windows NT server; then he ran setup.exe from that directory.

The installation program prompted Ted for the directories to use for the discussion groups and for access control files. These access files are used to record which users can access the various discussion areas. Ted finished the installation by entering a password for the administrator's ID that's used to manage the software.

Configuration

Workgroup Web Forum uses the term *forum* instead of conference. Ted used the web page in Figure 12-4 to set up a forum called Production Procedures. This forum will be used to share ideas on production practices. Employees can also use the forum to ask for help with manufacturing problems.

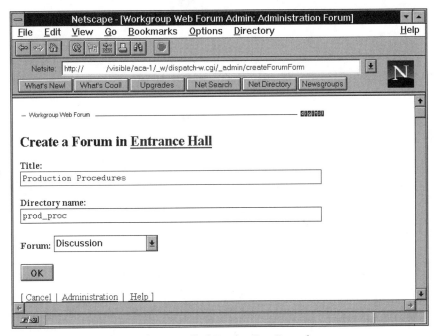

Figure 12-4: Ted set up a forum called Production Procedures.

Workgroup Web Forum has a category feature that helps you organize the topics in a forum. The software lets you assign categories to a forum. The categories appear as a drop-down list when users post a message. Users can assign a category to a message, then use Workgroup Web Forum's search engine to find all messages that match a given category.

Ted used the screen in Figure 12-5 to add a category called surface defects to the Production Procedures forum.

Build an Intranet on a Shoestring

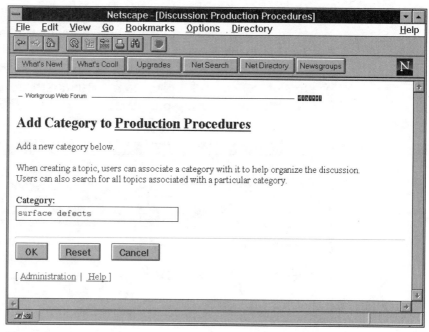

Figure 12-5: Ted added categories to the forum so users could search for related messages.

Workgroup Web Forum has a feature that allows the administrator to control the number of levels of replies in a forum. You can set up a read-only forum by selecting no replies. You can keep the replies to the point by limiting the forum to one level of replies. Ted set up the production procedures forum for five reply levels. This should allow for an exchange of ideas without letting the discussion get too far removed from the topic.

Ted finished the Workgroup Web Forum configuration, and intranet users could begin posting messages.

Discussion Group Messages

When you enter a forum in Workgroup Web Forum, you see a list of threaded topics. Figure 12-6 shows this screen. The topics are presented as hyperlinks. Clicking on a topic takes you to the messages in that thread.

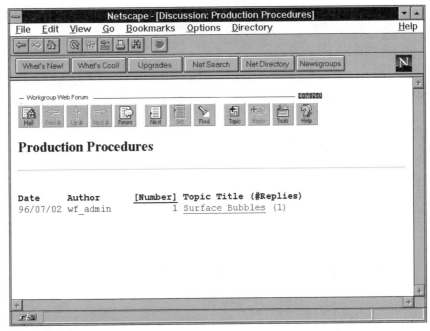

Figure 12-6: The topics in a forum are presented as hyperlinks. Clicking on a topic retrieves the message thread for that topic.

Figure 12-7 is an example of a message in Workgroup Web Forum. The message is about the bubble defects and has been assigned the category surface defects. Note the hyperlink that's embedded in the message. It points to a vendor's Internet site.

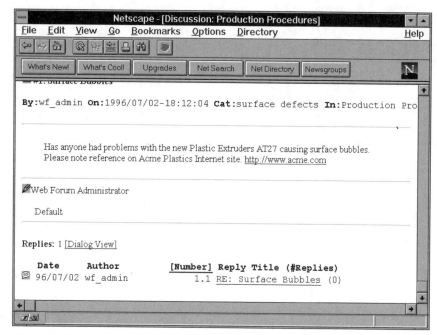

Figure 12-7: This message in a Workgroup Web Forum topic includes an embedded hyperlink.

There is a reply to the message. This appears below the original note. The software assigns a level number to each reply—it appears next to the subject of the reply. The level number of 1.1 indicates that this is the first reply to the original message. The level numbers help you determine the order of the messages.

Searching in Workgroup Web Forum

Most discussion group products provide search capability that lets you find all messages that include a certain word or phrase. Figure 12-8 shows the search screen in Workgroup Web Forum.

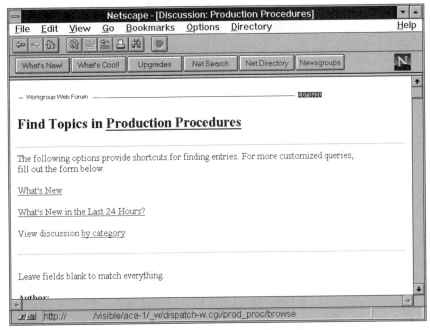

Figure 12-8: Employees use this screen to search through messages in Workgroup Web Forum.

The part of the search screen shown in Figure 12-8 lets you jump to documents that have been added since the last time you logged in, documents that have been added in the last 24 hours, or all documents matching a selected category. You can also scroll down to a search entry screen that will let you search by author, topic, or keywords in the body of messages.

Discussion Group Software Selection Criteria

Here are some key features to look for when selecting discussion group software for your intranet:

- ○ **Threaded discussions** help you keep track of the flow of information exchange. Most discussion group products let you divide messages into the equivalent of conferences and topics. They do vary, however, in how they display threaded discussions.

Some software uses indentation or level numbers to show the levels of replies in a topic. Some products simply list messages one right after another in the order they were posted, which makes it difficult to tell which reply goes with which message.

○ **Embedded hyperlinks** tie discussions to information stored on your intranet. This feature facilitates discussion. Employees can jump to a document or photo that illustrates the topic of a note, then return to the message and post a response.

Embedded links aid the exchange of information. You can put a link in a message that ensures everyone who reads the note can immediately jump to the same referenced information.

○ **Searching through messages**. Some products give you the capability to search through the messages in conferences. This extends the value of discussion groups because it lets employees quickly find crucial information hidden in various topics.

Some products add options to the search. For example, Digital's AltaVista Forum lets you add categories to notes, then search by these categories. It also allows you to search through only newly added messages.

Discussion Group Software Products

Here are some of the many discussion group products:

○ **Digital Corporation's AltaVista Forum**, formerly called Workgroup Web Forum, runs on Windows NT and Digital's UNIX. Prices start at $695 for one server with unlimited users.

You can visit http://webforum.research.digital.com/ info/wgwfinfo/wgwfinfo.html to download an evaluation copy or for more information. Digital maintains a list of customer case studies. Point your web browser to http:// altavista.software.digital.com/products/forum/whouse/ nfintro.htm to see this information.

○ **O'Reilly & Associates's WebBoard** is available for Windows 95 and Windows NT. WebBoard is priced at $149.

WebBoard's main menu shows you how many unread messages you have and gives you a hyperlink directly to these messages, as shown in Figure 12-9. You can also use the menu to select a conference or get information about discussion group users.

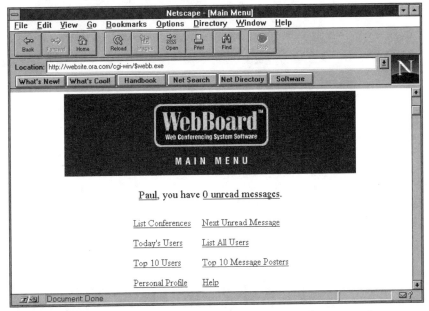

Figure 12-9: WebBoard's main menu lets you jump directly to unread messages.

WebBoard has a search capability that lets you look for all messages on a certain topic. You can select a conference to search, then indicate whether you want to find keywords in topic titles and messages or only in topic titles.

You can test drive WebBoard at O'Reilly's World Wide Web site (http://www.ora.com).

○ **Lundeen & Associates's Web Crossing** is available for Macintosh ($395), Windows NT ($495), and UNIX ($695) platforms.

Figure 12-10 shows a threaded discussion from one of the Web Crossing demos. Note the ability to embed a graphic right into a message.

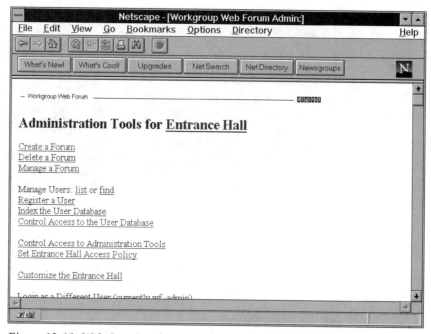

Figure 12-10: Web Crossing from Lundeen & Associates can display embedded graphics in messages.

Web Crossing displays the messages in a thread in the order they were posted, with no indenting or numbering to show the relationship of messages. Figure 12-10 is a good example of the problem this can cause. Is the third message a reply to the first or second message?

Lundeen & Associates maintains a Web page that contains an extensive link to customers who use Web Crossing. Figure 12-11 shows one of the customers, Napa County. You can visit these sites to get a feel for how people are using Web Crossing and discussion groups in general.

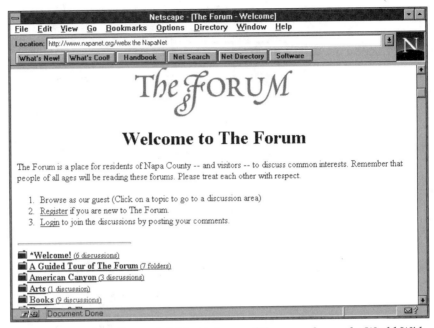

Figure 12-11: Napa County's Web site is one of the examples on the World Wide Web that shows discussion group software in action.

- ○ **Screen Porch, Inc.** offers Caucus, a discussion group program for Windows NT and UNIX. The product sells for $1,795 for unlimited users. See http://screenporch.com/ for more information.

- ○ **Web Threads** from inTouch Technologies is another discussion group product for Windows NT and UNIX. It's priced at $499. See http://www.in-touch.com/threads.html for more information.

Discussion Group Software Resources

Tietotie is an Internet Provider in Finland who maintains a list of over 20 discussion group products (http://www.tietotie.fi/pep/conference_tools.html).

Figure 12-12 shows part of this extensive list. The text briefly mentions product features and lists platforms. There is a hyperlink to vendor Web sites where you can see the product in action, download an evaluation, or get more information.

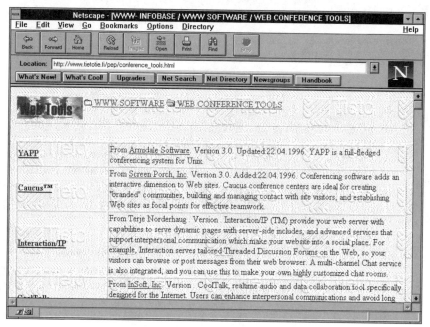

Figure 12-12: Tietotie maintains an extensive list of discussion group software at its World Wide Web site.

Moving On

Discussion group software adds value to your intranet. It lets your users easily share ideas across the organization. Best practices, help desk forums, and product feedback are three typical applications for this kind of software.

The next chapter shows you how to add value to your intranet by extending the capability of the client software. Helpers and plug-ins are two categories of products that give users features that go beyond the limits of web browsers.

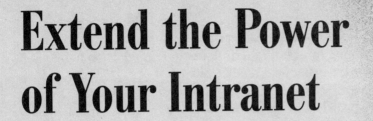

Extend the Power of Your Intranet

Your web browser is designed to display HTML documents. You've learned that you can use HTML to give your users live online versions of their information. Sometimes, however, you want to present data in its native format.

Your company has a lot of data in formats such as spreadsheets and word processing documents. While you can convert this information to HTML, it can be very difficult and time consuming to reproduce the exact appearance of these formats using HTML. And it would be extremely difficult to provide the functionality of these documents, especially an interactive spreadsheet, using HTML.

Your intranet users don't have to leave their spreadsheets behind. In this chapter you'll learn how to extend the capabilities of your web browsers to any file format, including spreadsheets, word processing documents, audio, and video. You'll learn how to use your intranet to serve up virtually any kind of information.

Take the West Coast plastics company as an example. The company has several Microsoft Excel spreadsheets that are designed to be used as templates for work processes. These include a spreadsheet used for expense reports, a seminar budget worksheet, marketing forecasting templates, and spreadsheets that perform employee benefit calculations.

When an employee wants to use one of these standard spreadsheets, he or she has to find it on the LAN. Since the spreadsheets are maintained by different departments, they are in multiple LAN directories. Finding the right spreadsheet can be a hassle.

Ted, the plastics company's intranet project leader, wanted to use the intranet to make access to these spreadsheets easier. He wanted to create a web page table of contents that pointed to the spreadsheets. Employees would click on a link to bring up a particular spreadsheet.

Figure 13-1 shows a web page that serves as a table of contents pointing to shared spreadsheets.

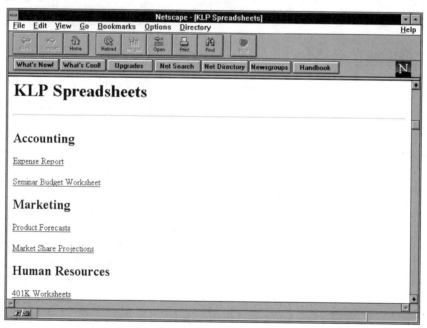

Figure 13-1: This web page allows employees to bring up a spreadsheet by clicking on a hyperlink.

Ted wanted users to be able to invoke the Excel spreadsheets in Excel, not as an HTML document that merely duplicates the data from a spreadsheet. He wanted intranet users to be able to enter and manipulate data, then print the spreadsheet and save it to their local hard drive.

A web browser's standard features don't include the ability to display spreadsheets, so Ted had to extend the capabilities of the intranet web browsers using a feature called a helper app.

Helper Apps

A web browser right out of the box can only handle a few file formats. Web browsers are designed to work with HTML files and text files. Most browsers also know how to deal with graphic images in the GIF and JPEG formats.

You can configure a web browser to handle file formats that are outside of its built-in capabilities by telling it to hand those formats off to other programs. The term for these other programs is helper apps.

A helper app is any program that a web browser has been instructed to associate with a given file format. This is done by referring to file extensions.

For example, Excel spreadsheets have an extension of XLS. You can add Excel as a browser helper app by adding a line to the browser configuration that tells the software to hand a file off to Excel whenever it has an XLS extension.

When a browser calls a helper app, the document is not displayed inside of the browser itself. The browser passes control to whatever software has been designated as a helper app for a given extension. When the user exits the helper app, control returns to the browser.

Before we look at how this works, we have to talk about how the web server lets the web browser know what kind of file to expect.

Configuring Your Web Server for Helper Apps

Web technology includes a standard way for the web server to let the Web browser know what kind of file the browser is about to receive. The server uses something called a Multipurpose Internet

Mail Extension (MIME) to identify file formats. MIME was initially set up to identify the types of files that could be sent as attachments to Internet mail. When the World Wide Web was designed, it used MIME as a way for the server to tell the browser what type of file was being transmitted.

Web servers have a file called mime.types. This file contains a list of file formats in the form of type/subtype. Examples of entries in a typical mime.types file are:

```
text/html      html htm
text/plain     txt
image/gif      gif
image/jpeg     jpeg jpg jpe
```

In the first line above, text is the type and html is the subtype. Following type/subtype entries are the extensions associated with the file format. The first line in the example above indicates that HTML files have either an HTML or HTM extension.

When a web server sends a file to a web browser, it first sends a header. The header includes an entry for the MIME type of the file.

If you want your intranet to have the capability to serve Microsoft Excel spreadsheets, you have to add a line to the mime.type file for this format. The entry would look like the following:

```
application/msexcel    xls xlc
```

The XLS extension is for Excel spreadsheets starting with version 5. The XLC extension is used with earlier versions.

Note
See the documentation of your web server for the directory location of the mime.type file. The file will be called something like mime.typ on servers that don't support long extensions.

This allows the web server to tell the web browser to expect an Excel spreadsheet, but it doesn't tell the browser which software to load for this file format. To set this up, you have to make the appropriate entry in the browser configuration.

Configuring Your Browser for Helper Apps

You can configure a browser to use just about any software as a
helper app. The exact method of configuring a helper app may
vary by browser, but basically you have to tell the browser two
things: which file extension to associate with which software and
the location of that software program.

Ted set up the company's Netscape browsers to use Excel as a
helper app by adding a line to the helper configurations in the
Netscape Navigator Preferences dialog box.

Figure 13-2 shows the screen Ted used to add Excel as a helper
app in Netscape Navigator. The dialog gave Ted three options for
handling a file of this type: the file could be saved directly to disk
for later use, the browser could prompt the user to specify the
name of the program to use (including the fully qualified path), or
the browser could launch the application. Ted selected the last
option and entered the name and location of Excel.

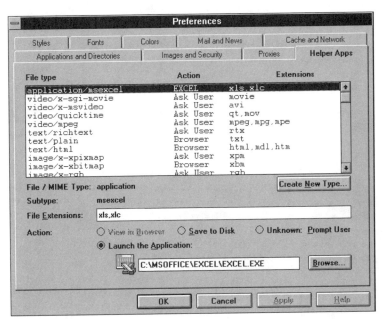

*Figure 13-2: You use this helper app dialog box in Netscape Navigator to add
Microsoft Excel to the list of helper apps.*

Now all that's left is creating an HTML document that contains hyperlinks pointing to Excel spreadsheets.

Coding a Link to Invoke a Helper App

You've seen how to configure the browser to associate a given file type with a helper app. When you want to include a file on your intranet that requires a helper app, you simply code a hyperlink that points to that file—with the appropriate extension. The browser automatically recognizes that a helper app is needed and passes the file to the proper software.

To create a link to a spreadsheet, for example, you use the standard HTML for a hyperlink. To link to the seminar budget spreadsheet, for example, you would code something like:

```
<A HREF="/acct/tools/sembudg.xls">Seminar Budget Worksheet</A>
```

This assumes that the Excel spreadsheet is in the same web server directory as the document containing the hyperlinks. If it's not, you will have to code the path in the hyperlink.

Although this example uses a spreadsheet, the results are the same for other software. If you configured a word processor as a helper app, users would have all the functionality of that software available when the browser invoked the helper app. The same is true for other software you might use as helper apps.

For example, the web page in Figure 13-1 contains a hyperlink to the seminar budget worksheet. If you click on this link, the browser will launch Excel and hand it the spreadsheet. The result will be the screen shown in Figure 13-3.

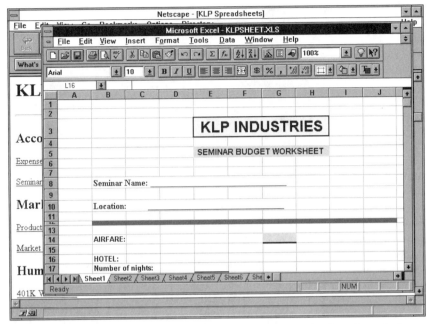

Figure 13-3: This screen shows an Excel spreadsheet that has been launched as a helper app from a Netscape browser.

When the spreadsheet appears, as shown in Figure 13-3, it's a fully functional spreadsheet. You can use this worksheet like you would if you had launched Excel directly, except that you can't save it back to the server. To save the worksheet, you have to use the Save As dialog box and save the file to your hard disk or a network directory.

Employees at the plastics company are required to use the seminar budget worksheet when they ask to attend a seminar. They enter the data pertaining to the seminar they want to attend, print it out, and attach the printout to their request. The intranet makes it easier for them to do this work process.

Why Bother?

Since employees can load spreadsheets, word processing documents, or other files directly using the original software, why go through the effort of adding these files to the intranet? What does the intranet add to the process?

The advantage of using the intranet is that it makes it easier to organize the company's shared files. You can add one document to the intranet that links to all the shared files that the company uses.

An example of this would be an intranet page containing links to the various spreadsheets that the company uses. This allows you to organize the spreadsheets by department or function, and makes it easy to highlight recently added files.

The intranet also shields the user from having to know the file location. This is coded in the hyperlink. The employee just clicks in the browser and the spreadsheet file appears.

You can use your intranet to put an easy-to-navigate map on top of your company's information. This can include spreadsheets, word processing documents, and other file formats.

Helper Application Examples

Just about any software can be set up as a helper app. Sometimes you'll want to use common office software as intranet helpers apps. There are also software products that provide a specialized function for intranet and
Internet applications.

Let's look at some examples of how helper apps are being used in intranets.

Word Processing Documents

Eli Lilly, the global pharmaceutical company, has set up Microsoft Word as a helper app. Eli Lilly information consultant John Swartzendruber said this allows the company to post some documents to the intranet without having to convert them to HTML.

Using Word as a helper app makes sense for some frequently updated documents, Swartzendruber said. Otherwise this is a two-step process. Someone makes the changes in Word, then converts the changed document to HTML. The helper app approach eliminates the ongoing conversion of these files and lets users edit the files in their word processors instead of an HTML editor.

Sometimes word processing documents have formatting that can't easily be translated to HTML. You can use your word processor as a helper app in these situations.

Adobe Acrobat

Sometimes you want a document to retain its original appearance, but you don't want to force users to launch a full-featured application just to view the information.

Adobe Systems, Inc. makes a software package called Acrobat that lets you take documents created in word processors, spreadsheets, and graphics programs and save them to a file called a Portable Document Format (PDF). The file retains its formatting, but it doesn't require you to launch the original application to view the document. You view the PDF in another Adobe software package, Acrobat Reader.

Acrobat Reader is available for Windows, Mac, and UNIX platforms. This cross-platform implementation makes PDF files suitable for your intranet (or the World Wide Web for that matter).

To use this technology on your intranet, capture some document with Adobe Acrobat Capture and save it to a file with a PDF extension. Then add Adobe Acrobat Reader as a helper app in employees' web browsers. When an employee clicks a hyperlink pointing to a PDF file, Acrobat Reader is launched. The employee can then scroll through a replica of the word processing document, spreadsheet, or graphic image.

Let's look at an example of this technology in action.

Arizona State University makes state tax forms available as Acrobat PDF files on the World Wide Web. Figure 13-4 shows the form that appears when you visit ASU's World Wide Web site (http://aspin.asu.edu/aztax/download.htm) and click on a hyperlink that points to one of these forms.

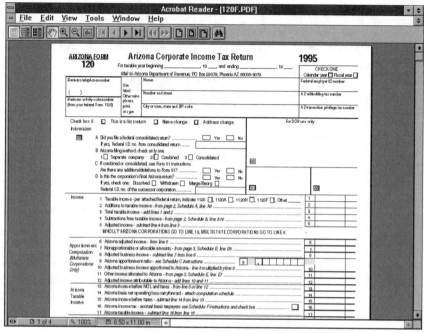

Figure 13-4: You can view an Arizona state tax form by using Adobe Acrobat Reader as a helper app.

The tax form in Figure 13-4 retains the appearance of the original, but you don't have to load a word processor or other software to view it. You can scroll through the form, zoom in to get a closer look, and print it.

The plastics company is using Adobe Acrobat Reader to display drawings of product labels. The zoom feature lets sales and marketing users zoom in to see fine print on the label. Employees can examine proposed labels online, then send comments back to the art department.

3M uses Adobe Acrobat to give intranet users access to reports in their original format. Employees convert spreadsheets, word processing documents, and other files to Acrobat PDF documents.

Adobe Acrobat Reader is freeware. You can download Acrobat Reader for the Windows, Mac, and UNIX platforms at Adobe's Web site (http://www.adobe.com). The software you use to create Acrobat PDF files is Adobe Acrobat. The software is priced at $295 and is also available for all platforms.

Adobe has a list of links to customer Web sites that use PDF files. Visit http://www.adobe.com/acrobat/coolpdf.html to see this list.

RealAudio

You can use a helper app to add audio to your intranet. A cross-platform product that was designed to provide audio on the World Wide Web, and on intranets, is RealAudio from Progressive Networks.

RealAudio provides streaming audio. This means that the audio player doesn't wait until the entire audio file arrives, but starts playing as soon as the connection is made.

A RealAudio server for five concurrent users costs $495 and is available for Windows, Mac, and UNIX platforms. The RealAudio player costs $15 per user for 500 users. See the company's Web site (http://www.realaudio.com) for more information on pricing.

To create audio content you'll need recording equipment and audio editing software. This is in addition to the RealAudio server and player.

Progressive Networks RealAudio Web site (http://www.realaudio.com/intranet/examples.html) contains case studies of companies that are using the technology for their intranets. Figure 13-5 shows one of these case studies, Hewlett Packard.

Figure 13-5: Hewlett Packard is one of the RealAudio case studies on Progressive Networks' Web site.

Hewlett Packard uses RealAudio on their intranet to allow employees who were not able to attend some company event to hear speeches from that event. Employees in other locations can be a part of corporate functions.

First Union National uses RealAudio to make aural copies of corporate reports available to branch locations. Charles Schwab uses RealAudio to provide training to customer representatives.

Intranet Video

You can use helper apps to add video to your intranet. Levi Strauss is using video on their intranet to let employees around the world view the latest product commercials and promotional videos. Levi Strauss uses this capability as part of a best practices approach. They want employees in all locations to learn from commercials and promotional videos produced by the various business units.

Apple Corporation's QuickTime is cross-platform video software for the World Wide Web and intranets. The QuickTime player runs on Windows, Mac, and UNIX platforms. The QuickTime editing software runs on Windows and Mac.

Intranet video requires the necessary video equipment and software. Because the cost of such equipment goes beyond the "shoestring" theme of this book, I won't discuss it further. You can get more information about Apple's QuickTime at their Web site (http://www.apple.com).

Finding & Installing Helper Apps

Netscape has a Web page that lists helper apps by platform (http://www.netscape.com/assist/helper_apps/index.html). You can find helper apps for presenting documents, audio, video, and more.

Netscape also has a Web page containing instructions for installing helper apps on all platforms. See http://www.netscape.com/assist/helper_apps/shorthelper.html for this information.

Helper App Pros & Cons

You can use helper apps to extend the capabilities of your intranet. You can make it possible for your intranet to serve up spreadsheets, word processing documents, and other types of files.

One of the advantages of helper apps is their ability to access information in its original format. This preserves the appearance of the information, reduces the amount of information that has to be converted to HTML, and lets employees uses the full functionality of software like spreadsheets and word processors.

There are disadvantages to using helper apps. When a browser makes a call to a helper program, the software is loaded into memory. This eats up resources, and the user has to wait while the software loads.

Helper apps also require setting up browser configurations on each desktop. This takes away some of the advantage a browser has as a universal client. It also means that you may have to purchase additional copies of desktop software. You may already have LAN copies of spreadsheets and word processing documents. If you don't, or you have insufficient licenses, you could incur a considerable expense making helper apps available throughout the company.

If you have a mixed platform computing environment, helper apps can cause another problem: incompatibility. If you have UNIX workstations, they won't be able to use Microsoft Excel as a helper app. In such a case, if you don't keep a backup copy of the information in some other format, UNIX users will not have access to the information.

In spite of the drawbacks of helper apps, they can bring considerable benefits to your intranet users. They allow you to increase the number of ways the intranet can present information and allow the company to continue harvesting its investment in desktop software.

Plug-ins

When a browser helper app is invoked, there is a disruption as the newly launched application takes control. One second you're looking at the browser, and the next second the screen has been taken over by some other software.

Netscape pioneered a solution to this problem. They designed a concept called a *plug-in*. A plug-in is similar to a helper app. It extends the capability of the browser by adding functionality that the browser doesn't have. The difference is that this functionality is activated within the browser itself. There is no disruptive launching of a second window. When you invoke a plug-in, the software appears within the browser window.

Microsoft recently added similar technology, called ActiveX. ActiveX controls also are browser add-ins that appear within the frame of the browser window.

Configuring Your Browser for Plug-ins

Most plug-ins are available for downloading from the World Wide Web. To set up a browser for a particular plug-in, download the file, then run the product's installation program. The installation program usually makes the appropriate configuration changes to the browser. If it doesn't, you'll be given instructions on how to configure the browser to associate the appropriate file type with the plug-in software.

A Spreadsheet Plug-in

You saw how you can include spreadsheets in your intranet by adding spreadsheet software as a helper app. Let's see how a spreadsheet could be implemented as a browser plug-in.

Visual Components makes a spreadsheet plug-in called Formula One/NET Pro. This product lets you embed a fully functional spreadsheet object inside of a web page.

Formula One/NET Pro costs $79 per copy. It's a working spreadsheet that can read and write Excel spreadsheets. The product is available for Windows 3.1, Windows 95, and Windows NT. You can download an evaluation copy of the product at the company's Web site (http://www.visualcomp.com/f1net/download.htm).

Visual Components has a Web page that links to examples of the product in action (http://www.visualcomp.com/f1net/example.htm). Figure 13-6 shows an example of a blank worksheet that can be embedded in a web page.

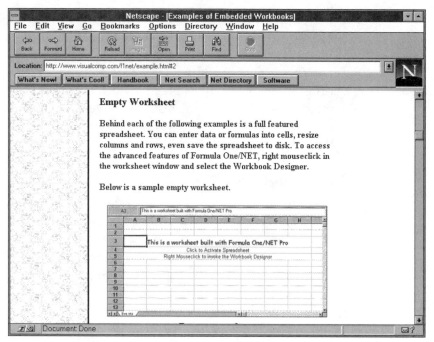

Figure 13-6: A Formula One/NET Pro worksheet can be embedded in a web page. It's a fully functional spreadsheet.

You can design a fairly advanced interactive application using Formula One/NET Pro and Excel spreadsheets. Figure 13-7 is a table of mutual funds. At the top is a data entry area where you enter the amount to invest. The spreadsheet calculates the estimated returns from each mutual fund.

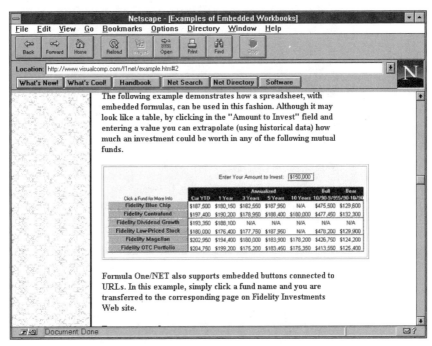

Figure 13-7: You can use Formula One/NET Pro to create sophisticated applications. Here you can enter an amount to invest and see the results by mutual fund.

The worksheet in Figure 13-7 also shows Formula One's ability to use embedded hyperlinks. The names of the mutual funds are actually buttons coded with hyperlinks. You can click on one of the buttons to jump to another web page.

This product allows you to give spreadsheet capabilities to intranet users without launching a separate application.

Embedding Objects in Web Pages

To use the plug-in software in your intranet, you have to embed objects in a web page that will invoke the plug-in. To embed a plug-in object, you use the HTML embed tag.

Here is how the Formula One mutual fund spreadsheet was embedded in the example shown in Figure 13-7.

```
<embed src="vtsfiles/funds.vts" width=690 height=220>
```

This code causes the browser to load the funds.vts worksheet and hand it off to the Formula One/NET plug-in. When the Formula One/NET plug-in was installed, it mapped the .VTS extension to the plug-in.

Adobe Acrobat Plug-in

Figure 13-4 showed a document viewed in Adobe Acrobat Reader. The software took control of the screen, and obscured the browser.

Adobe now makes a plug-in for Netscape browsers on all platforms. This plug-in lets you view PDF files within the browser frame and does not start up a separate window.

The Adobe plug-in was formerly called Amber. Now this product has been rolled into Adobe Acrobat 3.0. The list price of the software is $295 per use. See Adobe's Web site (http://www.adobe.com) for more details.

Autodesk, Inc.'s WHIP! Plug-in

Autodesk, Inc. makes drafting software called AutoCad. The company recently introduced Autodesk WHIP!, a plug-in for Netscape Navigator that allows World Wide Web or intranet users to view and manipulate AutoCad drawings.

Engineers at the plastics company use AutoCad for engineering blueprints. The company is interested in the WHIP! plug-in as a way to let engineers at the corporate offices and at each location share drawings.

WHIP! is still a beta product. You can download the product from a Web page at Autodesk's Web site (http://www.autodesk.com/products/autocad/whip/whip.htm). Pricing is not yet available.

Other Plug-ins

There are plug-ins for audio, video, and other functions. Netscape keeps a list of plug-ins at its Web site, as shown in Figure 13-8. This page divides the plug-ins into categories.

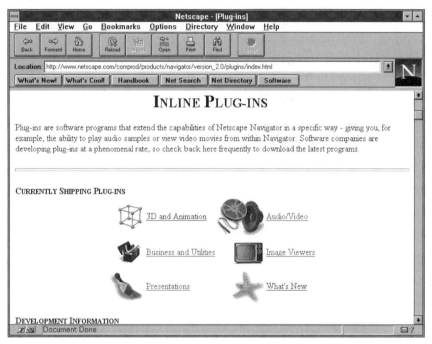

Figure 13-8: Netscape keeps a list of plug-ins organized by category at its Web site (http://www.netscape.com/comprod/products/navigator/version_2.0/plugins/index.html).

Yahoo! has a list of over 30 Netscape plug-ins. Part of their list is shown in Figure 13-9. Visit http://www.yahoo.com/Computers_and_Internet/Internet/World_Wide_Web/Browsers/Netscape_Navigator/Plug_Ins/ to scroll through the information.

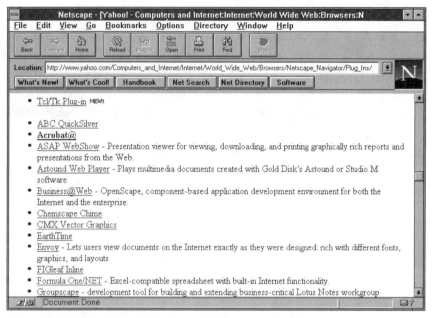

Figure 13-9: Yahoo! has a list of over 30 Netscape plug-ins.

Microsoft ActiveX Controls

Microsoft ActiveX controls are similar to Netscape plug-ins. They extend the capability of the browser without launching a separate window.

ActiveX is a new technology. There aren't yet as many ActiveX controls as Netscape plug-ins, but the list is growing.

Some products are available as both Netscape plug-ins and Microsoft ActiveX controls. These include Adobe Acrobat and Autodesk's WHIP!

Microsoft keeps a list of ActiveX controls on a page at its World Wide Web site (http://www.microsoft.com/ActiveX/).

Pros & Cons of Plug-ins & ActiveX Controls

Netscape browser plug-ins and Microsoft ActiveX controls extend the capability of Web browsers. They also keep the added capability within the browser window without requiring a distracting launch of another window.

Plug-ins and ActiveX controls have many disadvantages when used in an intranet. The majority of the products only run in the Windows environment. There are a few plug-ins for the Mac version of Netscape and only four for the UNIX version (at the time of this writing). If you have a mixed platform environment, plug-ins and ActiveX can present a problem.

The products require a certain browser. This completely overrides the open standards of Web technology and ties you into specific client software. If you can control which browsers are used throughout the organization, it may not cause a problem for you.

If you can overcome these disadvantages, you're still faced with the fact that plug-ins require you to purchase additional software for each client workstation that will use the technology. The aggregated costs of rolling out these products to intranet users will soon move beyond the "shoestring" category.

When to Use Browser Extensions

Helper applications are useful in a variety of situations. They let you add the ability to use existing information without conversion. They also let you use the hyperlinked, point-and-click environment of an intranet to deliver the functionality of desktop software. It's likely that you'll find at least a couple of applications for helper apps.

In my opinion, plug-ins and ActiveX controls are valuable in an intranet for limited, specialized use. The products allow you to use the intranet to deliver applications like engineering drawings to a select group and still take advantage of the ease of use hyperlinked documents provide.

The trick is to extend the functionality of your intranet browsers only where it adds value to your intranet.

Moving On

You've seen how to enhance the value of your intranet by extending the functionality of your users' web browsers. You have to be selective about when to use this capability, but helpers, plug-ins, and ActiveX controls can add to the features you offer your intranet users.

Another way to add value to your intranet is to give users the ability to access corporate data from within the intranet. In the next chapter, you'll learn about products that let you embed database queries in intranet web pages.

Connecting Your Intranet to Corporate Data

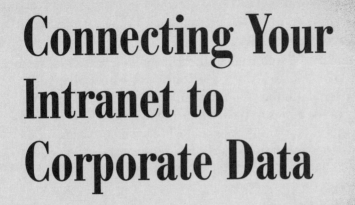

Chapter 13 showed you how to use your intranet to access company information stored in spreadsheets and word processing documents. In this chapter you'll learn how to connect intranet web pages to corporate databases.

When you create links from your intranet to the company's databases, you give employees the capability to access the core data of the business from within their web browsers. You add to the value of the intranet by giving users a point-and-click map to their data and shielding them from the sometimes messy details of querying databases.

Intranet Applications for Databases

How would you use a database in your intranet? Here are some examples of how companies are using links to corporate data in intranet web pages.

Checking Operational Data

Sun Microsystems has a web page in their intranet that links to fixed asset data stored in an Oracle database. Employees can look up asset information by serial number, tag number, or other keys. Managers can get listings of the assets in their department, link to further details, and even retire or transfer assets using a web browser.

You can link your intranet to application databases to let employees check on important data without leaving their browsers.

Multiple Search Criteria

Search engines are good at searching through intranet documents looking for words or phrases, but sometimes you want a more controlled search of some piece of information. When you link a web-page form to a database, you can create sophisticated query-by-example applications where users can search on a number of fields at once.

Netscape has a case study at its Web site (http://www.netscape.com/) that shows how one company uses a database to implement a multiple-criteria search. This company is the commercial real estate broker Cushman & Wakefield.

Cushman & Wakefield is building an intranet application that will let brokers around the country query a database of real estate properties. Brokers will use a web-page form that lets them specify the city to search, the desired square foot space, the rental price range, and other factors. This will return a hyperlinked list of properties meeting the criteria. Clicking on a property will bring up the details of that site.

You can match a database with web-page text and graphics to create a query-by-example application that lets users quickly narrow in on the exact data they are looking for.

Work Process Automation

Some companies use the intranet to allow employees to handle a work process from within their web browsers. An example of this is an intranet application that allows employees to order supplies. Employees can start by linking to an office supply database that shows them the on-hand balance and cost of various supplies. They can fill out a requisition and enter it directly into a database.

An intranet sometimes makes it easier to automate processes that require connections to databases. You don't have to install an application on each user's workstation. You just code a web page that connects to the database as needed, then make this page available on your intranet.

Reports on Demand

Companies sometimes create online reports by taking a pre-defined set of reports, converting them to HTML documents, and storing them on the intranet web server. The savings over a paper-based reporting system can be substantial.

You can create online reports for your intranet users—without the hassle of creating every possible report and storing the pre-formatted documents on the web server.

The trick is to build intranet documents that act as report templates. These documents offer drop-down lists, radio buttons, check boxes, and text input fields to allow employees to choose the data they want to see on a report. The reports don't exist on the server; they're created dynamically as each user requests a custom view of information. You do this by linking the report specification forms to databases.

You can have the savings of an online reporting system without the considerable hassle of creating reports ahead of time. You let the intranet create the reports on demand.

Dynamic, Data-driven Intranet Documents

One of the most exciting applications of databases is the ability to create entire web pages on the fly. These dynamic documents are created by assembling the text, graphics, and hyperlinks for the page based on the contents of a database.

An example of this would be a web page that serves as a clickable table of contents to your company's products. Let's say you have 10,000 items, and your company divides the products into 4 general product types, 50 product families, and 500 product categories. The relationship between the hierarchy of products is constantly changing, and items are continually added and deleted.

If you had to manually create and maintain the web pages that let employees navigate through a three level hierarchy into 10,000 ever-changing items, your work would never be done. It would be a maintenance nightmare. A better solution would be to create a system that uses the company's product database to automatically create the hierarchical web pages on demand. Employees would always see the most up-to-date product data, and you wouldn't have to manually maintain the structure.

There is software available that can automatically turn the data from a relational database into hyperlinks that point to the next level of information. You can use this type of software to create the data-driven web pages that would give employees easy access to product data.

Here's how the system works. When the user starts the application, a web page is displayed showing the four general types of products. When he or she clicks on one of these choices, the database retrieves all of the product families in that product type and places them as hyperlinks on the next web page. The user continues to browse into finer detail until the items themselves are displayed.

All of these web pages are created dynamically by the database program, and they always reflect the current data.

Some companies take the concept of data-driven intranet pages even further. They store all the elements of web pages—text, graphics, HTML tags—in a database and let the system generate entire collections of web pages dynamically. This might require more work initially, but it allows companies to change the design of whole sections of the intranet by making a few changes to the database and letting the system generate the redesigned web pages.

You can use databases to automate the creation and maintenance of intranet content.

Connecting Intranet Documents to Databases

What's the big deal about connecting intranet documents to databases? After all, there are only three components involved: the web browser, the web server, and the database.

Databases & Web Technology

The problem is that the web browser wants to send a request to the web server and get an HTML document in return. The web server receives a request and knows it has to return a file to the browser, but it doesn't have the capability to directly query the database. The web server has to pass the query to a program that handles the details of retrieving the data and creating the HTML file that the browser expects.

It's up to you to somehow implement a program that can take a request from a web browser, turn it into a database query, retrieve the data from the database, and format the results as an HTML document. You also have to code HTML documents so they send queries that this back-end program can understand.

Low-Level Programming

One way to create a link between the web server and a database is to write an interface program in a low-level language like C or Perl. There are freeware programs on the market in these languages that can parse a request from a web browser and turn it into an SQL query. It's still up to you to code the programming logic that takes the query results and creates an HTML page. This can be a tedious and time-consuming process.

A step up from programming the interface in C or Perl is to use the web-enabled features of enterprise databases like Oracle or sybase. These products take some of the complexity out of connecting web pages to databases, but they still require knowledge of their procedural languages. Plus, it's expensive to purchase the products for your intranet if you're not already using them for other applications.

Database Queries on a Shoestring

Fortunately, there are some inexpensive products on the market that simplify the process of connecting web pages to virtually any database. I'll show you three of them, explain how to use them, and show you examples of how they are used on the World Wide Web.

Allaire's Cold Fusion

Allaire's Cold Fusion is an Internet/intranet development product that lets you tie web pages to databases without programming. The software runs on Windows NT and Windows 95 and can link to most databases.

You use a template to tell Cold Fusion how you want to work with the database and how to format query results. The template contains a mixture of standard HTML and extensions to HTML that Allaire calls Database Markup Language (DBML). The DBML tags specify database queries and results page formatting. Templates are stored on the web server with a DBM extension.

Users kick off the Cold Fusion process by clicking on either a hyperlink or the Submit button in a form. Here are the steps in the process:

1. The browser sends the request from the form or hyperlink to the web server. In the HTML file, this is coded as a call to the Cold Fusion executable (dbml.exe) with the name of a template as a parameter.

2. The web server forwards the request to the dbml.exe program.

3. The Cold Fusion program reads the DBML commands in the template and uses them to send a query to the database.

4. The database sends the query results back to the Cold Fusion program.

5. Cold Fusion uses the DBML and HTML codes in the template to format the query results into an HTML document and sends it to the web server.

6. The web server returns the HTML document to the browser.

This process is extremely simple compared to writing low-level programs to carry out these tasks. All you have to do is code a call to the Cold Fusion program in an HTML document and format the template using HTML and DBML tags.

Let's take a look at a sample application from Allaire's Web site (http://www.allaire.com/), then examine some of the code behind this example.

Figure 14-1 is an example application that searches a database of national parks. You can use drop-down lists to limit the search to certain kinds of parks and/or regions. You can use a text input box to specify a state, and users can even enter the name of a park. The application will use whichever combination of fields are filled in to query the database.

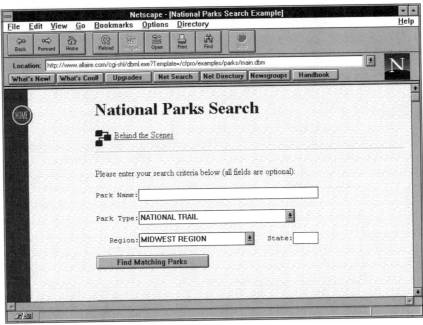

Figure 14-1: This Cold Fusion demo application shows how you can create a multiple-criteria search against a database.

The results of the query are returned from the database to a web page, as shown in Figure 14-2. The park names are formatted as hyperlinks. Clicking on a name brings up the details for that park, including a phone number, manager name, and the hours of operation.

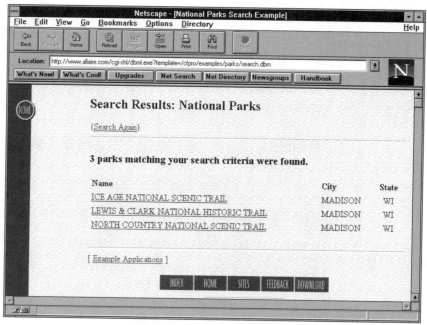

Figure 14-2: Cold Fusion has returned the query results as a list of hyperlinks pointing to further details.

> **Tip**
> The capability to return the records from a database as hyperlinks is powerful. You can use this feature to create dynamic intranet documents whose content depends on records in corporate databases.

Let's look at some of the template code behind the screens in Figures 14-1 and 14-2.

The search document in Figure 14-1 was created by a Cold Fusion template. The template is invoked by clicking on either a form button or a hyperlink.

The drop-down lists in Figure 14-1 are populated from the database. This requires two sections of code in the Cold Fusion template. The first section specifies the query that will populate the list. For the drop-down list of park types, the code looks like this:

```
<!-- Get information about the type of park -->
<DBQUERY NAME="GetType" DATASOURCE="CF Examples"
SQL="SELECT ParkType FROM Parks GROUP BY ParkType">
```

This code identifies a query called GetType. The query selects the column ParkType from a relational table called Parks and sorts the list of park types in alphabetical order.

The second section of code adds the list of park types to the HTML drop-down list:

```
Park Type:<SELECT NAME="ParkType">
 <OPTION VALUE="AllTypes" SELECTED>(All Park Types)
   <DBOUTPUT Query="GetType">
     <OPTION>#ParkType#
   </DBOUTPUT>
</SELECT>
```

Option value is standard HTML code. #ParkType# refers to the column returned from the database. This combination of HTML and DBML creates a drop-down list populated with data from a database.

The results screen in Figure 14-2 is based on another template. It uses another mixture of HTML and DBML to format the output. The city and state shown in the list were formatted by the following code:

```
<TD ALIGN=LEFT>#City#</TD>
<TD ALIGN="CENTER">#State#</TD>
```

Everything in this code is HTML except for the field names surrounded by pound signs. The pound signs act as placeholders in the template. Query results are inserted into the appropriate positions at runtime.

You can code Cold Fusion templates by hand or use one of the application wizards that come with the product to automatically generate a template. There is a wizard for creating a simple data entry page and another for a three-level data drill-down application.

MedSearch America has a Web site called Physician Finder Online. The site uses Cold Fusion to search a database of physicians, dentists, medical associations, and hospitals. The menu for Physician Finder is shown in Figure 14-3.

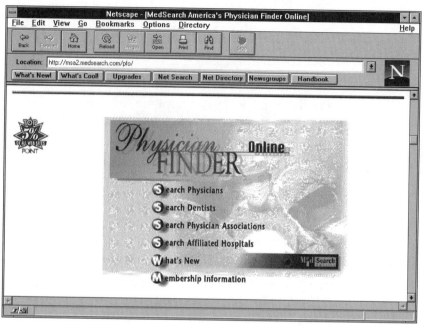

Figure 14-3: Physician Finder is a World Wide Web site that uses Cold Fusion to search a database of physicians (http://msa2.medsearch.com/).

If you click on Search Physicians in the screen in Figure 14-3, you'll get the search form shown in Figure 14-4. This is a query-by-example form that lets you search the database using any combination of several criteria.

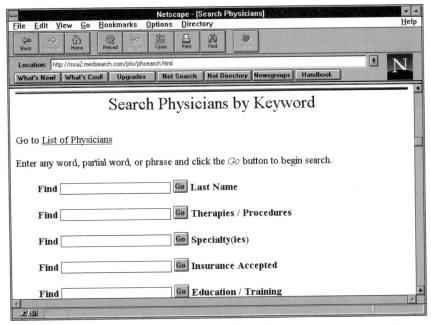

Figure 14-4: Physician Finder's search page is a query-by-example form allowing you to specify multiple search criteria.

If you scroll down the list of criteria and enter **spanish** as the language the doctor can speak, you'll get the results page shown in Figure 14-5.

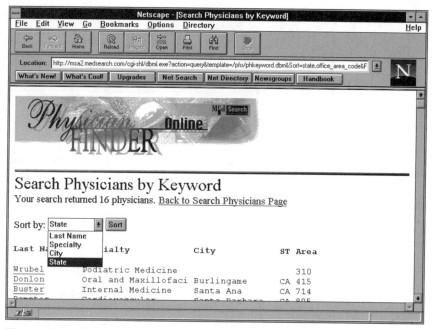

Figure 14-5: The search page used Cold Fusion to return this list of physicians meeting the criteria.

The doctors' names were returned as hyperlinks. Clicking on a name brings up another HTML document, which contains details about the doctor you selected.

Physician Finder Online is a good example of using multiple criteria to select a subset of a large set of data, then using hyperlinks to drill further into the detail. There are a lot of applications for this kind of processing.

Cold Fusion sells for $495. You can download a 30-day evaluation of the product from Allaire's Web site (http://www.allaire.com).

EveryWare Development's Tango

Tango, from EveryWare Development, is a Web-to-database development package for the Macintosh. It should be available for Windows NT and Solaris UNIX by the time you read this.

Tango is similar to Cold Fusion. It uses templates containing a mixture of HTML and database extensions to specify queries and results.

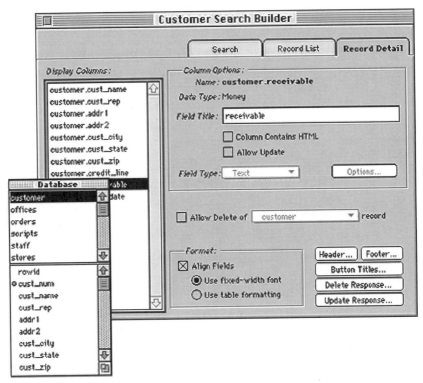

Figure 14-6: Tango uses GUI, point-and-click dialogs to build templates.

Tango uses wizards to build templates in a GUI, point-and-click environment. Figure 14-6 shows Tango's search builder dialog. You click to select database tables and columns to use in queries.

The code in a Tango template is similar to the code in Cold Fusion. The following code creates a list of branch locations:

```
<H3>Here are some branches that are close by:</H3>


<@ROWS>
<B>City:</B> <@COLUMN Contact.City>
<B>Street Address:</B>
<@COLUMN Contact.Address1>
<@COLUMN Contact.Address2>
<B>Phone #:</B>
<@COLUMN Contact.Telephone>
</@ROWS>
```

As in Cold Fusion, this code combines HTML tags with database extensions.

Figure 14-7 shows a Tango application, a Web site that lets you search for real estate in Virginia. The screen shows the search page that lets you use a number of criteria to find commercial properties. You can try this for yourself by starting from the Web site's home page (http://www.newcitymedia.com/realestate/).

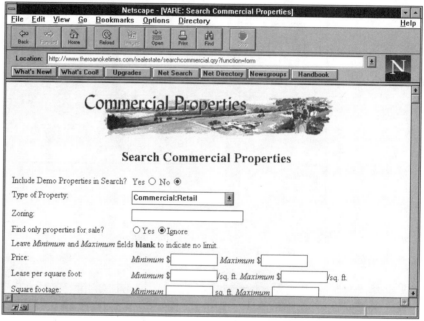

Figure 14-7: This screen uses Tango to search a database of commercial properties.

Tango costs $495 for a single-server, two concurrent user license. See EveryWare's Web site, http://www.everyware.com/Tango_Info/default.html, for more information.

BestWeb Pro by Best-Seller's, Inc.

BestWeb Pro, by Best-Seller's, Inc., is another product that connects web pages to databases, but it takes a different approach than either Cold Fusion or Tango.

BestWeb Pro does not provide a link to a live database. The product converts a database into a fully indexed document. You specify which fields from the database are indexed. BestWeb Pro also generates a search page that lets you search the converted database on any of the indexed fields.

The conversion program runs only in Windows, but the indexed document can be placed on a web server in either Windows or UNIX.

Because you have to convert a database to a proprietary file before you can search it, BestWeb Pro is not suited for use with constantly changing data. It is suitable for data that changes on a periodic basis, such as monthly sales data.

Figure 14-8 shows a BestWeb Pro application on the World Wide Web. This screen appears at the Web site of the BIA Companies (http://www.biacompanies.com/). It allows you to search a database of radio stations.

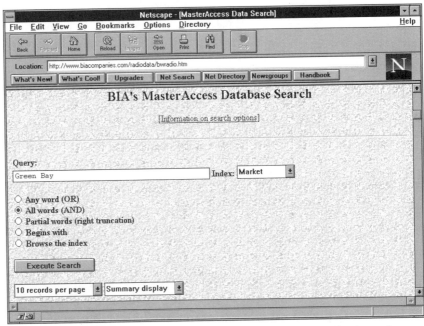

Figure 14-8: The BIA Companies use BestWeb Pro to search a database of radio stations.

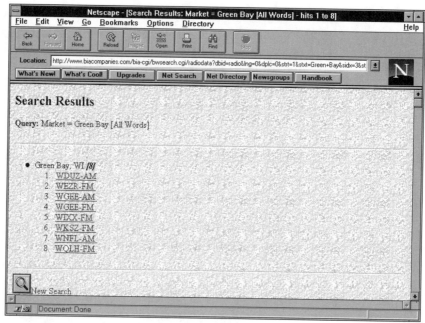

Figure 14-9: BestWeb Pro returns search results as a numbered list of hyperlinks.

In this application, BestWeb Pro returns the search results as a list of numbered hyperlinks, as shown in Figure 14-9.

BestWeb Pro sells for $349. For more information, visit the company's Web site (http://www.bestseller.com/home/weben/webprod.htm).

Web-Enabled Databases

The products covered so far in this chapter are database independent. They work with almost any database. Database vendors are adding features to their products that let you link web pages to their databases without having to buy a third-party software package.

Let's look at three examples of how database companies turn their products into web-enabled databases.

web.sql by sybase

The sybase database gateway, web.sql, sits between the database and the web server. It uses templates similar to the templates used by other products in this chapter.

The web.sql templates contain HTML codes and either code from sybase's procedural language, Transact-SQL, or Perl. This code appears between <SYB> tags in the template file. The files are stored with an .HTS extension, instead of the .HTM or .HTML extensions used for HTML files.

The sybase web.sql programmer's guide gives the following example of the syntax used to provide a list of stores within an HTML document:

```
<HTML>
<HEAD>
<TITLE>Stores<?TITLE>
</HEAD>
<BODY>
<H1>Stores</H1>
Stores found in $state:<P>
<SYB TYPE=SQL>
  select stor_name, stor_address, city, state
  from pubs2..stores
  where state = upper("$state")
  order by stor_name
</SYB>
</BODY>
</HTML>
```

Everything in this code is standard HTML except for the SQL statement between the <SYB> tags. The $state variable is used to pass information from a field on an HTML form to this code. It's used in the document text and to select the records for that state.

When web.sql processes this file, it executes any statements between the <SYB> tags and places the results in that position in the file. The result is returned to the web browser as an HTML file. Code between the <SYB> tags can be either SQL statements or Perl program code. This gives the programmer a lot of flexibility for creating dynamic output.

Silicon Graphics uses web.sql to read databases containing pricing and product information and to return a price quote to a Web browser.

web.sql pricing starts at $1,200. For more information, see sybase's Web site (http://www.sybase.com/).

Oracle Web Server

Oracle has a product called Oracle Web Server. This product adds HTML extensions to Oracle's procedural language, PL/SQL. You can use these extensions to write output from Oracle to HTML files.

To create a dynamic HTML document using Oracle Web Server, you code the PL/SQL program to retrieve and process records from an Oracle database, then use the HTML extensions to PL/SQL to embed the results in an HTML document.

To give an example of the syntax, the following would appear inside a PL/SQL block to create the title Branch Locations in an HTML document:

```
htp.htitle('Branch Locations');
```

The syntax to print to an HTML document from within a PL/SQL block is `htp.p`, followed by text, database columns, or both. Programmers would code PL/SQL procedures to create dynamic HTML documents that would be returned to web browsers.

Oracle Web Server 1.0 is available for most UNIX platforms. It is available free with the current version of Oracle. Oracle Web Server 2.0 is currently only available for the Sparc Solaris and SGI servers. It's priced at $2,495.

To download a copy of Oracle Web Server 1.0 or to get more information about the product, visit Oracle's Web site (http://www.oracle.com).

Informix Interface Kits

Informix has released a series of free interface kits that programmers can use to connect Informix databases to web pages. The interface kits allow Informix programmers to create web pages using either C or the Informix 4GL programming language.

To use the interface kits, you write procedural programs in either C or Informix 4GL that make the necessary calls to Informix databases; then format the results as an HTML file.

To download the interface kits, or for more information, visit Informix's Web site (http://www.informix.com/).

Advantages of Web-Enabled Databases

Oracle's Web Server, sybase's web.sql, and Informix's interface kits have a couple of advantages over products like Cold Fusion, Tango, and BestWeb Pro.

These products use the database's procedural language, which gives you a lot of flexibility for processing data before writing it to HTML documents. You have all the power of the database's built-in language.

Using the database's built-in language can be a huge advantage in some applications. Let's say you want users to use web browsers for price quote requests. Some companies have fairly complicated calculations behind their pricing. You might have to look up components in a bill of materials database, then apply some business rules to the data. A product like Cold Fusion is designed just to pass a simple query to a database and return the results as an HTML document. The procedural languages of the web-enabled databases are capable of more sophisticated processing.

If your company already has one of these databases, you probably have database developers who are very familiar with the procedural code. They can crank out some fairly sophisticated applications rather quickly.

Another advantage of using a web-enabled database is that you can take advantage of existing database code. If you already have a lot of database procedures that generate the data for some process, you can copy this and modify it to write to HTML files.

Disadvantages of Web-Enabled Databases

The strengths of these products can also be liabilities. Because you use each product's procedural language to code web pages, your formatting options are limited to the capabilities of those languages. Some of the database-independent software applications we mentioned earlier have extensive options for formatting data as HTML output—which is an advantage over using the built-in procedural languages of the web-enabled databases.

These products require more than a passing knowledge of the procedural languages. And in the end, you're cranking out code by hand instead of using a point-and-click wizard to generate templates for you.

If you have a lot of corporate data in a database like Oracle, sybase, or Informix, it might make sense to at least experiment with the web features of the product.

Resources for Web-to-Database Software

Jeff Rowe of COMSO, Inc. maintains an extensive list of software products that link web pages and databases (http://cscsun1. larc.nasa.gov/~beowulf/db/existing_products.html). The list can be separated by platform. The site lists software for Windows, Mac, and UNIX. Figure 14-10 shows the list of software for the PC platform.

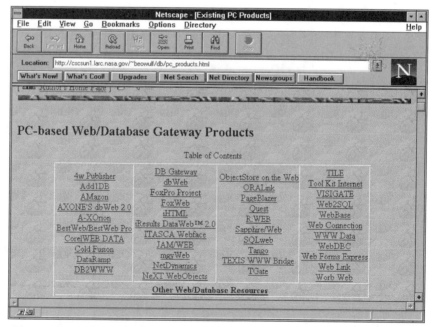

Figure 14-10: Jeff Rowe of COMSO, Inc. maintains an extensive list of web-to-database software. This screen shows the list for PC platforms.

Yahoo! also has a list of hyperlinks to information about web-page database software (http://www.yahoo.com/ Computers_and_Internet/Internet/World_Wide_Web/ Databases_and_Searching/).

Moving On

You can use one of several products to bring the benefits of dynamic, data-driven web pages to your intranet. Some inexpensive products make it easy to create templates that query the database and format results into HTML pages.

The last few chapters highlighted products that let you enhance the value of your intranet. The next chapter shows how companies are using the technology to bring real business benefits to their organizations.

SECTION 5

Building a High-Payback Intranet

Companies are rolling out intranets because they can provide significant business benefits for a modest investment. Chapter 15 shows you how companies are applying intranet technology and what they're getting out of it. In Chapter 16, you'll learn how to apply the lessons from the case studies to your own organization. Chapter 17 shows you why an intranet isn't the best solution for all applications. You'll learn how to avoid the high-effort, low-yield projects and start with the applications that can really pay off.

What Companies Are Doing With Intranets

So far you've seen how to assemble an intranet and how to add functionality that increases the value of your intranet. Now it's time to see what companies are doing with the technology.

In this chapter, you'll see which applications companies are putting on their intranets, and more importantly, what benefits they're reaping from their internal webs.

Mining Best Practices at Booz-Allen & Hamilton

Every company has a gold mine of knowledge. For far too many organizations this knowledge is stored only in the minds of employees and in reports hidden away in desk drawers. This knowledge is a vast, untapped resource.

The consulting firm Booz-Allen & Hamilton (BAH) tapped into their gold mine of knowledge and turned it into Knowledge On Line, a knowledge repository served up through the company's intranet.

Knowledge at Your Fingertips

The BAH intranet is a repository for consultants' reports, industry studies, research papers, and other documents. Employees in any of the 30 countries where BAH has offices use a search screen that takes queries in the form of English statements and returns hyperlinks that point to the company's knowledge.

When a BAH associate starts an assignment, he or she can turn to Knowledge On Line and call up the expertise on that topic from around the world.

BAH principal Aron Dutta said Knowledge On Line lets the company mine the best practices of employees anywhere in the corporation. "The intranet gives us global access to our best thinking," he said. "You can prevent people from reinventing the wheel."

The company also uses the intranet to store a directory of company experts. A BAH associate can access this directory to find out who is knowledgeable on a given topic. This helps when you've got to assemble a team for a project. "We map the knowledge to the people and create a directory of skills," Dutta said. "We've created a community of experts."

Dutta remembers doing research before the online knowledge repository or experts directory was available. "When you got an assignment, you might send out e-mails asking for help," he said. "People would send information to you, and you'd end up with a stack of documents on your desk. You might find that only 2 pages out of a 400-page report were appropriate to your assignment, but it was up to you to filter the information."

Dutta said this time-consuming process didn't always turn up useful information. "The data people sent me might help—if I was lucky and got to the right person."

How does Knowledge On Line change this process? Dutta said a recent project highlights the advantages of the intranet. A team of people from around the world had to put together a proposal for a client and meet a short deadline. They signed on to the intranet, used the skills directory to contact the appropriate experts, retrieved best practice and competitor data on the topic, and put the proposal together over a weekend.

"We capture, synthesize, and store our knowledge in a global knowledge base," Dutta said.

Learning From the Best

A company-wide knowledge base is part of a best practices application. You also have to find a way to bring the right people together to use that knowledge.

BAH uses discussion group software on its intranet to foster collaboration. There are discussion groups organized by topic, such as sourcing strategy. Other forums are created for various work teams.

Employees can use the discussion groups to tap into expert knowledge. There might be a forum on procurement processes, for example. The forum is monitored by the four or five BAH associates who spend time researching this topic. If you have a question in this area, you can post a message and get a response from one of the company's experts. Questions and responses are maintained in threaded discussions so employees can learn from the exchange of information.

BAH links the discussion groups to the company's knowledge repository. This makes the stored information more valuable, because employees can simultaneously access the data and company experts on the same topic. This also helps employees learn how to use the information.

"We can exchange dialogue with our experts throughout the world," Dutta said. "By collaborating, we're continually applying and enhancing the knowledge we've collected," Dutta said. "Knowledge is nothing unless it can be applied."

The Intranet is the System

The intranet isn't just an application at BAH. Employees use their web browsers to access all corporate information systems. This includes the knowledge base and forums, but also legacy databases, transaction processing, and other company information.

"Employees have one window into all BAH information—Netscape Navigator browsers," Dutta said. "We've reengineered the company, and the intranet is the conduit to fuse knowledge to people."

The Benefits of the Intranet

"The intranet provides connectiveness, transfer of knowledge, and an architecture that gives us flexibility," Dutta said. "It's a global system that lets us share information across 30 countries. The benefit is that we share our best knowledge. Knowledge is power. It gives us a competitive edge."

Open Communication & Collaboration at 3M

What do you think would happen if you built the infrastructure of an intranet, then turned it over to employees and said, "Here it is; do what you want with it."? That's exactly what 3M did. If you guessed that the result was chaos, you guessed wrong. The intranet that 3M employees built business unit by business unit turned out to be everything that the ideal intranet is supposed to be—a vehicle for open communication and collaboration.

This employee-driven system has also delivered real benefits to the corporation.

Open to Everyone

3M has designed an intranet that's open to just about everybody. As Jim Radford, Manager of Interactive Customer Communications, explains the setup. "Anyone who has e-mail has a browser. We can get to most of the company with TCP/IP."

3M allows employees to build their own intranet web sites. "Someone in a factory might want to host an intranet web site to post production schedules and personnel assignments," Radford said. "If that person has a PC hooked to the network and can keep it running 24 hours a day, they can mount a web site."

This openness has resulted in a lot of intranet web sites spread around the company. Radford estimates there are about 70 Netscape servers being used to host intranet sites for the various business units.

What about concerns that employees will put inappropriate material on the intranet? "We expect people to control their own content," Radford said. "The author has to decide the appropriateness of the content just as they would with a printed document that they would have slipped into interoffice mail."

Radford said employees putting information on the intranet have to consider their audience. "The information should be shareable company wide," he said. The majority of the content on 3M's intranet is open information, with the exception of some sales and marketing documents that are password protected.

> **Note**
>
> Intranet security is covered in Chapter 19.

Business Unit Participation

The list of hyperlinks on the 3M intranet home page tells a story— the company's business units have bought into the internal web in a big way. There are links to web pages for 3M factories, the Austin center has its own technical forum, and the Federal Systems Department has a home page, as does the 3M Pharmaceutical division.

The 3M Tape Group is a good example of what information business units are posting on the intranet. There is a hyperlink to industry information. This is valuable information for the group's engineers. The Tape Group's web page is also used to announce employee rewards and recognition. The site contains a Tape Group newsletter.

The intranet web pages built by the business units are not just isolated pockets of information. Radford said he's noticed that business units are connecting their web pages. "A lot of the web pages link to sites around the company," he said.

Using the Intranet for Collaboration

The intranet is becoming a tool for collaboration across boundaries. Radford gives an example: "There is a cross-function interest group for acoustics and vibrations," he said. "They use their web page to list meeting information, including minutes. They post a directory of members and equipment. They also list the skills and expertise of the members."

It's this last item, the list of skills, that shows how the intranet can benefit the company. "If you need someone to work on a project involving acoustics," Radford said, "you can just go to the list."

The 3M intranet is also a repository for online reports. Trend reports from 3M's Economic Services are an example. The department puts forecasts and analysis of global business conditions on the intranet. 3M employees from around the world can use the reports for their own forecasts.

Radford said the company uses Adobe Acrobat to convert spreadsheets and graphs used in the economic reports and puts them on the intranet as PDF documents. The reports retain the look that printed documents previously had, adding to their readability. Entire studies are posted on the intranet in their original formats.

The reports are organized so intranet users can start with summary information and drill down into the detail. Employees have a central source for the latest information and can get the detail they need, when they need it.

Customer service uses the intranet to post information that service reps can use when the customer is on the phone. "They've developed a list of frequently asked questions and posted the answers to these questions on the intranet," Radford said. The intranet gives the customer service reps instant access to this shared knowledge.

"A service rep can bring up that web page while the customer is on the phone," Radford said. "This results in consistent answers across the department and leads to good response time. Good response time translates to customer satisfaction."

Intranet Payback

3M opened the intranet up to employees. The result was not chaos, but collaboration. "The intranet lets us more effectively leverage knowledge within the company," Radford said. "The intranet is a vehicle for the distribution of information. It allows us to be responsive to our internal customers and ultimately our external customers."

Radford summarized the benefit of 3M's intranet: "It allows us to become an effective, knowledge-based enterprise."

> *Note*
> The issue of controlling who can update intranet content is covered in Chapter 19.

Silicon Graphics' Database-Driven Intranet

A few years ago Silicon Graphics, Inc. (SGI) recognized that it had a problem common to many companies. Key business data was safely locked away in corporate databases, but not everyone who needed to use this information had access to it.

Customer service reps had access to order information, but not manufacturing databases that held information about products. Manufacturing couldn't access the customer call tracking database. Sales reps couldn't access billing and commission information. Resellers couldn't connect to the databases that would allow them to put together price quotes.

People couldn't directly get the information they needed to do their jobs. They had to call around until they found someone who could call up the appropriate database. Sales reps and other employees wasted time playing telephone tag, and key people in customer service and accounting spent a lot of time looking up information for the rest of the company.

SGI wanted to design a common interface to corporate databases, an interface that wouldn't require a lot of training. Sales reps and resellers used a variety of workstations, so this system had to work across platforms.

SGI designed this cross-functional database access into their intranet, Silicon Junction.

Linking Databases Through the Intranet

Silicon Junction contains many tools that link employees and partners to databases. These include:

○ **A web-based sales order and shipping tool.** This tool allows employees to query order status. An order summary is displayed, then employees can drill down to see more and more of the details of the order.

○ **Online purchasing requisitions.** Employees use a web page form to enter a requisition and it goes directly into the database.

○ **Silicon Sales Desk and Partner Sales Desk.** Sales reps and resellers log in to this part of the intranet with a username and password. They can assemble components into a complete solution for a customer, then automatically fax the quote.

○ **Channel City.** Resellers log into this system to link to vital sales information such as competitive reports, sales presentations, and training materials. The system has an online product literature catalog. Resellers can call up a web-page form to submit an order for sales literature.

○ **Cross-referenced hyperlinks to corporate databases.** A customer service rep can call up the manufacturing database while the customer is on the phone and give information about product components. Manufacturing personnel can view customer information relating to the products they produce.

The intranet organizes all the company's data through one easy-to-use, cross-platform interface—a web browser.

Sales Data on Demand

When sales reps have to continually call headquarters for information, they lose time they could have spent serving customers. The SGI intranet lets sales reps directly access the data they need.

Kyle Brown is a consultant who helped SGI develop the links between intranet web pages and databases. He said the advantage of tying the intranet to live databases is that sales reps can access only relevant information. They don't have to wade through a hierarchy of hyperlinks to navigate to their data.

"Based on the user's ID and password, we present only the information they're interested in," Brown said. "Billings, backlog, commission statements can be viewed by the rep. This reduces the phone calls. Otherwise this takes commission accounting time as well as sales rep time because you play phone tag."

Web to Database Experts

Kyle Brown is director of Web technologies at ProjectSolutions. ProjectSolutions specializes in helping companies tie their intranets and World Wide Web sites to databases. Their clients include Silicon Graphics, Sony, Hewlett Packard, Hughes DataSystems, and Incyte Pharmaceuticals.

You can make your intranet a vital part of your company's information systems by integrating it with corporate databases. Consulting firms like ProjectSolutions can help streamline this process.

To learn more about the technology ProjectSolutions uses and the different ways they've linked intranets to databases, visit their site on the World Wide Web (http://www.projectsolutions.com).

Another advantage of linking the intranet to databases is providing users with a window on the most current information. "Sales and product information is online and up-to-date at all times," Brown said. "This encourages the sales reps to look at Silicon Sales on a regular basis to learn about the latest products and how to sell against competition."

Channel City is the section of SGI's intranet that speeds the flow of information to SGI sales partners. Channel City has a tool called Quote Configurator. Sales partners use Quote Configurator to access databases of product components and pricing. Reps configure the system that meets customer needs, then the system computes and formats a price quote that can be automatically faxed to the sales partner for presentation to the customer.

"This is where we get the most leverage," Brown said. "We extend access to our internal applications to our partners through the web."

Karilee Wirthlin managed the development of Channel City. "Our goal with this site is to make doing business with SGI easier for our resellers by providing them with information and tools they can access from anywhere at anytime," she said. "The web provides a common denominator for communicating information to our resellers."

The Benefits of Silicon Junction

SGI's intranet puts a single interface on top of the company's key databases. This makes vital data easily available to the people who need it.

"Better communication is probably the greatest benefit of an intranet," Brown said. "You save a lot of time looking up information on the internal web instead of calling people on the phone and having to track down data. We give people access to the data directly, using the web, which puts the power in the hands of the users requesting the information."

By giving employees direct access to their data, you benefit the whole company. "People who had to answer questions are happier, and the sales reps are happy because they now have access to information that previously only headquarters people could see. I feel the real benefits can be reaped by remote sales offices and manufacturing facilities because they can access the information and don't feel so isolated."

Wirthlin agreed, "I think the biggest benefit is centralized access to information. The web is not only a great technology for reaching the masses, it's a great vehicle for delivering on the promise of databases."

Bringing People Together at Comedy Central

Companies that have locations spread across the country often find it difficult to achieve effective collaboration between remote offices. It can be hard to build a feeling of teamwork with people who are thousands of miles away. An intranet can help by serving as a common source of information that can be accessed from any location at any time. The technology can be used to bring people together.

A Database of People

Information Systems project manager Al Holmes used an intranet to bring employees at the cable channel Comedy Central face-to-face. Literally.

Comedy Central, home of cable TV shows like Politically Incorrect, Dr. Katz, and Dream On, has offices in New York, Los Angeles, Chicago, and Detroit. Comedy Central was faced with a problem all multiple-site organizations face; how do you help people collaborate across the country?

Holmes started with what has proved to be the intranet's most popular application—the photo phone directory. Holmes created a database containing the company's phone directory. Nothing new about that. Then he added a twist. He circulated a digital camera around the company and collected electronic photos of employees. He stored these photos in the phone database along with the usual contact information. When users click in a web browser to search the phone directory, they see the employee's phone number and smiling face.

Holmes was surprised by the reaction to the directory. "The photo phone list is a big hit," he said. People like seeing who they've been dealing with over the phone. Holmes said when he put the directory on the company's intranet, employees immediately started calling up the photos of their colleagues from around the country.

The popularity of the photos has caused an unexpected problem for Holmes. "People are very picky about their photos," he said with a laugh. "I still haven't been able to pry photos away from some people."

Holmes said you'd be surprised at the number of people within the same location that have never come face-to-face with the people they work with. He plans to enhance the directory by including an image of each site's floor layout. When you call up a phone number, you can drill down to a graphic that shows you where that employee is located within the building.

Holmes developed the photo phone directory using Allaire's Cold Fusion to connect the database to an intranet web page. He built a query-by-example form that allows wildcards. An employee might want to reach someone, but is only able to remember part of the person's last name and that the person works in Los Angeles. He or she can enter this partial data and the system can find the information.

Working Together Through the Intranet

A challenge for a company with multiple locations is creating an environment that makes it easy for people to collaborate. Holmes used another product from Allaire, Allaire Forums, to create threaded discussion groups on the intranet.

The forums are organized by department or topic. There is a marketing forum, for example, and another for cable advertising. Holmes said this allows employees to gather ideas from around the company. Someone might post a note asking for ideas for one of Comedy Central's shows or promotional advertising. "People like it a lot," Holmes said. "It's good for brainstorming within a department and across departments."

The intranet is making it easier for people to discuss projects like promotional videos. Holmes put electronic versions of video clips on the intranet, then coded organized hyperlinks to the material. Users can click to download a film clip, and an Apple QuickTime helper app runs the video on their desktop. "People can see the latest version of a video," Holmes said. "This allows them to collaborate while it's being developed."

Payback From the Intranet

Holmes said the intranet brings people together, starting with the opening screen. The intranet home page is divided into two frames. On the left is a table of contents, which includes links to the photo phone directory, the discussion groups, and company news. There is also a link to an Excite For Webservers search engine from Excite, Inc., which finds information across departments and locations.

The rest of the intranet home page is an image of a building. In each window is the name of a department. An employee can click on a department to bring up its home page.

The very organization of the internal web helps unify the corporation.

Holmes sees another benefit from the intranet— very fast application development. "The applications you build won't have the bells and whistles of a PowerBuilder or Visual Basic application," he said. "But they're enterprise-wide applications and the rollout is fast. You do it in one place and it's available across the country."

The 200 intranet users at Comedy Central are on mixed platforms. Holmes said the mix is about 60 percent PCs and 40 percent Macs. "The multiple platforms of the intranet is a huge advantage," he said.

Holmes said the intranet's biggest payback for Comedy Central is that it brings people together. "There's a big drive within the organization for people to communicate with each other; to collaborate. This is the engine to drive that."

The Big-Payback Intranet Applications

I've studied over 50 intranets. While each company's implementation is unique, there are some common themes. The biggest benefits of intranets come from three types of applications:

○ Reducing the cost of publishing information.

○ Reducing the cost of accessing information.

○ Best practices.

Reducing the Cost of Publishing Information

One of the most common ways corporations use intranets is to replace printed copies of documents with paperless, online versions. This can result in huge savings.

Consider a procedures guide that goes to hundreds or even thousands of employees. The printed version of this document goes through the typical cycle of prepublication layout, printing, and distribution. Then the document is out-of-date within a few months, and the cycle is repeated.

If this same document is on an intranet, you eliminate printing, handling, and mailing costs. You also get the benefit of up-to-date information, since you can change the information in one place and it's immediately available throughout the organization.

Kyle Brown, the consultant who helped build Silicon Graphics' intranet, estimates that the company is saving $60,000 per quarter by having the price book online.

Let's see how other companies have benefited from putting documents on an intranet.

PC Week Online[1] reported that Los Alamos National Laboratory saved $500,000 in printing and distribution costs in its intranet's first year of operation. The lab saved $100,000 on one document alone.

> **Note**
> The references for sources quoted in the book appear in the Works Cited.

Hewlett Packard has deployed an intranet application called Electronic Sales Partner. This application makes over 13,000 sales and marketing documents available to employees around the world. *Internet World*[2] quotes one company official who says that sending this data out costs $10,000 per mailing. An article in *PC Week*[3] said HP has over one million documents on its intranet.

Tyson Foods, Inc., is using an intranet to reduce the cost of information. *PC Week*[4] reports that Tyson is saving $360,000 a year by putting its phone directory online. An article in *ComputerWorld*[5] said Tyson is saving $10 per copy by publishing an employee manual online.

Cracker Barrel was sending each store manager 10,000 pages per month of profit and loss statements, sales reports, and customer comments. Now the company stores these reports electronically on its intranet, and managers only access the information they want. (Source: *PC Week*[6].)

You can realize significant savings by putting documents on your intranet and eliminating the printing and distribution costs.

Reducing the Costs of Accessing Information

You've seen how Silicon Graphics, Inc. (SGI) uses its intranet to give employees access to data stored in company databases. Before the intranet, employees and resellers had to call someone at headquarters and track down the information they needed. Now they can get this information directly, through their web browsers.

It would be hard to put a precise dollar amount on the difference between the manual process and the intranet, but it's easy to see how the new process benefits the company. The cost of accessing information before the intranet included the sometimes considerable time of two people—the employee hunting for information and the person at headquarters taking the call. Now employees get the information directly and don't have to go through someone else to get it.

This reduces the cost of each information transaction. When you consider the number of times each employee looks up information and multiply that times the number of employees, you have considerably reduced the cost of information.

There is another side to the benefits that SGI realizes. When employees spend less time hunting for information, they can spend more time on their core responsibilities. This is an especially big payback to the company when the employees involved are sales reps, who can now spend more time on customers.

Employees who use the intranet to look up information are likely to have more of the information they need. When you have to constantly call for information, you don't ask for everything you should. It's too much of a hassle. With the intranet, the information is available at the employees' convenience.

An intranet also allows you to dramatically cut the cost of accessing information by using a hierarchy of hyperlinks to organize it and a search engine that allows employees to go directly to the information they need—without wading through mounds of paper.

The online reports that 3M makes available on its intranet are a good example of how hyperlinks can simplify information access. 3M's Jim Radford said that the economic updates are organized so that employees around the world can start at a summary level, then drill down into detail for particular markets or economic factors.

If these reports were in printed form only, you'd probably have to send out entire sets of data, since you couldn't predict in advance which data a given employee may need. Employees would have to flip through thick documents for data. The intranet lets 3M employees quickly drill down to only the data they need to do their jobs.

You'll recall from the Hollings Cancer Institute case study in Chapter 1 that the online versions of the thick protocols resulted in greatly improved information access. With the addition of simple hyperlinks, Dr. Afrin was able to allow medical personnel to jump directly to the document they wanted and then right to the appropriate section within that document. Compare this to the task of thumbing through binders of paper documents to find the few relevant pages.

Companies are speeding access to information by organizing their documents with hyperlinks.

The ability to do keyword searches through whole libraries of manuals, procedure guides, technical documents, customer reports, and other information also cuts the cost of information access.

Sandia National Laboratories is a research agency for the Department of Energy. The lab stores research reports, called SAND reports, on its intranet. The intranet enables engineers and scientists to do keyword searches on the information. The computer does the work of hunting down all references to a topic. Employees no longer have to comb through printed documents to draw on data they need for a project.

AT&T puts 5,000 technical documents per year on its intranet, according to a case study available on Netscape's World Wide Web site (http://www.netscape.com/). Employees can search this growing library of information using an intranet search engine.

The plastics company that I'm using as an example throughout the book is putting production facility newsletters on the intranet and giving employees the capability to search this collection with a search engine. This is a big improvement over having to sort through a stack of paper copies of the newsletter.

Companies are finding that a big benefit of an intranet is reducing the cost of accessing information.

Best Practices

A number of companies are using their intranet to implement the application known as best practices. You saw an example of this earlier in the chapter. Booz-Allen & Hamilton has one of the most advanced implementations of this application.

Best practices can have a huge payback for an organization. When employees have easy access to the best thinking of the company, the productivity of employees and the quality of the company's products can rise tremendously. Employees across the company learn the best techniques that the company has to offer and this knowledge spreads through the organization.

The dollar benefits of best practices can pay for an intranet many times over.

Taco Bell is using an intranet to share best practice data among regional and unit managers. There is a wide variance between the performance of individual units. Some stores have low turnover rates; others have exceptional operational efficiency. The company wants to use an intranet to spread the best ideas around the country.

The intranet is used as a repository for best practice tips. It is also used to share data on turnover rates, speed of service, and financial results for each unit. Managers use the intranet to share project information. (Source: *PC Week*[7].)

National Semiconductor is using an intranet to share information among its geographically dispersed production facilities. Design engineers, production managers, and other employees have centralized access to product information, regardless of where the data originated. This makes it easier to spot trends across production locations and helps everyone see the best ideas from around the world. (Source: Netscape customer case study [http://www.netscape.com].)

Levi Strauss has over 37,000 employees around the globe. The company is using an intranet to share best practices. Employees can use the intranet to view customer presentations that originated anywhere in the world. This lets employees in each country learn from the ideas of their global colleagues. (Source: *PC Week*[8].)

You can use your intranet to implement a high-payback best practices application.

Finding Intranet Case Studies

There are a number of intranet case studies available on the World Wide Web. Two of the best sources are *PC Week Online* and customer profiles at Netscape's Web site.

PC Week

While many monthly and weekly publications print intranet case studies, *PC Week* is a premier source for intranet case studies. The magazine publishes one intranet case study each week. The case studies have two regular sidebars. One called "Inside The Wall" gives the history of the subject's intranet—how it happened, the company's goals for the technology, staffing and expense where available, and favorite user applications. A second sidebar, called "The Toolbox," talks about the hardware and software used to build the subject's intranet.

Fortunately, *PC Week* has an archive of their case studies online. Visit their online magazine (http://www.pcweek.com/) to read through the collection.

Netscape's Intranet Profiles

Netscape offers a collection of intranet profiles at their Web site (http://www.netscape.com/). The profiles feature Netscape technology, of course, but they also detail the applications each company has implemented. There are quotes from customers on the benefits of their intranet.

Netscape also offers what it calls intranet demos. These are not working intranet screens, but representations of intranet pages at 3M, National Semiconductor, and other companies.

Other Case Study Sources

There are a number of sources of intranet case studies on the World Wide Web. Many computer hardware and software vendors, such as Sun Microsystems and Silicon Graphics, have white papers about intranets. There are some entire Web sites devoted to the topic.

The best way to find this information is to use a World Wide Web search engine. Start with "intranet" as a keyword to see the list of documents available. Then try limiting the search using phrases such as "intranet savings" or "intranet applications." You can pick up valuable tips by seeing how companies are using the technology.

Moving On

Companies use intranets in a variety of ways, but there are a few key applications that can yield big returns on a modest expense. You've seen how companies use intranets to reduce the cost of publishing and accessing information. You've also seen how the technology can be used to reap the benefits of best practices.

The next chapter gives you tips on implementing these big-payback applications on your intranet without spending a fortune to do it.

Building the Big-Payback Applications

16

You've seen how some intranet applications can return a big payback. This chapter contains some tips that will help you implement projects on your intranet that will yield a significant return to the corporation.

This book has two main objectives: to show you how to build a low-cost intranet and to show you how to reap the benefits of that technology. You've seen how to build an inexpensive intranet component by component. Now it's time to use the intranet to return benefits to the organization.

A Shoestring Intranet

Is it possible for an intranet to provide returns to the corporation that exceed its cost? Let's look at the cost of a typical intranet, then see what it would take to implement applications that would more than pay for the system.

Let's start by assuming you're going to roll out the intranet to 500 employees. (I'll use this number in savings estimates throughout the chapter.)

If you use existing hardware for the web server and a freeware browser, you can put together an intranet for under $2,000. Both Netscape's FastTrack Server and O'Reilly's WebSite web server sell for $295. O'Reilly's WebBoard discussion group software lists for $149. Excite, Inc.'s Excite for Web Servers search engine is free. You can buy a product to connect web pages to databases for $500 or less. You could get an HTML editor and a graphics editor for less than $400 combined.

> **Note**
> Please note that my use of specific products in the hypothetical intranet is for example only and does not signify endorsement.

While it's possible to build an intranet for under $2,000, studies have shown that the typical initial cost of an intranet is about $10,000. If you apply the $2,000 toward the cost of software for your initial intranet and add new hardware to house the web server, your cost would fall somewhere between $5,000 and $10,000. Let's use $10,000 as the cost of our hypothetical intranet.

Now let's see what it would take to bring more than $10,000 in benefits to the corporation.

Reduce the Cost of Publishing Information

You saw in the last chapter that some companies are saving substantial dollars by converting printed material to their intranet. You can bring the same type of savings to your company.

The Cost of a Document

The cost of a printed document includes the cycle of prepress layout, printing, handling, and mailing. Even if you print some documents yourself on laser printers, you incur the cost of the materials and the labor to print and distribute the information.

I've seen estimates that put the cost of a typical document somewhere between $.50 and $1.00. This would include documents like newsletters, product fact sheets, bulletins, and reports.

A large document like the company's human resources manual typically costs more. The benefits manual is usually a high-quality production. It comes in a binder with colored dividers for the various sections and contains a number of multicolor illustrations. I've seen estimates that put the cost of printing and distributing this kind of document somewhere between $10 and $20 per manual.

Note that I'm not including design time in this estimate. You'll incur equivalent design costs whether the document is printed or electronic. The cost to create an electronic copy suitable for printing and the cost to create an HTML document are roughly equal, so they're not included in these numbers.

Let's use the lower estimate of both of the example documents to calculate our intranet savings. This puts the typical document at $.50 each and a larger, high-quality document like a human resources manual at $10 each.

High-Payback Documents

Now you can see why many companies' first intranet applications are the corporate phone directory, the human resources manual, and procedure guides. Documents such as these are usually sent to everyone in the company, and they are expensive to produce and update.

Let's see what we could save by moving a couple of these documents to our hypothetical 500-user intranet.

Company policies and benefits change throughout the year. Some companies send the entire package out once a year, but then send enough updates to add up to a second copy of the entire set.

If you create an online human resources manual and it eliminates sending 2 copies a year to 500 people, the savings would be 2 times $10 times 500, or $10,000. You've paid for the intranet with your first application!

This not only saves money, but also offers an enhanced document to employees. You can provide hyperlink navigation to sections of the manual and from the manual to related documents. You can also offer employees the ability to do keyword searches on human resources policies and benefits.

You might also want to put the corporate phone directory on the intranet. This is an ideal application, since employee information changes constantly and the directory is sometimes out of date in a week.

If you put the phone directory on the intranet instead of sending it to 500 employees 6 times a year, you'll save $.50 times 6 times 500, or $1,500.

Another place to find some savings is a monthly newsletter. Putting this on the intranet saves $3,000 per year.

You've saved $14,500 per year for an expense of under $10,000; and you haven't even started down the list of potential applications. You've got monthly reports, product fact sheets, project updates, and a lot of other documents that can be accessed from the internal web, saving the cost of printing and distributing.

Starter Documents for Your Intranet

Some documents are better candidates for the first intranet applications than others. The initial content of your intranet will be driven by factors other than just savings, but you'll want to include at least a couple documents that have a high payback and are relatively easy to convert.

Here are the characteristics of ideal starter documents:

○ **Widely used**. A document that is printed and sent to every employee is a good candidate.

○ **Costly to produce and distribute**. A human resources manual is a good example.

○ **Frequently updated**. Information that goes out of date quickly is expensive to maintain in printed form.

○ **Relatively easy to convert**. A document that's already in electronic form and is simple text with a few images can be converted easily.

A document that is not in electronic form can still be converted to the intranet by running it through a scanner. This adds to the expense of the intranet—unless you already have scanning hardware and software.

> **Tip**
> Some print shops and computer stores will let you use their scanners for a per copy fee. This can be a cost effective way to convert a reasonable number of documents to electronic form if the conversion is one time only.

Think about the various printed documents that get routed around your company. You'll probably find that a lot of them are good candidates for conversion to online intranet documents.

Reducing the Cost of Accessing Information

You can bring benefits to your company by using the intranet to reduce the cost of looking up information. It's more difficult to put a precise dollar amount on this application, but there can be a huge payback from easier and quicker access to vital corporate information.

The Silicon Graphics case study in Chapter 15 showed you how an intranet dramatically reduced the amount of time people spent making phone calls to track down information. The intranet gave employees direct access to information and eliminated the need to tie up some centralized department with constant requests for data.

How do you put a dollar value on this? It's clear that the intranet applications at Silicon Graphics raise the productivity of the company, but what is this worth?

I've seen companies handle this in different ways. Some companies calculate the hours saved and multiply the result times an average dollar per hour. Other companies figure that the intranet reduces the need to hire additional administrative help, because the intranet makes it easier for employees to get information directly.

The cost of this chapter's hypothetical intranet is $10,000. If you assume the intranet reduces the administrative workload by 10 hours a week, and further assume a rate of $10/hour, you've just saved $5,000 a year—half the cost of the intranet.

Whether you assign a dollar value to the savings generated by more efficient information access or not, you should take advantage of the economic benefits this type of application can return.

Applications

What kind of applications fall under the category of reducing the costs of accessing information? The case studies in Chapter 1 and 15 give some examples.

The Hollings Cancer Institute's intranet, covered in Chapter 1, is a prime example of an application that increases the efficiency of information access. You'll recall that before the intranet was built, the institute kept paper copies of 50- to 100-page clinical protocols. The protocols were kept in large binders stored in bookcases.

If you wanted to cross reference some treatment across trials, you'd have to hunt through the bookcases to find the appropriate binders. Then you'd page through the thick documents to find the relevant material. Not very productive.

Dr. Afrin of the Hollings Cancer Institute greatly increased the efficiency of information access by organizing the protocols with hyperlinks. You can go to the correct protocol and the appropriate section in that protocol with a few mouse clicks.

The institute has also reduced the physical cost of storing information, since they no longer need to purchase protocol binders and bookshelves. You can multiply your savings by using the intranet to replace bulky, paper-based information. Is there any doubt that putting clinical trial information on the intranet has reduced the cost to access it?

The plastics company used as an example throughout the book put production facility newsletters on the intranet, then gave employees a search engine that allowed them to instantly find all newsletters containing some keyword or phrase. This reduced the cost of extracting valuable information from the newsletters.

Silicon Graphics linked intranet web pages to corporate databases, which opened up the information to a wide number of employees. The company benefits because employees get the data they need to do their jobs directly, without going through headquarters personnel to get it.

Let's look at how you can implement these high-payback applications on your intranet.

Simplify Access With Hyperlinks

You can simplify information access for your corporation significantly just by organizing the data scattered throughout the company. You do this by converting the data to HTML documents and organizing it with cross-referenced hyperlinks.

This strategy brought considerable benefits to Eli Lilly, the pharmaceutical company covered in a Chapter 1 case study. Regulations for putting new drugs on the market were scattered around the world. Eli Lilly put these documents on the intranet, then coded hyperlinks that gave employees anywhere in the company easy access to this vital information.

Before the intranet, employees scrambled to get the right contact on the phone. Then the data came in as e-mail messages. It was up to each person to organize the separate messages into a working document that could be used to coordinate projects between countries. After the intranet was implemented, employees could simply click in their web browser's window to accomplish the same task.

You can reduce the cost of accessing your company's data by using hyperlinks in two ways: as a table of contents to the information and to tie related documents together.

What you want to achieve is a structure that becomes an easy-to-use map to your company's information.

Simplify Access With a Search Engine

You can reduce the cost of accessing information by letting the intranet find it for employees—using a search engine. An intranet combined with a search engine can pay dividends for a corporation when it's applied to the right kind of information.

Some of the case studies in Chapter 15 showed how companies use a search engine to simplify access to technical documents, manuals, and product and customer information.

You can help the company mine the gold from documents by applying a search engine to certain sets of information.

The types of documents that can be enhanced with search capability include newsletters, technical reports, customer call reports, product fact sheets, competitor reports, and similar information.

Simplifying Access at 3M

Let's look at an example of using both hyperlinks and a search engine to reduce the cost of accessing information.

Consider 3M's World Wide Web site, which also turns out to be an example of structuring information for internal use. 3M keeps a lot of product information on their World Wide Web site. Rather than duplicate this information internally, they point hyperlinks in their intranet to the external Web pages. Employees can look up product data by following the links to this publicly available data.

Loke Crowfoot, 3M Marketing Services Supervisor, said that 3M employees account for 25 percent of the hits on the external Web site.

Using World Wide Web Pages Internally

A number of corporations use a mixture of intranet and Internet web pages for internal information access. Comedy Central's World Wide Web site contains information that is useful to employees, such as program schedules and announcements. Comedy Central's intranet project manager, Al Holmes, said not everyone with intranet access has Internet access, so they maintain a duplicate copy of the World Wide Web pages on the intranet.

Sun Microsystems and Silicon Graphics are two other examples of companies that use World Wide Web pages to provide information to internal employees.

3M has an information access problem. The company has over 60,000 products and wants to give both customers and employees easy access to data on all of them.

3M makes access available to this ton of information by organizing it with hyperlinks and offering a search engine that can find products matching search criteria.

Figure 16-1 shows how 3M simplifies the access to data on a large number of products. This screen links to four options to search for product information:

○ An alphabetical listing of product names. This is handy if
   you already know the name of the product you're looking
   for.

○ A search page that reads a database of company-defined
   keywords assigned to each product.

○ A Web page that divides products into markets, or how the
   product is used.

○ A full-text search engine that you can use to search through
   product data sheets.

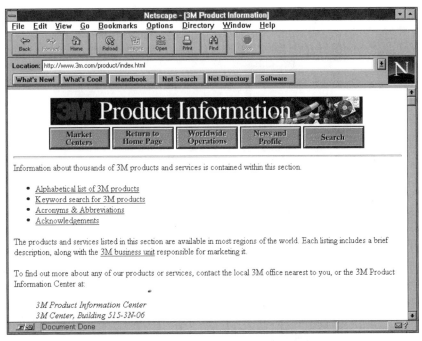

Figure 16-1: 3M uses web technology to offer multiple viewpoints into product data.

Figure 16-2 shows one of the two ways to search through 3M's
product data. This Web page is linked to a database of predefined
keywords assigned to each product. The database includes a noun
describing each product and the brand name. 3M uses this screen
to allow a more focused search than is possible by just searching
through the text of product fact sheets.

Build an Intranet on a Shoestring

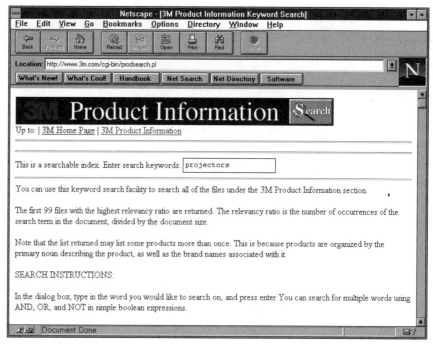

Figure 16-2: The 3M Web page that allows users to search by predefined keywords.

3M also offers the Excite search engine to allow users to comb through the text of product fact sheets. Figure 16-3 shows this screen. 3M improves this searching capability by offering a drop-down list of document collections to search. Users can search the entire Web site or the product section only. There is also a section, which 3M calls Market Centers, where users can search by type of product. The Market Centers section gives the user the ability to narrow the search to certain types of products before entering the search query.

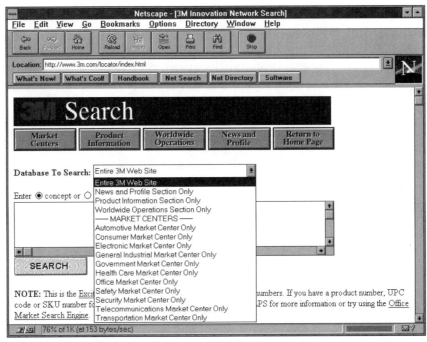

Figure 16-3: 3M uses the Excite search engine coupled with a drop-down list of document collections to help users find product information.

Jim Radford, Manager of Interactive Customer Communications at 3M, said that employees like Excite's ability to search by concept instead of keyword. A user can enter an English statement as a search query, and Excite will return a list of documents even if those documents don't contain the words in the query. Excite implements its search by concept by indexing how often certain words appear together in a document. It then calculates the possibility that separate words are part of the same concept and returns documents based on this possibility.

Radford said that employees sometimes know what a product does, but not what it's called. He gave as an example the query in Figure 16-4, which is "find a product that projects an image on a wall." I tried this query on 3M's Web site, and it returned a list of overhead projectors, panel projectors, and multimedia projectors.

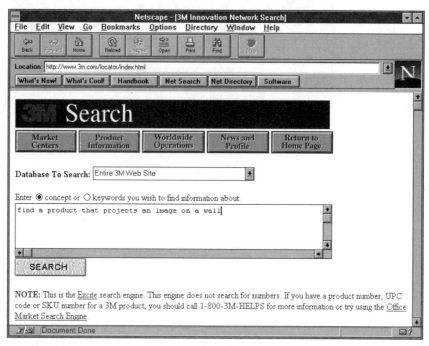

Figure 16-4: 3M employees can use Excite to search for product information by concept as well as keyword.

3M also uses hyperlinks to organize the 60,000 products by market centers or type of product (see Figure 16-5). This Web page is the first level of a multiple-level hierarchy of products. If you select the Automotive market center, you drill down into another set of hyperlinks, as shown in Figure 16-6.

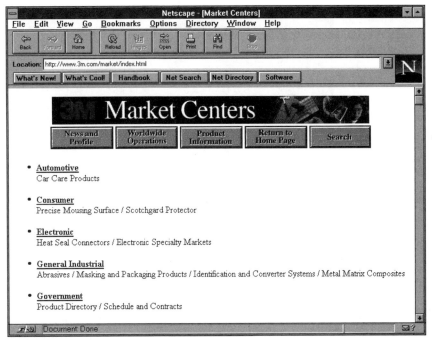

Figure 16-5: 3M uses hyperlinks to organize 60,000 products by how the product is used.

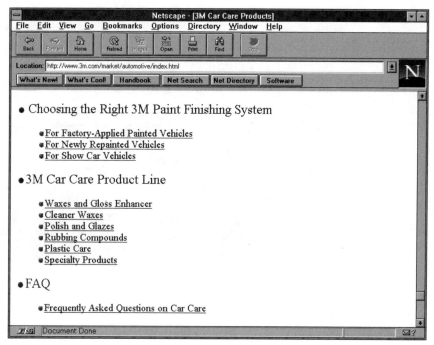

Figure 16-6: Clicking on the Automotive market center brings up another list of hyperlinks.

Selecting a link from the list of products brings up product information, which also might contain hyperlinks to appropriate documents. If you select Waxes and Gloss Enhancer from the hyperlinks in Figure 16-6, you see the product data shown in Figure 16-7. This screen gives product names, part numbers, and information about the product. There are hyperlinks to procedure guides for this group of products.

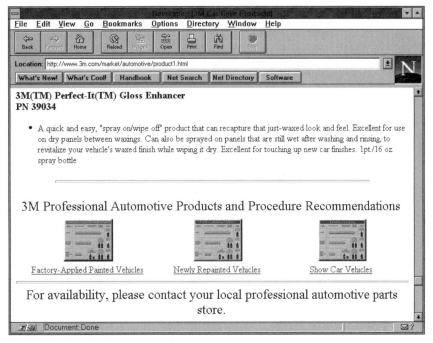

Figure 16-7: The 3M product fact sheets may contain hyperlinks to related documents.

3M's Web site is an example of how you can use intranet technology to provide quick and easy access to an overwhelmingly large collection of information.

Tip

Use the features of your intranet to provide multiple viewpoints into your company's data.

Bring the Benefits to Your Organization

You've seen how you can use hyperlinks and a search engine to reduce the cost of information access. You can use these intranet features to return a big payback to your company.

You'll want to start with the applications that have the most potential for increasing productivity. Look for collections of information that have the following characteristics:

○ The information is used by a large number of employees as part of their work processes.

○ The information contains a large group of data.

○ The information is not organized in the way people want to use it.

○ The ability to search the information can yield valuable results.

You can see how some of the case studies from previous chapters fit into this kind of application. The plastics company's production newsletters meet all of the criteria. When you consider the number of production facilities the company has and multiply it by 12 issues a year, there are a lot of newsletters in the collection. The printed newsletters are definitely not organized in a way that makes it easy to find information across months and plants.

The ability to search the newsletters is very valuable. If a production line runs into a problem, they can search through a couple years of newsletters across all facilities to see if anyone reported the same difficulty. What's the benefit of finding a quick solution to a production problem? This can result in huge savings.

Every company has information that's been faithfully collected, but not used to its full potential because of the way it's stored. You'll often find this situation with data that's captured on forms, then filed away. Customer call reports, product defect data, project updates, customer profiles, and product fact sheets are examples of this kind of data. The company goes through a great deal of time and expense to capture the details, but it doesn't get used as it should because it's hard to access.

This kind of data is like a buried treasure that no one digs up because they don't have the right tools. Your intranet is the tool that reveals the treasure hidden in the data that the corporation has collected. You've already spent the money to gather the information. Now you can put it on an intranet and reap the benefits of the company's information investment.

Implementing Best Practices Applications

What's the dollar return from a best practices application? The real question to ask is what's the value of spreading the company's best ideas throughout the organization?

It's hard to calculate the precise dollar benefits of a best practices application—harder than any other intranet application. Yet best practices projects have the highest potential for payback to the company. By far.

A well-implemented best practices application means the company will use the best techniques available, and this results in a better product. The dollar savings can often be measured in less scrap, lower product returns, reduced costs, and higher sales. The return to the organization from one good idea that spreads through the corporation can be priceless.

Implementing Best Practices on Your Intranet

The goal of a best practices application is quite simple. Enhance the collaboration throughout the company so everyone benefits from the best of the best. Your intranet offers some tools to help implement that kind of collaboration.

One of the best ways to enhance collaboration is with discussion group software. When you put topic-specific discussion groups on your intranet, you give employees an organized way to share ideas regardless of departmental or geographic boundaries.

The success of your discussion groups depends completely on whether employees see them as a resource they can benefit from. Work with the various departments to come up with the best candidates for starter forums.

The biggest payback for best practices comes in the work processes that can most benefit from a good idea. These are often manufacturing, R&D, sales, marketing, and customer service. You'll want to start with forums that will bring immediate returns to the company by helping employees solve production problems, improve the design of the product, or better serve the customer.

Go for the big return in the first few months of the intranet. Then as the whole organization can see the benefits of best practices, you can create forums for other parts of the corporation.

Another tool you can use in a best practices application is a search engine directed toward a specific collection of documents. The plastics company used a search engine that enabled employees to mine best practices tips from the company's newsletters.

You can implement best practices by creating online collections of knowledge and expertise. These include newsletters, research papers, project reports, and procedure guides. Create a repository of your company's expertise, then organize it with hyperlinks and allow employees to tap into this valuable data with a search engine.

You can also use the power of hyperlinks to help implement best practices. If the content on your intranet is cross-referenced in a useful way, employees can benefit from the work of others by following the chain of related documents.

The return to your organization from a well-designed best practices application can be enormous.

Putting It All Together

This chapter has covered the big-payback intranet applications in three categories: publishing information, accessing information, and best practices. When you build your intranet, you'll blend these three types of savings into one system.

The Three Types of Savings in One Application

The plastics company intranet that I've used as a prototype throughout the book is a good example of how a company uses the three types of savings in one application.

The plastics company's manufacturing division will use the intranet to simultaneously reduce the cost of publishing newsletters and make the information in those newsletters much easier to access. Hyperlinks will be used to link articles in the newsletters to other data from around the company—including customer comments about the products being produced and marketing reports on new items. The content from other departments will link back to the newsletters where appropriate.

Employees will be able to use a search engine to find keywords or phrases in any issue of the newsletter. There will also be hyperlinks from newsletter articles to the relevant discussion group forums. Someone who is reading a newsletter can follow a hyperlink to a threaded discussion, post a question or idea about the topic in the article, then click the Back button in the browser to return to the newsletter.

The company will put this one piece of data, the production newsletters, on the intranet. This will result in a reduction in publishing costs and easier access to the information, and it will serve as part of a best practices application.

It's very likely that this one application by itself will more than pay for the cost of the intranet.

Find Triple-Payback Applications

Do you have any of these triple-payback applications for your intranet? Look for information that's:

- widely used.
- costly to publish and revise.
- difficult to access in its current form.
- a core business process.

Many of our case studies had applications that met the criteria on this list. The Hollings Cancer Institute protocols were certainly widely used, costly to distribute to 10 or more locations, difficult to use, and were part of the core process. The regulatory data used by Eli Lilly fits this description. So do the consultant reports that Booz-Allen & Hamilton stored in their best practices application.

Start with these kinds of applications and you'll have no trouble reaping big benefits from your intranet.

Moving On

You can use your intranet to bring incredible benefits to your organization. You can implement applications that reduce the cost of information and spread the concept of best practices throughout the company. Many corporations are reporting sizable savings after implementing intranets. You can follow a few simple tips to bring these types of savings to your company.

An intranet can handle some kinds of applications better than any other technology, but it's not the best choice for every application. Chapter 17 shows you why some applications are just not suited for an internal web. You'll learn to use your intranet's strengths and avoid its weaknesses.

17

When the Intranet Isn't a Good Fit

An intranet is the best solution for many applications. You can build it for a low cost, then implement high-payback applications. But it isn't the best solution for everything.

HTML has limitations. You'll find that HTML is not well suited for building data entry-intense, high-transaction applications like order entry, general ledger, or accounts payable.

I've talked to developers who have had trouble getting their intranets started because management wanted the first applications to be mission critical client/server systems. One company's CEO insisted that a high-transaction data entry system would be the internal web's first application. Employees were initially excited about the intranet, but lost interest because the project dragged on as developers struggled to convert the mandated system. The intranet was never rolled out.

An information systems manager at another company was enthusiastic about intranet technology and thought it had real potential for the company. She was told that the project would not be approved unless all applications could be converted to the intranet.

If these examples sound illogical, remember that to many people outside of the Information Systems department, an intranet is just another computer system. It's easy for people to get caught up in the hype about web technology without understanding how it's different from currently deployed systems.

You don't want to be put in the situation where management has unrealistic expectations for the intranet that will doom it from the beginning. Be prepared to explain why some applications just aren't good candidates for the intranet. Address this issue from the start so you can cash in on high user excitement and implement the most beneficial applications.

Standard Web Technology & Data Entry Applications

Imagine entering orders into a client/server order entry application. The top half of the screen has customer information. The bottom half is a scrolling display of the items on a particular order. As you enter each item code, the description and price are automatically retrieved from the database and displayed on the screen. When you enter a quantity, the program extends the quantity times the price, displays this number, and updates order totals at the bottom of the display.

How does this differ from a web page form? Remember that a standard web page can not do client-side processing. If you created a web page to duplicate this order entry process, the user would have to fill out the item code and quantity for all items, then click a Submit button. The input data would be sent to the server, and an HTML page would be returned containing the extended dollar amounts and order totals.

Going Beyond the Shoestring

This chapter discusses the types of applications that you would have trouble designing using standard HTML. These applications are not impossible to do on intranets. In Chapter 20 you'll see that it's possible to develop sophisticated applications using recently released web-enabled development environments and languages like Java and JavaScript.

The purpose of this chapter is to show you the types of applications that will not be easy to implement using standard web technology.

Client-Side Processing

Those two scenarios, the client/server order entry process and the same process with a web page, might seem similar. After all, they both produce the same results in the end. But a customer service rep with a customer on the other end of the phone is used to instant, on-screen results. To this person, having to fill out the entire form, then wait for the results to be returned from the server, is a step backwards.

There are other subtle differences. What happens if the rep keys an invalid item code? The traditional order entry application is constantly verifying input and does not allow invalid codes to be entered. With the web version of this application, errors are not caught until the entire form is sent to the server for processing.

The client/server application gives constant feedback to the user by displaying item description and price as soon as an item is entered, and by popping up error messages when invalid data has been keyed in.

The web page is static. The user receives no feedback at all during entry. This is not what employees are used to from their data entry applications. Users of high transaction count data entry applications will not view a static data entry screen very favorably.

Ensuring Data Integrity

Another subtle difference between the two technologies can result in a very dangerous situation. In a traditional order entry application, the system doesn't let the user exit with unsaved changes. If the user enters or changes some data, then clicks on exit, the program typically pops up a warning dialog telling the user there are unsaved changes to the data.

This is a very important feature. It ensures the integrity of the data. The user never inadvertently leaves a data entry screen unaware that some input has only been partially completed.

With a web version of the same application, nothing prevents the operator from clicking on the Back button of the browser before submitting the data for processing. This can lead to disastrous results.

Head-Down Data Entry

If you've watched an experienced order entry or payroll operator in action you've probably noticed that their hands leave the keyboard as little as possible. Well-designed client/server applications let operators invoke menu choices with the keyboard. Frequently used options are often assigned to shortcut keys. These applications are designed for maximum productivity.

A standard HTML web page doesn't offer client-side processing, so it can't offer keyboard shortcuts that let employees speed through data entry chores.

It's not only tough to duplicate the look and feel of a client/server application in a web page, but it's impossible to provide the same processing that users expect without expending the dollars and time it would take to implement client-side programming in your web pages.

Low Payback Applications

You can use the new generation of web-enabled programming software to recreate the look and functionality of client/server applications, as you'll see in Chapter 20. It just isn't worth it for a lot of applications.

If you have an order entry program already in place, what's the benefit of converting this application to the intranet? It's tough to justify the time and expense it takes to move high-transaction data entry applications from their current technology to your internal web.

Some of the new software that you'll see in Chapter 20 will make it easy to put data entry applications in web pages. But the payback for moving this to the intranet will be low compared to the other intranet applications that you've seen in earlier chapters.

When you pick the first round of applications for your intranet, client/server data entry systems should usually fall to the bottom of the list.

Complementary Technologies

The fact that HTML isn't well suited for client/server data entry applications isn't a fault of web technology. HTML was created to provide a way of serving documents across platforms. It was not designed as an application programming environment. Web technology and client/server software are complementary technologies. The strengths of one are the weaknesses of the other.

Client/server software is great for retrieving, manipulating, and displaying a mass quantity of individual data records. It's not at all good at manipulating entire documents. A client/server application has been programmed to expect certain types of data, and instructed to display that data in predefined screen locations. It's tough to handle free format documents in this kind of software.

Web technology excels in manipulating entire documents. The client browser does not have to know ahead of time what kind of information is coming or how to display it. The HTML standard allows the browser to format the display based on the document itself, not predefined program code stored on the client. The technology is well suited for document manipulations, but not good for order entry, payroll, and similar data entry applications.

Most companies don't program document handling systems in application development software like PowerBuilder or Visual Basic. You can do it, but the effort isn't worth it. The same can be said about programming a data entry application using standard web technology.

You'll want to select applications for your intranet that match the strengths of the technology.

Selecting Intranet Applications

When you pick the first set of applications for your intranet, avoid the mission critical data entry applications like order entry and payroll. Any application that uses heads-down data entry is not a good candidate for your initial intranet applications.

What about letting users query databases from web pages? This is a good application for your intranet. It allows you to easily give employees cross-platform access to your corporate data, and enables the company to reduce the cost of accessing information.

So how does this differ from the kinds of client/server applications covered in this chapter? The kinds of database applications that companies are implementing on their intranets are usually fairly simple applications. There are database query applications, such as checking order status from a web page. There are also low transaction data entry systems like ordering supplies.

These types of database applications make sense for an intranet. They're not all that difficult to implement and they can mean big payback for the corporation.

What you want to avoid, especially when you first roll out your intranet, are the sophisticated, high-volume, mission-critical applications that require a lot of effort to convert and don't take advantage of the strengths of web technology.

When the Subject Comes Up

Sooner or later you'll come up against the "in-flight magazine syndrome." This occurs when someone from your company reads a quick overview of intranet technology, the kind of article that appears in airline magazines, and concludes that client/server is out and intranets are in. They'll come to you and ask if you can convert the company's mission-critical systems to this wonderful thing called an intranet. So what do you do then?

Point out that traditional client/server software and intranet technology have different, complementary strengths. It's not that the intranet can't handle mission-critical data entry systems; it's just that other applications will return a much better payback for the dollars and time that the company will expend to implement them.

Start your intranet with quick hit applications that have real benefits for the organization.

Moving On

Some applications just aren't well suited for an intranet. You've learned to recognize these kind of applications and can explain why the company should convert other systems first.

You'll want to get your intranet off to a good start by picking the appropriate applications for the initial phase of the system.

In the next chapter, you'll pick up some more tips for the early days of your intranet. You'll learn how to roll out a low-cost, low-risk pilot intranet.

SECTION 6

Making Sure Your Intranet Is a Success

The goal of this section is to help you make your intranet a success. Chapter 18 shows you how to roll out a successful pilot intranet, and in Chapter 19 you'll pick up some tips from intranet veterans. The book ends with a look at the new generation of intranet application development software.

Implement a Successful Intranet Pilot

You've learned how to build a low-cost intranet. You've also seen how an intranet can bring substantial benefits to your company. If you're skeptical, that's good. One of the main attractions of an intranet is that you can test the concept at little cost and almost no risk.

You can get freeware, shareware, or evaluation copies of every intranet component. Can you think of any other type of system where this is the case? The key is to take advantage of this situation and do a low-risk proof of concept for an intranet at your company. This chapter shows you how to do that.

In a way, your intranet pilot is the most important step in the whole project. You not only have to prove that an intranet has value for your corporation, you also have to make sure that employees will use the new system. This chapter gives you some tips for making your intranet a hit from the very beginning.

Start Informally

In many companies, any information technology project that will be rolled out across the company must go through a formal appropriation request process before work can begin. The requesting or sponsoring department has to submit a detailed financial analysis of the expenses versus the savings. The projected return on investment must justify the project or it won't be approved.

Numerous case studies show that intranets often are an exception to this process.

An article in *ComputerWorld*[1] shows that many companies allow a pilot intranet to be constructed without the need for a formal payback study. The article quotes a *ComputerWorld* survey revealing that 63 percent of companies surveyed did not require cost justification for their intranets.

The article points out that companies forego the more formal approval process because intranets use existing hardware and the software is so inexpensive. A full-featured web server costs little more than a single night in a hotel in some American cities.

An intranet pilot doesn't represent much of a risk for your company. Take advantage of this to test the benefits before trying to estimate the cost/benefit ratio of your internal web.

A Low Cost/Low Risk Intranet Pilot

One key to a successful intranet pilot is to minimize the risk to the corporation while you're testing the concept. The technology of an intranet allows you to do just that. Here are some tips to help you keep the risk low while still providing a fully functional intranet.

Keep Software Costs Low

You've got a great selection of freeware, shareware, and low cost commercial software to choose from to assemble your pilot intranet. You can also get an evaluation copy of just about any commercial intranet software on the market.

You have to use a little strategy to keep costs down without sacrificing the functionality of your pilot.

Many software companies put a time limit on evaluation software. Typical arrangements are 30, 45, or 60 day trials, with the 45 day trial being pretty common. You have to figure this into your pilot plan. You may have to arrange with your pilot users to test some function, such as a search engine or discussion group software, during the short evaluation time that the software company allows.

You have to decide what mix of freeware, shareware, evaluation, and commercial software you're going to use in the pilot.

In my opinion, many of the commercial products are so reasonably priced that you shouldn't settle for a lesser product just to save a couple hundred dollars during the pilot. Some freeware and shareware software is excellent, but if you have a choice between $295 commercial software and a product that's missing some functionality, spend the money.

Use evaluation copies of software whenever you can during the pilot, but don't be afraid to purchase some of the inexpensive commercial products as necessary.

Should You Switch Products?

When you put together the software for your intranet pilot you're going to face a tough question. Should you use a software package during the test that you know you won't use when you roll out your intranet?

For some components, like the web server, users might never know the difference. But other products are highly visible, including the web browser, search engine, and discussion group software.

You might face this decision if you think you're going to go with one of the higher-cost search engines or discussion group products. You probably want to go with shareware or a lower-cost product during the pilot. This lets you show what a search engine or discussion group product can do, but still keeps the cost of the pilot low. The intranet's web browser is a different story.

As I said in Chapter 6, to your users the browser *is* the intranet. While it might be okay to use one browser for the pilot, then switch to another when you roll the intranet out to a wider audience, be careful. Don't use a browser during the pilot that limits what employees can do. To them, the browser is very much a part of the evaluation.

You might have some tough decisions when you design your pilot intranet. You want it to be representative of what the real thing can do, but you don't want to run up a lot of costs during the pilot. With careful planning and well-timed use of evaluation software, you should be able to conduct a low-cost, but realistic trial.

Keeping the Risks Low

Part of implementing a low-risk intranet pilot is keeping the cost down. You also keep the risks low by careful selection of the applications you implement during the test period.

Don't convert a large quantity of documents to the intranet during the pilot. You'll want to build content that helps employees evaluate the pilot, but you don't want to convert a tremendous number of documents only to decide they'll have to be redesigned or scrapped later. Keep the labor investment in the pilot, as well as the software costs, reasonable.

Don't migrate a mission-critical application to your pilot intranet. You want to use the pilot to evaluate whether an intranet will be beneficial to the company. Don't create a situation where some employees depend on the pilot intranet to do their jobs—a situation in which the company would suffer if the intranet was not available for some period. This creates too much risk and is not the purpose of the pilot.

Involve Users From the Start

I've got a secret for you. One of the best ways to ensure the success of your intranet is to build excitement for the technology early in the process. You do this by both involving employees in the pilot from the beginning and by actively soliciting suggestions for intranet applications.

Build Excitement Early

A friend of mine was responsible for implementing an intranet at a manufacturing company. He put together the structure of the intranet, then started asking users what applications they wanted.

My friend thought the intranet was a good idea for the company, but he was worried that he wouldn't find enough applications for it. He was pleasantly surprised by the reaction to the idea. His intranet demos were met by excited employees throughout the company. He was soon flooded with suggestions for intranet applications. People not only had good ideas, but they often suggested applications that would solve some long-time problem and provide real value to the company.

An intranet can give employees capabilities they've never had. You can build a lot of excitement by involving employees in the design of the pilot.

Build an Intranet Demo

You'll want to give a demo of the intranet to users and get their feedback before you get too far along in the pilot. To do that, you have to start with a small-scale intranet demo.

Build the intranet infrastructure, then add enough software to be able to show what the technology can do. I recommend that you include a search engine and possibly discussion group software in the demo. After all, you can't get feedback from employees if you can't show them the capabilities your intranet can provide.

An alternative to building a full-featured intranet demo is to use the World Wide Web in the first round of feedback sessions. Gather some employees together and walk them through some Web sites, highlighting the capabilities. Bring up a search engine and discussion group from somewhere on the Web and demonstrate the full capability of the technology.

If you use the World Wide Web for early feedback, be sure to give them some ideas on how the technology might be used inside the company.

Gather User Input

Your goal is to design a pilot intranet that employees want to use. You'll want to include them in the planning for the pilot by getting their input on what applications they'd like to see on the intranet and how they would use the technology.

I've seen a number of approaches to getting user feedback. In some companies, intranet developers visit employee staff meetings, give a demo, then ask for input. Other companies put together a council of users, with no more than a couple of contacts from each functional area meeting to brainstorm ideas for the intranet. Another method is to set up a demo room. Put the word out that you've got an intranet set up in some room and let employees visit and play with it.

When you visit with employees, encourage them to suggest intranet ideas by throwing out a few example applications. Mention the ideas suggested by other areas so people can see what kinds of things this new system might be able to do.

The key is to start building excitement among employees over what the intranet can do for them, while at the same time collecting the suggestions people offer, to help you design an intranet pilot that has a high likelihood of being used.

Selecting Applications for the Pilot

You want employees to find the intranet useful. You'll want to build a pilot that makes it clear that the intranet makes it easier for them to do their jobs. Start by including the appropriate applications during the trial.

The initial content of the intranet pilot doesn't necessarily have to be the applications that provide the huge dollar payback, but the content has to be useful and serve a need.

Pick Low-Hanging Fruit

When you build the content for the pilot, start with "low-hanging fruit." Pick something that's relatively easy to implement, but also provides clear benefits to employees.

Pick applications that highlight the benefits of the technology and interest users at the same time. A good example of this is the plastics company's production newsletters. The newsletters contain information that help people do their jobs.

If you have information like the newsletters, you can convert it to the intranet, then use the features of the technology to demonstrate the benefits of the internal web. You could code hyperlinks connecting issues of the newsletter and also point articles to related documents. You could even add the ability to use a search engine against the information.

Take something that's fairly easy to convert to HTML and make it easier to access than it was before the intranet. Show employees that the intranet enables them to easily point and click through information that was once difficult to access. You'll be surprised by their reaction.

Avoid the Dental Benefits Syndrome

When you select content for the intranet pilot, try and look at it from the employees' point of view. Avoid what I call the "dental benefits syndrome." Even though you can save substantial dollars by putting the human resources manual online, this is not such a good application for the pilot. Employees won't get too excited about the ability to drill down to dental benefits.

For the pilot, stick with applications that will be more heavily used. These can include applications like the company phone book, procedure manuals, and project status updates.

Designing the Pilot Intranet's Web Pages

As you get application suggestions from users, you might be tempted to jump right in and start creating the content. This can result in a hodgepodge of documents that either have to be redesigned or that leave gaps in the flow of information.

Design It on Paper First

Even though your pilot intranet will be less formal than the version you roll out to the company, don't neglect to do some planning before you start building content. While you have a good idea how the finished system will function, users don't. Your pilot has to be representative of the real thing—not just a few, unrelated HTML documents.

Put some thought into how you want the information to flow in the pilot intranet so that it will clearly demonstrate the operation of a full-scale internal web. Draw a map of the proposed intranet on paper before you start setting up the physical structure and converting documents.

Provide a Complete Set of Web Pages

When you design the pilot intranet, don't assume that employees will intuitively know how to navigate web pages. Design a home page that provides a clear map to the content of the intranet. Use navigation buttons on interior web pages to show employees what options are available. Make it easy; first impressions can last a long time.

If you're going to include content from different departments, design home pages for each of the functional areas. This helps employees form a mental map of the information. They can see how the intranet will be structured to match the way they think about the company's information.

If you have a search engine and discussion group software on your intranet pilot, add hyperlinks to them from more than one web page. If you have marketing content and have started a marketing forum, make sure users can jump between the two sections of the intranet.

You want to make it as easy as possible for employees to envision how the intranet can tie the company's data together. Don't throw up isolated pieces of information. Design the intranet's structure so it provides intuitive navigation to all of the available information.

Implementing the Pilot

Once you've gathered user feedback and designed the pilot intranet, it's time to make it available. It's important to control the scope of the pilot and set up a process where you get regular feedback from employees.

Control the Scope of the Pilot

As you progress from the initial stages of the pilot through the first year of the intranet, you'll want to control the scope of the intranet if possible. Start the pilot with a predetermined, limited set of users. Then have a plan for adding employees to the pilot.

If you've done a good job and created an intranet pilot that clearly demonstrates its value to employees, you may find favorable impressions spreading throughout the company by word of mouth. Don't let the number of intranet users snowball out of control too early in the project. The purpose of the pilot is to test the value of the intranet, but it also provides valuable feedback that influences the final design. Don't find yourself in the situation where users are added to the intranet far ahead of content that interests them. You want employees to find the intranet useful from the beginning.

Start by selecting a pilot group. You can limit the initial phase to certain departments only or pick representatives from each area. Keep the initial user count manageable so you can keep in contact with them and learn from their experiences.

Get Feedback Throughout the Pilot

Set up mechanisms to collect constant feedback from intranet users. One popular technique is to put mail-to buttons on web pages. If you spend time on the World Wide Web, you've seen this in action. You code a button or a text hyperlink that allows users to send comments to someone on the intranet team. Encourage employees to use this feature by acknowledging their messages.

If your pilot intranet has discussion group software, set up a forum for feedback on the intranet itself. This is a good way to collect feedback and spark discussions at the same time.

You might want to use the traditional methods of gathering feedback as well. Send out surveys. Do selective interviews. Attend meetings and ask for input.

Your intranet will be a success if you learn from employee feedback, and then use what you've learned to design the intranet that employees want.

Get Approval, Then Take Action

You'll reach a point where you know the pilot has been successful. You'll know that the intranet has proven its value to the corporation.

When you reach this point, it's time to get approval to roll the internal web out to the rest of the company and start treating it like a production system.

It's vital that you keep the momentum going. Don't let enthusiasm for the intranet die. Keep adding the applications and content that provide the intranet's usefulness and value.

Moving On

One of the most attractive features of intranets is the ability to test the concept with little risk to the corporation. You've learned how to test the intranet concept without a significant investment. You've also picked up some tips on keeping employees excited about the new system.

When you move beyond the pilot and roll the intranet out, you'll confront a few more issues. The next chapter shows you how to involve users in updating the content of the intranet. You'll pick up some tips on designing the intranet so employees make it a part of their daily work processes.

When your intranet becomes an official system, you'll have some administrative issues to settle. You'll have to determine who can add and update intranet content. You'll also have to make decisions on standards for web-page design.

The next chapter also briefly discusses security. The chances are good that you'll either have confidential information on the intranet that you want to protect or that you'll want to connect the intranet to the Intranet. You'll learn how it's possible to provide adequate security in these situations.

You've learned how to make your intranet pilot a success. The next step is to ensure that it remains a successful part of your company's information systems.

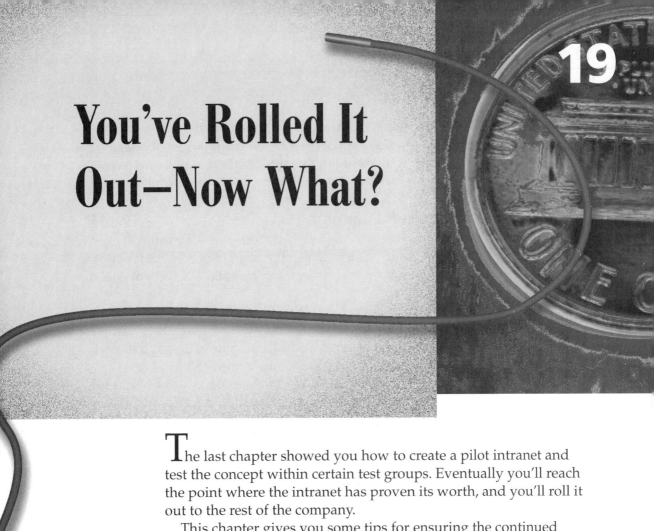

19

You've Rolled It Out—Now What?

The last chapter showed you how to create a pilot intranet and test the concept within certain test groups. Eventually you'll reach the point where the intranet has proven its worth, and you'll roll it out to the rest of the company.

This chapter gives you some tips for ensuring the continued success of your intranet. You'll pick up some pointers from intranet veterans and learn how to deal with some of the issues you'll confront. These issues include controlling who can add information to the internal web and how to handle security.

Keep Them Coming Back for More

When your intranet makes it past the pilot stage, you know you've got a system that employees find useful. Now you've got to work to continually provide a system that employees will make a part of their daily work processes.

Your intranet may attract a lot of attention at first simply because it uses the same interface as the World Wide Web. The novelty will soon wear off, though. Employees will only keep visiting your intranet as long as it holds useful information.

Provide Useful Content

The first secret to maintaining the success of your intranet is providing useful content. This may seem obvious, but it's easy to get caught up in the technology and lose sight of the real goal of the internal web.

Kyle Brown is Director of Web Technology for ProjectSolutions. He has developed intranets for a number of companies, including Silicon Graphics, Hewlett Packard, and Sony. He said the key to a successful intranet is simple—it's all in the content.

"In order for an intranet project to be successful," Brown said, "a company must ensure that content is king. Graphics are pretty, but they don't keep employees coming back for more. Sites that have ever-changing information or information that helps get the job done faster and easier are the most useful and the most visited."

> ### Note
> Some of the material in this chapter originally appeared in an article I wrote for *Internet Advisor* called "Steps to Intranet Success."

Dr. Lawrence Afrin, who built the intranet for the Hollings Cancer Institute, agreed that content is very important to the success of an intranet. He said intranet developers sometimes forget this fact.

"Far too much work goes into worthless content," Dr. Afrin said. He added that too much effort is put into designing web pages that look cool, but don't provide any function for employees. "The sole purpose of the site is to get information to or from the users as efficiently as possible, so that they can perform their jobs more efficiently," he said.

Don't forget to add work process tools to the intranet. These can include web pages to order supplies, sign up for training, or check order status. Karilee Wirthlin helped build Silicon Graphics' intranet. She believes an intranet must include work tools to remain a success. "An intranet site needs to be tool-oriented or transaction-based," she said. "An intranet is something that employees will use every day if new information is highlighted regularly and transactions can be done via the web."

Continually seek to load the intranet with information that employees will find useful, and the intranet will be a success.

Keep the Content Up-to-Date

One thing that can doom your intranet to failure more than anything else is out-of-date information. You just can't have a successful intranet if employees can't rely on the timeliness of the information.

Dr. Afrin said current information is a must. "Obsolete, out-of-date, inaccurate content is much worse than no content at all," he said. "If you can't afford the resources to keep the content of your site current, then you shouldn't even start site construction."

Brown said you have to be prepared to support intranet content. "Since content is everything," he said, "a company must be prepared to dedicate the resources required to maintain the information. Intranet content must change weekly, if not daily. Technical resources must be committed to create dynamic information and link to legacy databases."

Intranet developers recommend a couple of tricks you can use to get employees into the habit of checking the intranet every day. "One method I have seen used successfully to keep employees tuning into the corporate web page each day is to put the company stock price on the page," Brown said. "Employees will check it daily and will notice new links or news items."

The home page of Silicon Graphics' intranet is designed like a newspaper. Wirthlin says the company uses the headline and article banners to keep employees interested in the internal web. "The main banner changes every couple of days," she said, "and sub-bullets change daily, or even hourly. Other important banners can be highlighted via randomly changing banners."

Keep content fresh and structure the opening screens of the intranet to highlight new information.

Strategies for Maintaining Content

One of the most difficult tasks you'll face after you roll out your intranet is coming up with a workable strategy for maintaining content. You'll face an interesting paradox—you want users to maintain their own information, but you also want to have some control over who updates content, what they post to the internal web, and the look and feel of the web pages they create.

You want each department to take charge of their own content, but you don't want the intranet to turn into an information free-for-all that will end in chaos.

Controlling Content

It's usually a good idea to have some kind of guidelines on who can update the intranet and what information can be posted. This is tricky. You don't want to discourage employees from maintaining their own information, but you also want to maintain some logic to the structure and content of the intranet.

Companies are coming up with some good solutions to this dilemma. Some companies create a committee or team that is ultimately responsible for intranet content. This team usually has representatives from each functional area of the company along with intranet developers. Employees are allowed to design their own web pages, but the intranet team reviews all designs and ensures that they meet standards for content, functionality, and appearance.

Other companies implement a solution that isn't as centralized. Each department appoints an intranet contact. The contact is given access to the intranet's directories and can freely add or maintain departmental web pages. The department's content is not reviewed by a team or committee.

This second solution strikes a reasonable balance between control and individual responsibility. The company can make sure that each department's representative has adequate training and understands the intranet's goals and purpose. Then it's up to that person (or persons) to create the content the department wants. The rep is also responsible for working with other reps to ensure that the company takes advantage of cross-referencing information with hyperlinks.

Some companies allow individuals to add and maintain their own content, but appoint a team to periodically review the intranet's web pages for consistency. This team can ask a person or department to change their web pages to maintain a uniform look and feel across the company. Other companies let employees have almost complete freedom in what they do with the intranet, as you saw in the 3M case study in Chapter 15.

It might be a good idea to start out with more centralized control in the early months of your intranet, then allow more freedom as employees get a feel for the intranet's purpose and design.

It will be much easier for your company to keep the intranet content fresh if each department is responsible for their own web-page maintenance.

Web-Page Standards

You'll want to design an intranet that is intuitive and easy for employees to use. You'll probably want to develop web-page standards to maintain a consistent look and feel across web documents.

You can make the various web pages in the intranet feel like part of an integrated system if you enforce standards for web-page appearance, navigation, and hyperlinks. Here are some of the issues companies have addressed with their web-page standards:

❍ How to use white space and graphics to break up documents with an abundance of text.

❍ The proper use of hyperlinks. Some people go hyperlink crazy and turn a word or phrase in every other sentence into a hyperlink. This detracts from the ability of a hyperlink to highlight information.

❍ The proper use of graphics. You can cut down on the number of pages that are heavy on attractive, but useless, graphics.

❍ Guidelines for using titles and headings in web pages.

❍ Guidelines for navigation.

Some companies include a standard that requires "signing" all web pages. Web-page authors must identify themselves somewhere on each web page they create, and some companies even require that each page have a Mail-to button so other employees can send comments or questions to the person who designed it.

Getting Users Involved With Content

You don't want to be single-handedly responsible for intranet content. Another secret to intranet success is getting employees to maintain their own content.

Here's a trick you can use to make it easy for users to build their own content and maintain standards at the same time. Give users an intranet kit that includes content creation software; a collection of graphic elements like buttons, bars, and images; and web-page templates that will get them started.

This makes it more likely that they'll create and maintain their own content, but it also subtly enforces a standard look and feel. You can give them web-page templates that already include navigation bars, logos, and hyperlinks to your search engine and discussion group software.

Another technique for getting employees to maintain their own information is to offer classes in web-page creation. You can show them how easy it is to create web pages using some of the latest, point-and-click HTML editing software. You can also provide training on HTML converters they can use to convert their existing documents to web pages.

An intranet content course is also a good way to spread the word about web-page standards and procedures.

Use the Intranet to Collect Feedback

Your company's employees can participate in ensuring the success of the intranet. Use the features of the technology to continually collect their questions and concerns about the internal web and their suggestions for making it even better.

Make it easy for employees to send you comments about the intranet. Put hyperlinks on several web pages that allow employees to send you a message. Make it clear that you welcome their comments and ideas.

If you have added discussion-group software to your intranet, start a forum in which the topic is the intranet itself. You might want to start the discussion by posting a message that asks questions like, What do you like about the intranet?, and What can be improved? Highlight the forum by putting a link to it on your intranet's home page. You'll learn a lot from the exchange of messages that occurs in the forum.

Here's another secret for making your intranet a success—implement some of the best suggestions you get from employees. Then use an intranet-based newsletter or other means to announce the change and thank the people who suggested it. Employees will learn that their participation matters, that this really is their system, and they will remain enthusiastic about the intranet.

Intranet Security

An intranet makes it easy to share information. Sometimes, though, you want to limit access to certain pieces of data. Intranet security is a tough issue at some companies. You want to prevent unauthorized people from seeing sensitive information, but there is such a thing as too much security. You can create a security layer that's so complex that the burden of maintaining it outweighs the value of putting the information on the intranet.

In this section you'll learn how to implement security on your intranet. You'll also see how to recognize situations where the cost of securing some particular information isn't worth the benefit of putting that information on your intranet.

When Security Is Necessary

Intranet security is required in three situations:

○ When you put internal information on the intranet that is for selected employees only.

○ When you allow company partners, such as resellers or vendors, to access part of the intranet.

○ When you connect your intranet to the Internet.

There are times when you want to use the intranet to post confidential internal information. You might want to use the intranet to serve as a repository for online reports, and some of the reports might contain sensitive information such as financial results. You might also put pricing information online. You'll want to limit this type of information to a predefined list of employees. You'll need to establish security that lets employees see all of the open information, but limits who can access the typically small section of the internal web that contains confidential information.

If you build a section of the intranet for outside partners such as sales distributors or vendors, you'll want to build security that allows them to access only this small portion of the intranet. The logic here is the opposite of the logic regarding security for employees. You allow employees to see the majority of the intranet, but limit access to certain documents. Partners can only see a small portion of the intranet and are excluded from the majority of data.

Many companies have found advantages to linking the intranet to the Internet, such as allowing intranet web pages to contain links to Internet Web sites. Employees can be directed to external information about customers, vendors, competitors, and the industry. When you link your intranet to the Internet, you must provide heavy security that prevents the general public from accessing your intranet information.

Let's start by looking at different security techniques you can use on your intranet, then apply them to the three situations: internal employees accessing confidential documents, partners accessing part of the intranet, and Internet access.

Intranet Security Features

There are four basic forms of security you can implement on your intranet:

○ The security features of the web server can be used to limit access to the entire server, server directories, or individual files.

○ Programs called by the server can be designed with their own security. For example, a database procedure can check user ID and password before returning data.

○ HTML documents can be encrypted so the document can only be read by the intended audience.

○ A firewall can be implemented to filter access from the Internet or from partners. A firewall is software that is placed between two networks to control access.

Web Server Security Rules

Many web servers have security features that allow you to limit access based on the workstation's IP address, the host computer of the user, user ID and password, and the user's security group. You can use any combination of these methods to secure the entire server, selected directories, or individual documents.

Various web servers use different syntax for security rules, but the concept is the same. The syntax used by some web servers uses the keywords allow, deny, and order. Here is an example.

To use web-server security rules to allow only internal employees and selected IP addresses access to the server, you can code:

```
order deny, allow
deny from all
allow from mycomany.com
allow from 11.111.11.111
```

> ### Note
> The actual security syntax varies by web server.

This excludes everyone from the web server except people coming from one of the internal workstations and one selected IP address. An employee calling in using a laptop would be allowed access, for example. The *order* keyword is used so *deny* takes precedence over *allow*.

In addition to limiting access by IP address, you can also use name and password authentication to limit access to the server, directories, and files. Some web servers let you set up a database of names and passwords. There are also web servers that allow you to set up security groups, where you not only establish individual names and passwords but can also design groups of people and limit access by group.

> **Note**
>
> Most web servers that allow you to limit access by ID and password require that you create a complete ID and password database just for the web server. This can create redundant security efforts and become an administrative nightmare. We'll discuss this more at the end of the security section.

Enforcing Security With a Program

You can also enforce intranet security within programs that are called by the web server. Silicon Graphics' sales tools are an example of this method. Sales reps can use the intranet to request bookings and commissions data. The web page calls a database procedure that uses the rep's ID and password to determine which data that person can see.

This type of security can be easier to maintain than using the web server's security to protect directories and files. The database can contain a table that includes rep ID and the associated district or customer codes. The processing can then dynamically create the reports the rep wants by only retrieving data matching those codes. This is much easier than coding individual security rules for each of several HTML documents.

HTML Document Encryption

A solution that provides an extra layer of security is to encrypt the information on the server and decrypt it with a program on the client. Some companies are experimenting with this technique for their intranets. It gives an additional security step for very sensitive documents. You can store data on the server in encrypted form so that even if unauthorized users get past the web server security, they can't see the information. It's useless until it's decrypted.

An intranet consulting company called ProjectSolutions has developed a product that can encrypt HTML documents. You can contact them for more information at their Web site (http://www.projectsolutions.com).

Securing the Intranet With a Firewall

Firewall is the name applied to the software that controls the access between networks. If you connect your intranet to the Internet, you'll want to use a firewall to protect your internal data from Internet access.

To implement a firewall, you set up a server that's outside of your intranet. Then you put firewall software on the server and run a connection to your intranet. The connection to the Internet is made from the server that's outside of the intranet. The firewall sits between the intranet and the Internet. Firewall software lets you code access rules that limit who, if anyone, can pass through the firewall into your intranet.

Firewall software is relatively expensive. It ranges from $4,000 to $40,000 with some upper-end packages going for as much as $100,000.

Here are some sources of information on firewalls:

○ **Cathy Fulmer's List of Firewall Products.** Cathy Fulmer maintains a list of firewall products on the Web site of an Internet consulting firm, Great Circle Associates. The list contains over 50 commercial products and 5 freeware/ shareware products. Visit http://www.greatcircle.com/ firewalls/vendors.html for more information.

○ **Yahoo! Firewall Information.** Yahoo! has a category for firewalls (http://www.yahoo.com/ Computers_and_Internet/Security_and_Encryption/ Firewalls/). This collection contains links to firewall white papers and tutorials and pointers to 30 firewall products.

○ **Firewall Frequently Asked Questions.** Marcus J. Ranum has put together a list of Frequently Asked Questions (http:// www.v-one.com/pubs/fw-faq/faq.htm) containing hints for selecting and implementing firewalls.

Applying Intranet Security

Here are some security techniques you can apply to the three situations requiring security:

○ **Internal users accessing sensitive information.** To limit internal employee access to sensitive information, you can use web server ID and password authentication that limits access to either whole directories or individual files. You can also provide this security by coding a database program to return information on IDs and passwords.

○ **External partner and vendor access.** You can limit partner and vendor access in a couple of ways. You can set up the web server to deny access to everyone, then code security rules that let all internal employees access most of the intranet and external users access very limited sections. You probably also want to force partners and vendors to come in through a firewall. Then external users will have to pass through the firewall and will be subject to an additional layer of security.

○ **Connecting the intranet to the Internet.** If you connect the intranet to the Internet, you really don't have much choice. You'll have to use a firewall to protect your internal data.

When Do You Have Too Much Security?

An intranet's strength is its ability to make information easily available across your organization. While you can secure confidential information, you shouldn't place yourself in the situation where you create a security scheme so cumbersome that the cost to maintain it exceeds the value of the information.

I've talked to a company that wants to secure just about every piece of information on their intranet based on the workgroup employees are in. They want to put documents on the intranet, then code an intricate scheme that specifies which users can see which document. The company wants to apply this group-by-group security to most of the intranet's information.

The company is thinking of building an ID and password database on the web server that replicates their existing network scheme. Unless they can find some way of easily passing the ID and password settings from the network to the web server, the administration required to keep the two systems in sync will be redundant. And they still have to code the security rules for directories and files.

Even if the company can somehow simplify the administration of their security scheme, they'll run into other problems. They want to use hyperlinks extensively to tie together related information. They also want to use a search engine to help employees find data. How will their complex security structure effect these features of the intranet? Will employees try to follow hyperlinks only to get security violations? How will the search engine handle documents that the employee can't see?

Use common sense when applying security to your intranet. It makes sense to limit access to a small set of confidential documents. If some application requires you to set up complicated security rules for every employee, it might not belong on the intranet. Don't implement intranet applications that will cause administrative headaches with little return to the company.

Moving On

After you've rolled out your intranet, there are some things you can do to ensure that it's a continued success. You've learned techniques you can use to keep employees interested in the intranet and make them feel like they're part of the system. You've also learned how to handle some of the issues you'll face, such as who will maintain intranet content and how to implement security.

So far this book has discussed how to build an intranet "on a shoestring." You've seen the things you can do with standard web technology. The next chapter shows you the new generation of software that will let you take your intranet beyond the limitations of HTML. You'll see how you can design intranet applications that are more like your existing information systems.

20

Going Beyond the Shoestring

You've learned to put together a low-cost intranet. You start with a web server and web browser, then add a search engine, discussion group software, and maybe a product that links web pages to databases. You take some information and turn it into HTML documents, and you've got an intranet.

This system you've assembled can bring some benefits to your company better than any other type of system, but there are also some things it can't do very well. You learned in Chapter 17 that the standard intranet design has some limitations.

This chapter shows you how to go beyond the "shoestring" intranet and overcome the limitations of the standard intranet design.

The Limitations of Standard Intranet

Let's look at the typical intranet design. Employees click in their web browsers to retrieve a document. The web server receives the request, finds the document, and returns it to the browser. The employee can view the document in the browser.

There are two subtle limitations in this scenario. The first is that the web server merely retrieves an already formatted document and passes it to the browser. The second limitation is that the browser interprets and displays the document, but it is essentially static information. The browser doesn't interact with the data contained in the document.

The intranet I've just described is different from other information technology because *it is not a programmable system.*

You've seen how this limits what you can do on an intranet. Chapter 17 explained that standard intranet technology is not well-suited to certain applications. The standard intranet described above is not good at handling traditional client/server applications because it lacks programmable processing in two key places:

○ When information is retrieved by the server and sent to the browser or when data from the browser is sent from the server to a database.

○ On the client browser.

Processing Data on the Server

You learned in Chapter 14 that some products can put data from a database into a web page and take data from a web page form and save it back to the database. While this provides the ability to pass data dynamically between the client browser and the database, it is not really programmable. You create a web-page template that contains placeholders for the data and code a query that extracts the data from the database. The process is not reacting to the data from either direction; it's just passing it through.

What you want is software that lets you program logic for both manipulating the data and creating the HTML that's returned to the client. You could program this by hand in something like C or Perl, but that's likely to be a step back from the point-and-click software you use to design all of your other applications. You want an integrated development environment that lets you code processing for the data and screenpaint the resulting HTML document.

Processing on the Client

In the standard web-page design, the client browser doesn't manipulate the web page but merely displays it. This means the client can't validate input, perform calculations, or update the display without going back to the server. It also means that the look and feel of the web page is limited to whatever can be produced by HTML.

To go beyond the limitations of the standard web design, you need some way to design and implement processing on the client browser. You also want this programming to be done with a point-and-click software product.

Software That Takes You Beyond the Limitations

This chapter shows you the latest application development software for intranets. You'll see a couple of software products already on the market that make it easy for you to program server-side processing of both data and web-page documents. Then you'll see three newly introduced products that take three different approaches to creating a fully programmable intranet.

The title of this chapter is "Going Beyond the Shoestring" because these application development products take you beyond standard intranet technology in a couple of ways. They offer capabilities that can't be matched by standard web design. They also require more time and effort for developing intranet content than is required for static HTML documents. This new software extends the types of applications your intranet can handle, but it also requires the same amount of work that it takes to design traditional client/server systems in a product like PowerBuilder, Visual Basic, or Delphi.

The applications you develop with these products will be more involved than the typical intranet applications, but in many cases the capabilities you can offer your users will be worth it.

Java & JavaScript

Four of the five products covered in this chapter use either Java or JavaScript or both. Let's briefly look at these intranet/Internet client-side programming languages.

The Need for a Cross-Platform Programming Language

Remember that the World Wide Web was originally designed to be primarily a system to exchange documents. The system was designed so that the documents themselves were not platform dependent. The client software running on any type of computer could interpret and display the document.

It wasn't too hard to design a markup language that could be used on any platform. HTML is not really a programming language; it's just a series of formatting instructions that the browser deciphers. It's much more difficult to design a standard programming language to run on all platforms, and since this really didn't add much to the original purpose of the Web, the Web designers didn't attempt it.

After forms were added to the HTML standard and more businesses started using the Web, there was a need for a programming language to provide client-side processing.

Java

Sun Microsystems, Inc. designed a cross-platform intranet/ Internet programming language called Java. Sun managed to make Java perform across platforms by designing it so it didn't compile to the native code of an operating system. Java compiles to something called bytecode, which is interpreted by software in the browser. This means that you compile a Java program once, and it's available for all platforms.

A Java program designed for a web page is called an applet. You invoke an applet inside of a web page by referring to it in HTML, just like you refer to a graphic image. When the browser sees the Java applet reference, it loads the applet file, interprets the bytecodes, and runs the program.

Java is an object-oriented language that borrows heavily from C++. It is purposely limited so that it doesn't have access to system resources. A Java applet can't read or write the client's disk drives or run amok in memory. An applet is a well-behaved application. This design prevents malicious programmers from serving viruses via applets.

Let's take a look at some Java code. The following code prints "hello world" inside of the browser:

```
import java.applet.Applet;
import java.awt.Graphics;

public class HelloWorld extends Applet {
    public void paint(Graphics g) {
        g.drawString("Hello world!", 50, 25);
    }
}
```

The following HTML code invokes the hello world applet within a web page:

```
<HTML>
<HEAD>
<TITLE> A Simple Program </TITLE>
</HEAD>
 <BODY>

The applet message should appear here:
<APPLET CODE="HelloWorld.class" WIDTH=150 HEIGHT=25>
 </APPLET>
 </BODY>
 </HTML>
```

Java can do just about anything that C++ can do; the only difference is the safety restraints placed on Java. This means it can make a web page appear and function just about any way you can imagine. You can design Java-driven web pages to have the look and processing ability of an application that is very close to a traditional client/server program.

Java can also be compiled to a stand-alone program and run on the server. In this case it's called an application, not an applet.

JavaScript

Java is a complex, low-level language. If you haven't learned C++, you'll likely face a long learning curve before you master it. Since it is a low-level language, it can require a lot of code to implement an application.

Netscape introduced JavaScript so intranet/Internet developers could add client-side processing to web pages without the amount of programming required by Java. JavaScript is a scripting language that resides in an HTML document and interacts with the objects on the web page.

The hello world program in JavaScript would look like this:

```
<HTML>
<HEAD><TITLE>Hello World JavaScript</TITLE></HEAD>
  <BODY>
  The greeting will appear below:<P>
  <SCRIPT LANGUAGE="JavaScript">
    document.write('Hello World')
  </SCRIPT>
  </BODY></HTML>
```

The JavaScript program is not stored on the server as a separate object; it is part of the HTML document itself. A browser that is capable of handling JavaScript interprets anything between the SCRIPT tags as JavaScript and runs it. You can see that this code is simpler than the Java equivalent.

JavaScript code to validate the entry in an HTML form would look similar to this:

```
function submit_page(form) {
   foundError = false;
   // Make sure the city field is not blank
      if(isFieldBlank(form.City)) {
         alert("City is a required field.");
   foundError = true;
      }
```

You would call this function before letting the user submit the form to the server. It would validate data entry before sending the data.

JavaScript is easier to learn than Java, but not as powerful. You can use JavaScript to validate data entry, do calculations, and conditionally change part of the page based on user input. Java is the better choice when you want complete control of the appearance of the screen or want some sophisticated animation or other function that requires low-level control of the display.

You could design server-side intranet processing by hand-coding in Java, C, C++, or Perl. You could design client-side intranet processing by writing Java or JavaScript programs. Let's look at some of the new generation of intranet/Internet application development programs that let you create server-side and/or client-side processing from an integrated, visual environment.

Point-and-Click Server-Side Programming

There are a few products on the market that bring a traditional GUI application development environment to the task of programming the processing on your intranet server. Let's look at a couple.

Bluestone, Inc.'s Sapphire/Web

Sapphire/Web gives you a point-and-click interface for designing your server-side processing. Figure 20-1 shows an example of the Sapphire/Web programming environment.

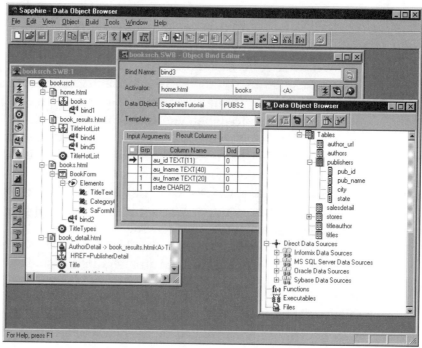

Figure 20-1: Sapphire/Web lets you point and click to design your server-side processing.

On the left side of Figure 20-1 is an outline of your application. Each item in the outline is an HTML file with various web-page elements. On the right side of the screen is the Data Object Browser. This contains a list of database tables, functions, executable programs, and flat files.

In the middle of Figure 20-1 is the Sapphire/Web Object Bind Editor. This connects HTML page components to data objects.

To create an application using Sapphire/Web, you create HTML pages; then you drag and drop database columns, functions, executable programs, or flat files to connect these objects to elements in the web-page documents. After the connections are made, you can add processing logic that processes the data before it's passed to the browser from the database or vice versa.

When the design is final, Sapphire/Web generates C or C++ code that will be called by the web server upon a request from the browser. The program will make the necessary database calls, process the data, and dynamically create web pages.

If you want to add client-side processing to the application, you can add JavaScript to the HTML files or call a Java applet. You have to code this manually, however.

Sapphire/Web sells for $2,495 and is available for Windows 95, Windows NT, and a number of UNIX platforms. To download an evaluation copy, visit Bluestone's Web site (http://www.bluestone.com).

Spider Technologies, Inc.'s NetDynamics

NetDynamics is similar in operation to Sapphire/Web, but the software generates Java instead of the C or C++ that Sapphire/Web creates.

You use a visual interface in NetDynamics to select database objects, as you do in Sapphire/Web. NetDynamics integrates web-page development into the design process where Sapphire/Web requires you to use an HTML editor to define web pages outside of the application development process.

Figure 20-2 shows the NetDynamics web-page wizard you use to specify what kind of web page you want the program to create. You can select a single page, a master/detail page that will divide the display into two sections, or multiple linked pages.

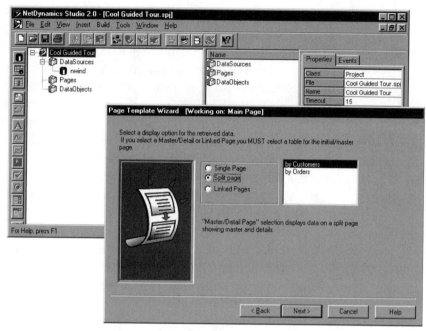

Figure 20-2: NetDynamics' page wizard gives you options for displaying related data from multiple tables.

NetDynamics has a page wizard that lets you assign database actions to web-page buttons (see Figure 20-3). The actions include data navigation, insert, delete, update, and search. The software will add the buttons to the web page.

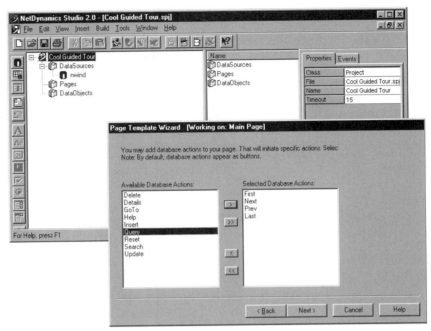

Figure 20-3: NetDynamics has a page wizard that lets you assign database actions to web-page buttons.

The action buttons in a web page generated by NetDynamics will make calls to Java code on the server, which can process the data, interact with the database, and generate dynamic web pages. Figure 20-4 shows the screen you use to create the application logic you want to assign to action buttons. The logic is coded in Java. The product comes with a number of prebuilt objects you can choose from to create your processing.

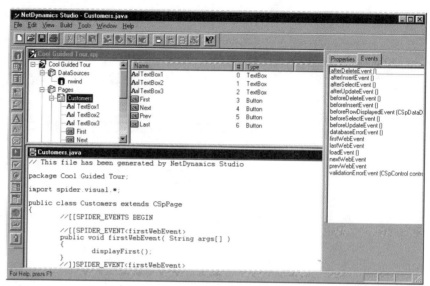

Figure 20-4: You can select from prebuilt Java objects to assign processing to web-page elements using NetDynamics.

Spider Technologies plans to add the ability to generate client-side Java applets to the NetDynamics software. This will result in a development environment that uses Java for processing on both client and server.

NetDynamics is priced at $1,295. It's available for Windows 95, Windows NT, and several UNIX platforms. Visit Spider Technologies's Web site (http://www.w3spider.com/) for more information.

Point-and-Click Client-Side Programming

Sapphire/Web and NetDynamics bring a point-and-click interface to server-side intranet development, but you still have to code your client-side processing by hand. Software companies have recently announced integrated development packages that bring a visual interface to the development of the entire intranet application, client and server.

These exciting new tools open intranet programming to a whole new group of developers and lead to a wide range of intranet applications.

Lets look at three products that take different approaches to intranet application development.

Borland International, Inc.'s Latte

Borland sells a visual development environment called Delphi that uses object-oriented Pascal as its language, provides database connectivity, and offers drag-and-drop screen design. Borland has taken that same interface and used it to create a visual programming environment for Java. The product is called Latte.

Figure 20-5 shows one of the screens from Latte. There is a form in the bottom left corner of the screen. It's not HTML, but a form that is generated at run time on the client browser by a Java applet. This frees the developer from the design limitations of HTML and results in a screen that looks more like a traditional client/server application than HTML allows.

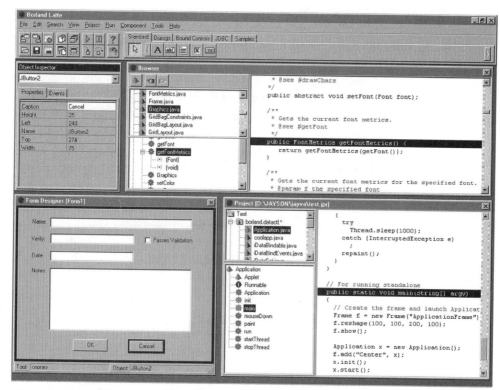

Figure 20-5: In this screen, the developer is using Borland's Latte to design a Java-based web page.

Latte has many of the features of Delphi. You use the Object Inspector, shown in the upper left corner of Figure 20-5, to change object properties and events. You can see the hierarchy of classes. And you can open multiple code windows. Latte simplifies the process of designing Java-based applications.

Latte is scheduled to ship by the end of 1996. No pricing is available. For information, visit Borland's Web site (http://www.borland.com).

Borland International, Inc.'s IntraBuilder

Borland's IntraBuilder takes a different approach to intranet development than Latte. Where Latte builds Java applets to automate client-side processing, IntraBuilder brings a visual environment to the development of HTML web pages with embedded JavaScript for processing.

IntraBuilder gives you an interface that makes building sophisticated web pages as easy as dragging components from a design pallet and dropping them on a web-page canvas.

Figure 20-6 shows IntraBuilder's web-page design mode. Here the developer is designing a home page by dragging elements from a list of available items. At the bottom of the screen is a code window that shows the JavaScript processing the programmer has assigned to one of the web page's buttons. Figure 20-7 shows the finished web page in a browser.

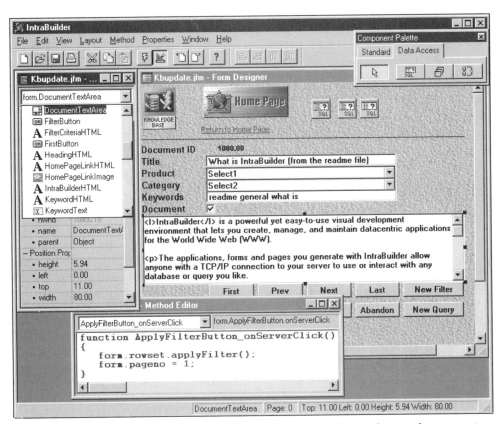

Figure 20-6: You use IntraBuilder's web-page design mode to drop web-page elements onto your document.

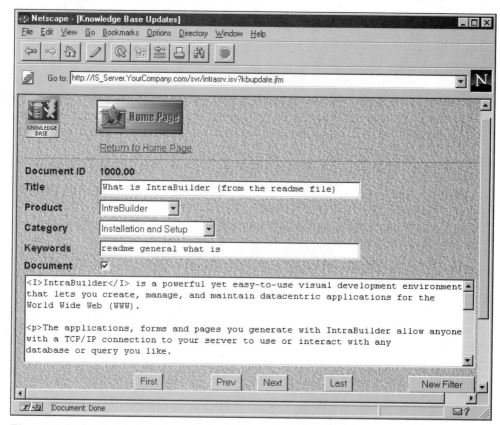

Figure 20-7: The finished web page looks the same in the browser as it did during design.

When you need to insert data from a database table into a web page, you can use IntraBuilder's Report Designer, shown in Figure 20-8. This banded report writer lets you easily organize the data into sorted groups. In the lower right corner of the screen is the Field Palette. You place fields by dragging them from the palette and dropping them somewhere on the Report Designer canvas. You can turn a column from the database into a hyperlink by highlighting the column, then clicking on hyperlink for the text property of the field.

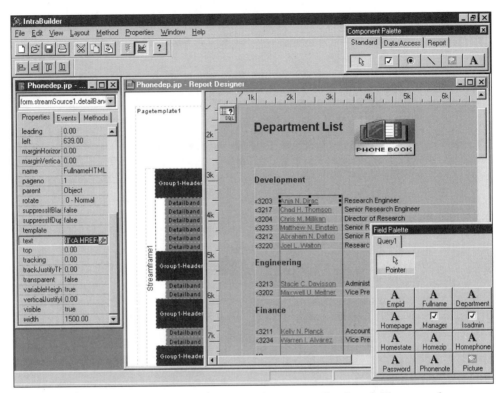

Figure 20-8: The IntraBuilder Report Designer lets you easily place fields on a web page, create groups of data, and turn any field into a hyperlink.

Figure 20-9 is the phone directory created in the Report Designer shown in Figure 20-8. The data is displayed as an HTML table, with highlighted department names over each group of employees.

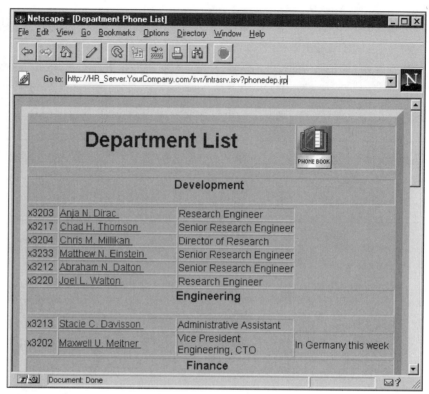

Figure 20-9: This phone directory is the result of the Report Designer layout shown in Figure 20-8.

IntraBuilder makes application design easy through extensive use of wizards. Figure 20-10 shows a form wizard that lets you select form buttons for navigation, updating, searching, and filtering. You indicate whether the buttons should be standard HTML buttons or images, and where to place the row of buttons on the HTML form.

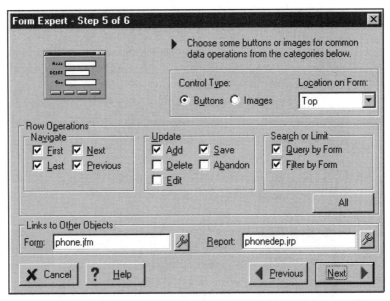

Figure 20-10: IntraBuilder makes extensive use of wizards to simplify web page creation. Here a form wizard lets you quickly design an HTML form.

Borland's Latte will appeal to programmers who feel comfortable with Java's C++ style syntax. IntraBuilder allows you to design intranet applications using the less demanding JavaScript.

IntraBuilder runs on Windows 95 and Windows NT. The product lists for $495, and you can download an evaluation copy of the product from Borland's Web site (http://www.borland.com).

Powersoft's PowerBuilder Browser Plug-in

Three of the products you've seen so far in this chapter create HTML documents. Only Latte is able to create web pages that can go beyond the limitations of HTML. Latte's Java applets can approach the look and feel of traditional client/server applications, but require programming in the low-level Java language.

A new product from Powersoft approaches the problem from a totally different angle. Powersoft figures that the best way to get a web page to look and feel like a client/server application is to let it run existing applications inside of the browser, as is.

Powersoft is about to release a PowerBuilder browser plug-in that lets PowerBuilder applications run as designed inside the browser. This truly brings client/server processing to an intranet.

The PowerBuilder browser plug-in will greatly extend the features you can offer intranet users. Figure 20-11 shows a PowerBuilder application that lets you drill down into detail by clicking on a graph. Clicking on a department on the upper half of the screen updates the bar chart in the lower half with employee detail.

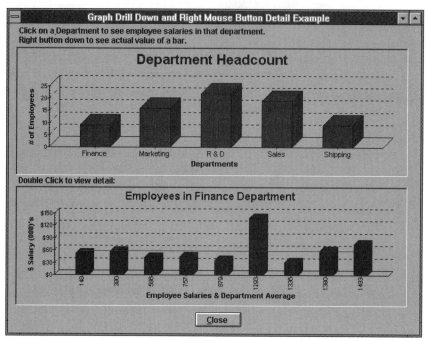

Figure 20-11: This graphical drill-down application is an example of the type of application you'll be able to offer users with the PowerBuilder browser plug-in.

An advantage this product has over the others is the ability to instantly use existing applications in an intranet. If the product works as expected, there will be practically no limit to the applications you can deploy on your internal web.

The PowerBuilder plug-in is available for download from Powersoft's Web site (http://www.powersoft.com). Pricing is not yet available.

Applications Beyond the Shoestring

What kind of intranet applications would you build with these software packages? Here are some examples:

○ **Product Incident Tracking system.** Chapter 9, on web page forms, used an example application called Product Incident Tracking (PIT). Employees could use this system to record every complaint and comment made about one of the company's products. Chapter 9 showed you how to use a standard HTML form to create a data entry web page for this system.

The PIT form created with standard HTML has some limitations. There is an entry field for both product ID and description, for example. It would be nice to enter the ID, then have the system automatically look up the product, and display the description right on the form, or display an error message if the ID was not found. Standard HTML can't accomplish this, but you can program this feature with software that lets you create client-side processing. You can also have the application validate other fields and prevent the user from submitting the data until all required fields have been entered.

○ **Daily Order Report.** Some companies distribute daily reports that give a snapshot of the day's orders. Employees often only spend a few minutes looking at this data, then if there are no surprises they either file the information or discard it. This could be a good application for the intranet. You could use the software discussed in this chapter to create a system that displays a summary of orders, with the products and/or customers presented as hyperlinks. If something unusual catches your attention, you could click on it to call up the detail behind the summary information.

You could apply this same design to other daily, weekly, or monthly reports. Employees can use the intranet to point and click to get a quick update, then dive into the detail when necessary. This eliminates paper, and makes the information interactive.

○ **Sales Rep Commission.** You can use the intranet to automate work processes that require time-consuming phone calls. One example of this is a system that gives a sales rep an update on commissions earned. The rep would log into an intranet application that would return a customized report, based on their ID and password. You could use one of the products discussed in this chapter to design a system that automatically generates web pages based on the contents of a database.

Conclusion

The products highlighted in this chapter show the range of solutions to the problem of making the intranet a programmable technology. You will see a number of these kinds of products over the next few months as software companies convert their products for intranet and Internet development.

If the reality of this software matches the promise, you'll be able to develop an intranet that combines the easy navigation of hyperlinked web pages with all the power of traditional client/server applications. The result will be an information system with incredible potential for handling the company's documents and data.

This book stepped through the process of building an inexpensive intranet that can bring real business benefits to your organization. Take advantage of the technology to build a low-cost, low-risk internal web and prove it to yourself.

About the Companion CD-ROM

The CD-ROM included with your copy of *Build an Intranet on a Shoestring* contains valuable software programs for Windows, Macintosh, and UNIX computers.

To view the CD-ROM:

○ **Windows:** Double-click on the LAUNCHME.EXE file from your Windows Explorer or File Manager.

○ **Macintosh:** Double-click on LAUNCHME file.

You'll see a menu screen offering several choices. See "Navigating the CD-ROM" below for your option choices.

If the viewer does not run properly on your machine, follow these instructions for optimum performance:

Windows

1. Copy the LAUNCHME.EXE and LAUNCHME.INI files to the same directory on your hard drive.

2. Open the LAUNCHME.INI file in a text editor such as Notepad.

3. Find the section in the .INI file that reads:

   [Memory]
   ;ExtraMemory=400
   ; Amount of kBytes over and above physical memory for
   use by a projector.

4. If your computer has enough memory to do so, delete the semicolon from the ExtraMemory line, and change the ExtraMemory setting to a higher number.

5. Save the changes to the LAUNCHME.INI file, and close the text editor.

6. With the CD-ROM still inserted, launch the viewer from the hard drive.

If the viewer still does not run properly on your machine, you can access the material on the CD-ROM directly through File Manager (Windows 3.x) or Windows Explorer (Windows 95).

Macintosh

1. Copy the Launch Me file to your hard drive.

2. Click once on the Launch Me file.

3. Select Get Info from the File menu.

4. If your computer has enough memory to do so, change the amount in the Preferred size field to a higher number.

5. Close the info box.

6. With the CD-ROM still inserted, launch the viewer from the hard drive.

If the viewer still does not run properly, you can access the contents of the CD-ROM directly by double-clicking on its icon in the Finder.

Navigating the CD-ROM

Your choices for navigating the CD-ROM appear on the opening screen. You can read about and install the Software, browse the Hot Picks, learn more about Ventana, or quit the CD-ROM. A complete listing of the programs follows in Table B-1.

Special Notes for UNIX Users:

The UNIX programs on this CD-ROM are in the UNIX directory in .TAR format. To decompress and install them, follow these steps: First, copy [filename].tar to a local directory. Then, at the UNIX prompt, type **tar xvf [filename].tar**

Also, the UNIX programs on this CD-ROM were unable to be tested and are presented "as-is." If you have problems running a program, you should contact the software manufacturer for help

Program	Description
PolyForm	PolyForm™ is a Web form GUI software tool kit that allows you to easily create and manage interactive web pages with forms that collect, process, and respond to each user's specific needs. For example, with PolyForm, you can create forms to allow your users to order products, request information, provide customer feedback, or answer surveys. Each form can be configured separately, so you can collect and store form data as well as transaction information. Information submitted on a form can be sent to specified e-mail addresses, and data can be sent back to the user. With PolyForm, building forms and managing form data is effortless and requires no CGI or Perl programming. PolyForm runs on WebSite™ or any Win-CGI 1.1 or ISAPI compliant server.
WebSTAR	WebSTAR™ is an easy-to-use, full-fledged Web Server for Macintosh. It helps you publish hypertext documents to millions of Web users around the world. You can also use WebSTAR to put any Macintosh file on the Web, including GIF and JPEG images, Shockwave movies, QuickTime VR, and Java applets. Using WebSTAR is as easy as double-clicking. Plus, it's faster than many Web servers running on UNIX.

Program	Description
	WebSTAR is completely compatible with all Web clients including Netscape Navigator and Microsoft's Internet Explorer. To activate the version of WebSTAR on this CD, you will have to e-mail a request for a key to: keys@starnine.com. Detailed instructions are in the program's README file.
O'Reilly Web Site	WebSite™ 1.1 is a 32-bit multi-threaded World Wide Web server that combines power and flexibility with ease of use. Its intuitive graphical interface and easy installation make it a natural for Windows NT and Windows 95 users.
	In a corporate LAN environment, you can use WebSite to publish project information, on-line training material, corporate policies, and company news. WebSite's powerful server engine allows you to publish large sets of corporate data, including sophisticated CGI forms, with excellent performance and reliability. With WebSite's access control features, you can ensure that confidential information is accessible only to people in a specific group or department.
	Using WebSite on the Internet, you can reach a large and growing audience on the Web. Documents on your WebSite server can include text, graphics, forms, sound, video, and hypertext links. With these dynamic elements, businesses can use WebSite to present product literature, technical updates, interactive surveys, and promotions.
HTML Assistant Pro 3	HTML Assistant Pro 3 is a point-and-click editor for making World Wide Web pages that runs under Microsoft Windows (Version 3.x or Windows 95). HTML Assistant Pro 3 greatly simplifies the process of creating a Web page. You begin with a blank screen and an idea and start typing. Mark up your page using push button tools so you don't have to remember complicated codes. Including

Program	Description
	hypertext links (highlighted words that link your page to other Web pages), is simply a matter of copying and pasting the URL (Uniform Resource Locator) for the page you want to point to. Whatever you want to do: share interests or research, advertise your product or service, or publish your ideas, HTML Assistant Pro 3 gets you on the Web easily and quickly.
PageSpinner for Macintosh	PageSpinner is an HTML Editor for MacOS. It supports HTML 2.0, HTML 3.2, plus additional Netscape extensions and is useful for both beginning and advanced web authors. The editor gives you quick access to often-used formatting and also supports interactive help with AppleGuide and an HTML Assistant to help you create your own HTML pages. PageSpinner also includes support for the latest Web technologies, such as Frames, Embedded Objects, autoload of HTML files, WorldScript, Java, and JavaScript.
asWedit	asWedit is a comprehensive and easy-to-use HTML 2, HTML 3, and text editor for X Window System and Motif. It offers three independent modes: a plain text editing mode and two context-sensitive, validating modes for authoring of HyperText Markup Language documents (HTML 2 and HTML 3) as used on the World Wide Web and enterprise networks. A partial list of asWedit features includes: full support for all HTML 2 tags and attributes based on the RFC 1866; full support for all HTML 3 tags and attributes based on the HTML 3 Document Type Definition (DTD) as of March 24, 1995; support in our HTML 2x and HTML 3x extended modes for client-side image maps, form-based file upload, Java applets, and the widely used Netscape extensions; customizable colors for different HTML tags; text-to-table and -to-list converters; a table

Program	Description
	of contents generator, ready to use and test Form examples; spell checking that skips HTML tags; and keyboard shortcuts for the most common HTML tags.
Paint Shop Pro	Paint Shop Pro is the complete Windows graphics program for image creation, viewing, and manipulation. Features include painting, photo retouching, image enhancement and editing, color enhancement, image browsing, batch conversion, and TWAIN scanner support. Included are 20 standard image-processing filters and 12 deformations. Supports Adobe-style image-processing plug-in filters. Over 30 file formats are supported, including JPEG, Kodak Photo-CD, PBM, and GIF.
LView Pro	LView Pro 1.7 is an image file editor/viewer/converter for Microsoft Windows 3.1, Windows 95, and Windows NT. LView Pro loads and saves image files in: JPEG, JFIF, GIF 87a/89a, Truevision TARGA, Windows, and OS/2 BMP formats. LView Pro performs batch compression, batch printing, contact-sheet image merging, and slideshow viewing. Supported retouch operations include: Cropping, Resizing, Rotating, RGB, Contrast, HSV, YCrCb, Gamma, conversion to Grayscale, photo Negative, Interactive RGB editing with algebraic-function mapping definitions, individual-palette-entry edition, editable image filters, adding text and full support for cutting, pasting, and moving image pieces. LView Pro supports 24-bit images and 8-bit images.
Image Alchemy	Image Alchemy, the leader in graphic/image file format conversion programs, guarantees successful conversion to and from 75+ supported formats and 150 flavors of TIFF including Web formats: PDF (Acrobat), transparent-GIF,

Program	Description
	interleaved-GIF, progressive-JPEG, and PNG. Image Alchemy also offers superior dithering algorithms, resizing, batch processing, customized palette control, spiffing, DPI specification, and color management.
Mapedit	A graphical editor for World Wide Web clickable-image maps. Mapedit simplifies the creation of client-side and server-side image maps. Mapedit allows the creation of image maps using GIF, JPEG, and PNG format images.
Mac-ImageMap	Mac-ImageMap is a tool which makes it easy to install clickable maps on a Macintosh WWW Server which runs with the software WebSTAR or MacHTTP (both from StarNine Technologies, Inc., developed by Chuck Shotton) or NetPresenz (by Peter Lewis). Mac-ImageMap runs as a CGI-program, or as a user-action handler with WebSTAR. No scripting software is needed to use this utility! The map-definition files may be compatible with image-map-definition files for the NCSA-httpd image map program, which runs under UNIX. 　　Mac-ImageMap has been released as freeware. The actual version supports rectangular regions, elliptic (such as circle) regions, arbitrary polygon regions, and nearest points. For details, see the README file of the current distribution.
Apache Web Server for UNIX	A free plug-in replacement server for NCSA-httpd 1.3. The Apache Web Server offers faster performance, better security, more stability, and better compliance with HTTP specifications than the NCSA server it replaces. You can download the latest version of the Apache Web Server at http://www.apache.org.
InContext Spider	InContext Spider is an easy-to-use, Windows-based HTML authoring tool for the World Wide Web. Unlike enhanced-text-editor and word-

Program	Description
	processor add-ons, InContext Spider has features for users of any level. A near-WYSIWYG editor and quick-start templates help novice and intermediate Wed authors, while advanced users can take advantage of support for all versions of HTML, including the Netscape and Microsoft Internet Explorer extensions. Features include: integration with our built-in Web browser, an interactive Windows help file for HTML 2.0 and Netscape and Microsoft Internet Explorer extensions, automatic HTML validation, and drag-and-drop links and images.
Graphics Tools! for Macintosh	Graphics Tools! for Macintosh includes the Media Manager with the ability to capture, catalog, view, and convert JPEG, GIF, and Macintosh PICT images.
Graphics Tools! for Windows	Graphics Tools! for Windows includes the Media Manager with the ability to capture, catalog, trace, view, and convert JPEG, GIF, and BMP images.
QuickSite	QuickSite is constantly updated to keep up with the ever-changing Web. You can download the most current 30-day trial version of QuickSite from http://www.deltapoint.com. QuickSite for Windows is the fastest and most powerful way to create and manage your Internet Web Site. QuickSite wizards lead you through the entire Web site-building process, so even new users can create their own Web sites. Includes one-click updating and uploading of your site, making revising easy.

Table A-1: Programs on the Companion CD-ROM.

Technical Support

Technical support is available for installation-related problems only. The technical support office is open from 8:00 A.M. to 6:00 P.M., Monday through Friday and can be reached via the following methods:

Phone: (919) 544-9404 extension 81

Faxback Answer System: (919) 544-9404 extension 85

E-mail: help@vmedia.com

FAX: (919) 544-9472

World Wide Web: **http://www.vmedia.com/support**

America Online: keyword *Ventana*

Limits of Liability & Disclaimer of Warranty

The authors and publisher of this book have made their best efforts in preparing the CD-ROM and the programs contained in it. These efforts include the development, research, and testing of the theories and programs to determine their effectiveness. The authors and publisher make no warranty of any kind expressed or implied, with regard to these programs or the documentation contained in this book.

The authors and publisher shall not be liable in the event of incidental or consequential damages in connection with, or arising out of, the furnishing, performance, or use of the programs, associated instructions, and/or claims of productivity gains.

Some of the software on this CD-ROM is shareware; there may be additional charges (owed to the software authors/makers) incurred for their registration and continued use. See individual program's README or VREADME.TXT files for more information.

Works Cited

Chapter 15

[1]Wilkerson, Robert. *PC Week Online*. April 4, 1996. This article can be seen online (http://www.pcweek.com/sr/0401/01exper.html).

[2]Murphy, Kathleen. *Internet World*, online version. March 1996. (http://pubs.iworld.com/ww-online/96Mar/intranet/hp.html). Reprinted from *Web Week*, volume 2, issue 3, March 1996.

[3]Gibbons Paul, Lauren. *PC Week*, June 3, 1996. pgs. 46, 50.

[4]Mullich, Joe. *PC Week*, June 10, 1996. pgs. 42, 46.
[5]*ComputerWorld*, June 24, 1996. Intranets insert, pg 3.

[6]Callaway, Erin. *PC Week*, April 29, 1996. Pgs 53, 59.

[7]Gibbons Paul, Lauren. *PC Week*, May 20, 1996. Pgs. 52, 58.

[8]Gibbons Paul, Lauren. *PC Week*, May 13, 1996. Pgs. 53, 56.

Chapter 18

[1]Nash, Kim S. *ComputerWorld*, May 27, 1996. Pgs. 1, 109.

Index

Empower

yourself with up-to-date tools for navigating the Net—in-depth reviews, where to find them and how to use them.

Enhance

your online experience—get to know the latest plug-ins that let you experience animation, video, virtual reality and sound...live, over the Internet.

Enliven

your Web pages—tips from experienced Web designers help you create pages with punch, spiced with multimedia and organized for easy navigation.

Enchant

your Web site visitors—learn to create interactive pages with JavaScript applets, program your own Internet applications and build added functionality into your site.

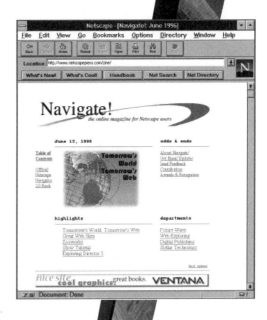

http://www.netscapepress.com/zine

Add Power to Web Pages

Official Netscape JavaScript Book

$29.99, 520 pages, illustrated, part #: 465-0

Add life to Web pages—animated logos, text-in-motion
sequences, live updating and calculations—quickly and
easily. Sample code and step-by-step instructions show how
to put JavaScript to real-world, practical use.

Java Programming for the Internet

$49.95, 806 pages, illustrated, part #: 355-7

Create dynamic, interactive Internet applications. Expand
the scope of your online development with this
comprehensive, step-by-step guide to creating Java
applets. Includes four real-world, start-to-finish tutorials.
The CD-ROM has all the programs, samples and applets
from the book, plus shareware. Continual updates on
Ventana's *Online Companion* will keep this information
on the cutting edge.

The Comprehensive Guide to VBScript

$34.99, 408 pages, illustrated, part #: 470-7

The only encyclopedic reference to VBScript and HTML
commands and features. Complete with practical examples
for plugging directly into programs. The companion CD-
ROM features a hypertext version of the book, along with
shareware, templates, utilities and more.

 Books marked with this logo include a free Internet *Online
Companion*™, featuring archives of free utilities plus a
software archive and links to other Internet resources.

Make it Multimedia

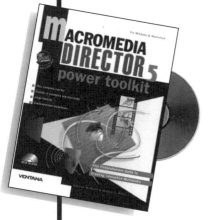

Macromedia Director 5 Power Toolkit

$49.95, 800 pages, illustrated, part #: 289-5

Macromedia Director 5 Power Toolkit views the industry's hottest multimedia authoring environment from the inside out. Features tools, tips and professional tricks for producing power-packed projects for CD-ROM and Internet distribution. Dozens of exercises detail the principles behind successful multimedia presentations and the steps to achieve professional results. The companion CD-ROM includes utilities, sample presentations, animations, scripts and files.

Shockwave!

$49.95, 400 pages, illustrated, part #: 441-3

Breathe new life into your web pages with Macromedia Shockwave. Ventana's *Shockwave!* teaches you how to enliven and animate your Web sites with online movies. Beginning with step-by-step exercises and examples, and ending with in-depth excursions into the use of Shockwave Lingo extensions, *Shockwave!* is a must-buy for both novices and experienced Director developers. Plus, tap into current Macromedia resources on the Internet with Ventana's *Online Companion*. The companion CD-ROM includes the Shockwave player plug-in, sample Director movies and tutorials, and much more!

The Comprehensive Guide to Lingo

$49.99, 700 pages, illustrated, part #: 463-4

Master the Lingo of Macromedia Director's scripting language for adding interactivity to presentations. Covers beginning scripts to advanced techniques, including creating movies for the Web and problem solving. The companion CD-ROM features demo movies of all scripts in the book, plus numerous examples, a searchable database of problems and solutions, and much more!

Follow the leader!

250,000+ in its first edition!

Hot on the heels of the runaway international bestseller comes the complete Netscape Press line—easy-to-follow tutorials; savvy, results-oriented guidelines; and targeted titles that zero in on your special interests.

All with the official Netscape seal of approval!

Official Netscape Navigator Gold 3.0 Book
$39.95
Windows 420-0
Macintosh 421-9

956 pages

Official Netscape Navigator 3.0 Book
$39.99
Windows 500-2
Macintosh 512-6

696 pages

"Destined to become the bible to the world's most popular browser."
—*PC Magazine*

OFFICIAL

Netscape Navigator 3.0 BOOK

The definitive guide to the world's most popular Internet navigator

BY PHIL JAMES
FOREWORD BY MARC ANDREESSEN

International Bestseller!
More than 250,000 in print!

OFFICIAL

Netscape Navigator GOLD 3.0 BOOK

The official guide to the premiere Web navigator and HTML editor

ALAN SIMPSON

Web Favorites

Voodoo Windows 95

$24.95, 504 pages, illustrated, part #: 145-7

Users will need voodoo to make the move to Windows 95! Nelson is back with more secrets, shortcuts and spells than ever. Scores of tips—many never before published—on installing, customizing, editing, printing, virtual memory, Internet connections and much more. Organized by task for easy reference. The companion disk contains shareware utilities, fonts and magic!

The Windows 95 Book

$39.95, 1232 pages, illustrated, part #: 154-6

The anxiously awaited revamp of Windows means new working styles for PC users. This new handbook offers an insider's look at the all-new interface–arming users with tips and techniques for file management, desktop design, optimizing and more. A must-have for a prosperous '95! The companion CD-ROM features tutorials, demos, previous and online help plus utilities, screensavers, wallpaper and sounds.

Windows 95 Power Toolkit

$49.95, 744 pages, illustrated, part #: 319-0

If Windows 95 includes everything but the kitchen sink, get ready to get your hands wet! Maximize the customizing capabilities of Windows 95 with ready-to-use tools, applications and tutorials, including a guide to VBA. CD-ROM: the complete toolkit, plus additional graphics, sounds and applications.Online Companion: updated versions of software, hyper-linked listings and links to helpful resources on the Internet.

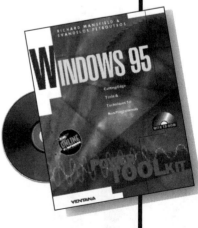

To order any Ventana title, complete this order form and mail or fax it to us, with payment, for quick shipment.

TITLE	PART #	QTY	PRICE	TOTAL

SHIPPING

For all standard orders, please ADD $4.50/first book, $1.35/each additional.
For software kit orders, ADD $6.50/first kit, $2.00/each additional.
For "two-day air," ADD $8.25/first book, $2.25/each additional.
For "two-day air" on the kits, ADD $10.50/first kit, $4.00/each additional.
For orders to Canada, ADD $6.50/book.
For orders sent C.O.D., ADD $4.50 to your shipping rate.
North Carolina residents must ADD 6% sales tax.
International orders require additional shipping charges.

SUBTOTAL = $ _____
SHIPPING = $ _____
TAX   = $ _____
TOTAL   = $ _____

Or, save 15%–order online.
http://www.vmedia.com

Mail to: Ventana • PO Box 13964 • Research Triangle Park, NC 27709-3964 ☎ 800/743-5369 • Fax 919/544-9472

Name _____

E-mail _____ Daytime phone _____

Company _____

Address (No PO Box) _____

City _____ State _____ Zip _____

Payment enclosed ___VISA ___MC ___ Acc't # _____ Exp. date _____

Signature _____ Exact name on card _____

Check your local bookstore or software retailer for these and other bestselling titles, or call toll free: **800/743-5369**

All technical support for this product is available from Ventana.
The technical support office is open from 8:00 A.M. to 6:00 P.M. (EST) Monday through
Friday and can be reached via the following methods:

World Wide Web: http://www.netscapepress.com/support

E–mail: help@vmedia.com

Phone: (919) 544-9404 extension 81

FAX: (919) 544-9472

America Online: keyword **Ventana**